Theories of Va

Most expressions in natural language are vague. But what is the best semantic treatment of terms like 'heap', 'red' and 'child'? And what is the logic of arguments involving this kind of vague expression? These questions are receiving increasing philosophical attention, and in this timely book Rosanna Keefe explores the questions of what we should want from an account of vagueness and how we should assess rival theories. Her discussion ranges widely and comprehensively over the main theories of vagueness and their supporting arguments, and she offers a powerful and original defence of a form of supervaluationism, a theory that requires almost no deviation from standard logic yet can accommodate the lack of sharp boundaries to vague predicates and deal with the paradoxes of vagueness in a methodologically satisfying way. Her study will be of particular interest to readers in philosophy of language and of mind, philosophical logic, epistemology and metaphysics.

ROSANNA KEEFE is Lecturer in Philosophy at the University of Sheffield. She is co-editor (with Peter Smith) of *Vagueness: A Reader* (1997).

CAMBRIDGE STUDIES IN PHILOSOPHY

Theories of Vagueness

CAMBRIDGE STUDIES IN PHILOSOPHY

General editor ERNEST SOSA

Advisory editors
JONATHAN DANCY *University of Reading*
JOHN HALDANE *University of St Andrews*
GILBERT HARMAN *Princeton University*
FRANK JACKSON *Australian National University*
WILLIAM G. LYCAN *University of North Carolina, Chapel Hill*
SYDNEY SHOEMAKER *Cornell University*
JUDITH J. THOMSON *Massachusetts Institute of Technology*

Theories of Vagueness

Rosanna Keefe
University of Sheffield

CAMBRIDGE
UNIVERSITY PRESS

CAMBRIDGE UNIVERSITY PRESS
Cambridge, New York, Melbourne, Madrid, Cape Town, Singapore, São Paulo

Cambridge University Press
The Edinburgh Building, Cambridge CB2 2RU, UK

Published in the United States of America by Cambridge University Press, New York

www.cambridge.org
Information on this title: www.cambridge.org/9780521650670

First published 2000
This digitally printed first paperback version 2006

A catalogue record for this publication is available from the British Library

Library of Congress Cataloguing in Publication data
Keefe, Rosanna.
Theories of vagueness / Rosanna Keefe.
p. cm.
Includes bibliographical references and index.
ISBN 0 521 65067 4 (hardback)
1. Vagueness (Philosophy) I. Title.
B105.V33 K44 2000
160–dc21

ISBN-13 978-0-521-65067-0 hardback
ISBN-10 0-521-65067-4 hardback

ISBN-13 978-0-521-03389-3 paperback
ISBN-10 0-521-03389-6 paperback

For my parents, Sheila and Terry

Contents

Acknowledgements

Chapter 5 is a slightly revised version of my paper 'Vagueness by numbers' in *Mind* 107, and a version of chapter 6 appeared in *The Australasian Journal of Philosophy* 76 as 'Vagueness and language clusters'; I am grateful to Oxford University Press for permission to use this material. Parts of the introduction to *Vagueness: A Reader*, ed. Rosanna Keefe and Peter Smith (MIT Press 1997) also appear in this book (particularly in chapter 1).

A large number of people have helped and influenced me since I started working on vagueness. My doctoral thesis on the topic was supervised by Timothy Smiley and examined by Alex Oliver and Mark Sainsbury: I am much obliged to them for constructive criticism and many helpful suggestions. Thanks too to Chris Daly and Joseph Melia, who were both there at the beginning of my doctorate and have continued to give me help and advice ever since. Peter Smith has generously discussed various drafts of my work since we began co-editing *Vagueness: A Reader*. And for perceptive comments and much fruitful informal chat I am very grateful to Dominic Gregory, who nevertheless always appreciates when the day's philosophy is over.

A wide range of useful comments have also been made by Linda Burns, Jeremy Butterfield, Bob Hanna, Katherine Hawley, David Hemp, Richard Holton, Terry Keefe, Jochen Runde, Timothy Williamson, an anonymous reader for Cambridge University Press, and audiences for my talks at the Universities of Sheffield, Cambridge, Leeds, York and Bristol as well as at the conference on vagueness in Bled, Slovenia (June 1998). I am indebted to Hilary Gaskin of Cambridge University Press for general help with preparation of the book.

I am extremely grateful to Jesus College, Cambridge, which supported me for three years in a Research Fellowship. This provided an excellent environment in which to write and rewrite large portions of this book. I also offer the warmest of thanks to the Philosophy Department at the University of Sheffield, which not only allowed me to complete the Jesus Fellowship before taking up a lectureship, but also provided substantial criticism and advice on this book in a series of intensive seminars in November 1998.

Introduction

The aim of this book is to formulate and defend the best possible theory of vagueness. First, I explore some general questions. What is vagueness and what are theories of vagueness? What should such theories be aiming to do? And how should we assess them?

My project is primarily one in the philosophy of logic and language. The focus is on finding the logic and semantics of vague language rather than, for example, illuminating the psychology of our use of it. But I am less concerned with formal modelling than with the philosophical rationale for any chosen type of model. Consequently, I minimise the technical discussion of complex logical material. This book should be accessible to anyone who has a grasp of elementary formal logic.

If you remove a single grain of sand from a heap of sand, you surely still have a heap of sand. But if you take a heap and remove grains one by one, you can apply that principle at each stage, which will commit you to counting even the solitary final grain as a heap. This is a sorites paradox. Arguments of a parallel form can typically be constructed for any vague term. For example, the generalisation 'anyone one hundredth of an inch shorter than a tall man is also tall' can be used to argue that a three-foot man is tall given that a seven-foot man is, by considering a series of men each one hundredth of an inch shorter than the previous one. And a tadpole does not become a frog in the space of one hundredth of a second, which invites an argument to the conclusion that a tadpole can never become a frog. No straightforward answer to this persistent type of paradox looks promising: the premises are highly plausible, the inference seems valid but the conclusions are absurd.

The paradox is best dealt with in the context of a theory of vagueness more generally – a theory which answers a range of other questions. Consider Tek, who is a borderline case of 'tall'. We may

1

be inclined to say it is indeterminate whether or not Tek is tall: the meaning of 'tall' is too vague to fix a specific height marking the boundary between the tall and the not-tall. But what does this borderline status amount to? What should we say about the truth-value of the sentence 'Tek is tall'? To call it true or call it false seems to misrepresent the apparent indeterminacy that characterises border-line cases. But can we allow sentences that are neither true nor false? And, if we do, are we just creating a new semantic category (containing those sentences that are neither true nor false) and committing ourselves to, for example, a sharp division between those things which are tall and those which neither are nor aren't? A theory of vagueness must provide an account of borderline cases and of the (at least apparent) indeterminacy characterising vague predicates. And this is closely related to the need to provide a logic and semantics of vague language. For classical logic and semantics are committed to the principle that every statement is either true or false (the principle of bivalence) and borderline cases thus threaten the applicability to vague language of that familiar system. Perhaps a new logic or a new semantics is required.

The theory I seek to defend – supervaluationism – classifies border-line case predications as neither true nor false, and yet it yields a logical system that agrees with standard classical logic in the classifica-tion of logical truths and valid inferences (with some explicable exceptions). The essence of the theory is to evaluate vague sentences by reference to all ways of making them precise. Though there is no exact height that is the minimum height for counting as tall, 'tall' could be made precise by selecting such a height boundary among the borderline heights, without thereby altering the classification of the uncontentious cases. There is substantial choice available over such precise boundaries and if we are to avoid privileging a single one, we should count 'Tek is tall' as true if and only if it is true for all the choices. Similarly, 'Tek is tall' is false if and only if false on all ways of making it precise. So 'a single grain forms a heap' is false, because false on all ways of making 'heap' precise. But when x is a borderline heap, 'x is a heap' is not true on all ways of making it precise nor false on all those ways, so it counts as neither true nor false.

Supervaluationism has been recognised as a serious contender for a theory of vagueness since Fine's highly influential defence of it (see his 1975). Passing comments and endorsements from philosophers in

2

a variety of different contexts suggest that the theory is philosophically plausible and attractive. But among those tackling vagueness in more detail, supporters have been more rare, and a range of objections to the theory has gained popularity. It is time for a systematic defence of the theory. I argue that the standard objections fail and that the theory is much better than its rivals, and I concentrate on the philosophical justification of my position, leaving aside some details of its formalisation.

The first two chapters are devoted to foundational issues. The wide range of vague expressions is emphasised: most of our language is vague. This increases the urgency of providing a theory of the phenomena and an account of good reasoning in vague language. As well as providing an overview of the area, chapter 1 explores, partly in abstraction from particular theories of vagueness, some key issues which play a recurrent role in the rest of the book. For example it introduces higher-order vagueness, emphasising how the range of borderline cases for a vague predicate is itself not precisely determined. This phenomenon provides a revealing test which weeds out superficial treatments that ignore the persistence and depth of vagueness.

Chapter 2 addresses crucial questions of methodology which have been surprisingly ignored in the literature. It offers an account of how competing theories should be (and generally are) assessed and what constraints are imposed on theorising. I recommend seeking a reflective equilibrium that achieves the best balance between preserving as many as possible of our judgements or opinions of various kinds (intuitive and pre-philosophical ones among others) and meeting theoretical requirements such as simplicity. Having an explicit methodology to hand helps situate the subsequent discussions of individual theories, putting criticisms in perspective and aiding comparative judgements. The final section of chapter 2 will also help in similar ways: I there examine the attitude displayed by theorists who hope to avoid worries about certain elements of their theory by casually remarking that what they offer is 'only a model'. I argue that in many circumstances this is unacceptable.

In conformity with my methodology, to defend a supervaluationist theory of vagueness I must show that rival theories either fail to reach a reflective equilibrium, or can only reach one that violates considerably more of our intuitions and opinions than my favoured alter-native. The major rival theories are dealt with in detail in chapters 3 to 6, and at various points along the way other candidates are rejected (including Unger's nihilism, intuitionistic accounts, and hybrids of and variants on the main contenders).

Chapter 3 considers the epistemic view, according to which a borderline heap *does* either truly or falsely count as a heap, though we do not know which. Being a borderline case, it is *unclear* whether or not it is a heap, but this lack of clarity is owed to a special and unavoidable kind of ignorance. There is a particular instant in the process of removing grains at which you cease to have a heap, and all vague predicates are similarly sharply bounded. Classical logic and semantics are retained in their entirety. Although this theory is initially implausible, it has received an extremely thorough and influential defence in Williamson 1994. I offer objections to Wil-liamson. Nevertheless, I do not claim to show that his theory is not viable: bullet-biting responses are generally available, though with each such response, the theory becomes less and less appealing. Williamson himself rests much of his case for the view on his criticisms of its rivals, and I show in chapters 7 and 8 that his criticisms of supervaluationism fail. In short, I think there is a much better alternative to the epistemic view.

If it is not viable to retain classical logic and semantics or accept that our vague predicates are sharply bounded, perhaps the leap from truth to falsity is avoided because borderline case predications have some other non-classical value. A popular approach to vagueness adopts this line and employs a many-valued logic which generalises the logic of two-values to accommodate the extra values. Chapters 4 and 5 are directed against these theories and I amass a number of different objections. The moral is that we cannot just assign an interpretation to a predicate – even a many-valued interpretation – and then use truth-functional definitions of the connectives to capture the logic. A different approach is needed.

Chapter 6 considers the pragmatic view, which treats vagueness, not as a feature of a language, but as a matter of the relation between users and language. The hope of its advocates is that classical logic and semantics can be retained, but without the commitments of the epistemic view, since there is no unique sharp language which is used by all English-speakers. I show that,

4

depending on how the proposal is understood, either the theory fails or it collapses into supervaluationism.

The remaining alternative is thus to modify classical semantics and give up trying to treat the usual logical connectives truth-functionally. Supervaluationism takes this path. A vague predicate such as 'tall' need not then have a unique sharply bounded extension, nor need it be associated with a function from people to a set of more than two values. Instead, sentences involving that predicate are assessed by reference to the range of alternative precise extensions corresponding to ways of making the predicate precise. As well as the account I defend, I survey and reject some alternative ways to employ the same, or a similar, framework, including ones that deviate from classical logic. The discussion of my own theory spans chapters 7 and 8.

1

The phenomena of vagueness

I. CENTRAL FEATURES OF VAGUE EXPRESSIONS

The parties to the vigorous debates about vagueness largely agree about which predicates are vague: paradigm cases include 'tall', 'red', 'bald', 'heap', 'tadpole' and 'child'. Such predicates share three interrelated features that intuitively are closely bound up with their vagueness: they admit borderline cases, they lack (or at least apparently lack) sharp boundaries and they are susceptible to sorites paradoxes. I begin by describing these characteristics.

Borderline cases are cases where it is unclear whether or not the predicate applies. Some people are borderline tall: not clearly tall and not clearly not tall. Certain reddish-orange patches are borderline red. And during a creature's transition from tadpole to frog, there will be stages at which it is a borderline case of a tadpole. To offer at this stage a more informative characterisation of borderline cases and the unclarity involved would sacrifice neutrality between various competing theories of vagueness. Nonetheless, when Tek is borderline tall, it does seem that the unclarity about whether he is tall is not merely epistemic (i.e. such that there is a fact of the matter, we just do not know it). For a start, no amount of further information about his exact height (and the heights of others) could help us decide whether he *is* tall. More controversially, it seems that there is no fact of the matter here about which we are ignorant: rather, it is *indeterminate* whether Tek is tall. And this indeterminacy is often thought to amount to the sentence 'Tek is tall' being neither true nor false, which violates the classical principle of bivalence. The law of excluded middle may also come into question when we consider instances such as 'either Tek is tall or he is not tall'.

Second, vague predicates apparently lack well-defined extensions. On a scale of heights there appears to be no sharp boundary between the tall people and the rest, nor is there an exact point at which our growing creature ceases to be a tadpole. More generally, if we imagine possible candidates for satisfying some vague *F* to be arranged with spatial closeness reflecting similarity, no sharp line can be drawn round the cases to which *F* applies. Instead, vague predicates are naturally described as having fuzzy, or blurred, boundaries. But according to classical logic and semantics all predicates have well-defined extensions: they cannot have fuzzy boundaries. So again this suggests that a departure from the classical conception is needed to accommodate vagueness.

Clearly, having fuzzy boundaries is closely related to having borderline cases. More specifically, it is the *possibility* of borderline cases that counts for vagueness and fuzzy boundaries, for if all actually borderline tall people were destroyed, 'tall' would still lack sharp boundaries. It might be argued that for there to be no sharp boundary between the *F*s and the not-*F*s just *is* for there to be a region of possible borderline cases of *F* (sometimes known as the penumbra). On the other hand, if the range of possible borderline cases between the *F*s and the not-*F*s was itself sharply bounded, then *F* would have a sharp boundary too, albeit one which was shared with the border-line *F*s, not with the things that were definitely not *F*. The thought that our vague predicates are not in fact like this – their borderline cases are not sharply bounded – is closely bound up with the key issue of higher-order vagueness, which will be discussed in more detail in §6.

Third, typically vague predicates are susceptible to sorites para-doxes. Intuitively, a hundredth of an inch cannot make a difference to whether or not a man counts as tall – such tiny variations, undetectable using the naked eye and everyday measuring instru-ments, are just too small to matter. This seems part of what it is for 'tall' to be a *vague* height term lacking sharp boundaries. So we have the principle [S_1] if *x* is tall, and *y* is only a hundredth of an inch shorter than *x*, then *y* is also tall. But imagine a line of men, starting with someone seven feet tall, and each of the rest a hundredth of an inch shorter than the man in front of him. Repeated applications of [S_1] as we move down the line imply that each man we encounter is tall, however far we continue. And this yields a conclusion which is clearly false, namely that a man less than five feet tall, reached after three thousand steps along the line, is also tall.

Similarly there is the ancient example of the heap (Greek *soros*, from which the paradox derives its name). Plausibly, [S₂] if *x* is a heap of sand, then the result *y* of removing one grain will still be a heap – recognising the vagueness of 'heap' seems to commit us to this principle. So take a heap and remove grains one by one; repeated applications of [S₂] imply absurdly that the solitary last grain is a heap. The paradox is supposedly owed to Eubulides, to whom the liar paradox is also attributed. (See Barnes 1982 and Burnyeat 1982 for detailed discussion of the role of the paradox in the ancient world.)

Arguments with a sorites structure are not mere curiosities: they feature, for example, in some familiar ethical 'slippery slope' arguments (see e.g. Walton 1992 and Williams 1995). Consider the principle [S₃] if it is wrong to kill something at time *t* after conception, then it would be wrong to kill it at time *t* minus one second. And suppose we agree that it is wrong to kill a baby nine months after conception. Repeated applications of [S₃] would lead to the conclusion that abortion even immediately after conception would be wrong. The need to assess this kind of practical argumentation increases the urgency of examining reasoning with vague predicates.

Wright (1975, p. 333) coined the phrase *tolerant* to describe predicates for which there is 'a notion of degree of change too small to make any difference' to their applicability. Take '[is] tall' (for simplicity, in mentioning predicates I shall continue, in general, to omit the copula). This predicate will count as tolerant if, as [S₁] claims, a change of one hundredth of an inch never affects its applicability. A tolerant predicate must lack sharp boundaries; for if *F* has sharp boundaries, then a boundary-crossing change, however small, will always make a difference to whether *F* applies.[1] Moreover, a statement of the tolerance of *F* can characteristically serve as the inductive premise of a sorites paradox for *F* (as in the example of 'tall' again).

Russell provides one kind of argument that predicates of a given class are tolerant: if the application of a word (a colour predicate, for example) is paradigmatically based on unaided sense perception, it surely cannot be applicable to only one of an indiscriminable pair (1923, p. 87). So such 'observational' predicates will be tolerant with

---

[1] Note that throughout this book, when there is no potential for confusion I am casual about omitting quotation marks when natural language expressions are not involved, e.g. when talking about the predicate *F* or the sentence *p* & ¬*p*.

respect to changes too small for us to detect. And Wright develops, in detail, arguments supporting the thesis that many of our predicates are tolerant (1975 and 1976). In particular, consideration of the role of ostension and memory in mastering the use of such predicates appears to undermine the idea that they have sharp boundaries which could not be shown by the teacher or remembered by the learner. Arguments of this kind are widely regarded as persuasive: I shall refer to them as 'typical arguments for tolerance'. A theory of vagueness must address these arguments and establish what, if anything, they succeed in showing, and in particular whether they show that the inductive premise of the sorites paradox holds.

Considerations like Russell's and Wright's help explain why vague predicates are so common (whatever we say about the sorites premise). And they also seem to suggest that we *could* not operate with a language free of vagueness. They make it difficult to see vagueness as a merely optional or eliminable feature of language. This contrasts with the view of vagueness as a defect of natural languages found in Frege (1903, §56) and perhaps in Russell's uncharitable suggestion (1923, p. 84) that language is vague because our ancestors were lazy. A belief that vagueness is inessential and therefore unimportant may comfort those who ignore the phenomenon. But their complacency is unjustified. Even if we could reduce the vagueness in our language (as science is often described as striving to do by producing sharper definitions, and as legal processes can accomplish via appeal to precedents), our efforts could not in practice eliminate it entirely. (Russell himself stresses the persistent vagueness in scientific terms, p. 86; and it is clear that the legal process could never reach absolute precision either.) Moreover, in natural language vague predicates are ubiquitous, and this alone motivates study of the phenomenon irrespective of whether there could be usable languages entirely free of vagueness. Even if 'heap' could be replaced by some term 'heap*' with perfectly sharp boundaries and for which no sorites paradox would arise, the paradox facing our actual vague term would remain.[2] And everyday reasoning takes place in vague language, so no account of good ordinary reasoning can ignore vagueness.

[2] See Carnap 1950, chapter 1, Haack 1974, chapter 6 and Quine 1981 on the replacement of vague expressions by precise ones, and see Grim 1982 for some difficulties facing the idea. Certain predicates frequently prompt the response that there *is* in fact a sharp boundary for their strict application, though we use them more loosely – in par-

In the next section I shall discuss the variety of vague expressions – a variety which is not brought out by the general form of arguments for tolerance. First, I clarify the phenomenon by mentioning three things that vagueness in our sense (probably) is not.

(a) The remark 'Someone said something' is naturally described as vague (who said what?). Similarly, '*X* is an integer greater than thirty' is an unhelpfully vague hint about the value of *X*. Vagueness in this sense is underspecificity, a matter of being less than adequately informative for the purposes in hand. This seems to have nothing to do with borderline cases or with the lack of sharp boundaries: 'is an integer greater than thirty' has sharp boundaries, has no borderline cases, and is not susceptible to sorites paradoxes. And it is not because of any possibility of borderline people or borderline cases of saying something that 'someone said something' counts as vague in the alternative sense. I shall ignore the idea of vagueness as underspecificity: in philosophical contexts, 'vague' has come to be reserved for the phenomenon I have described.

(b) Vagueness must not be straightforwardly identified with paradigm context-dependence (i.e. having a different extension in different contexts), even though many terms have both features (e.g. 'tall'). Fix on a context which can be made as definite as you like (in particular, choose a specific comparison class, e.g. current professional American basketball players): 'tall' will remain vague, with borderline cases and fuzzy boundaries, and the sorites paradox will retain its force. This indicates that we are unlikely to understand vagueness or solve the paradox by concentrating on context-dependence.[3]

(c) We can also distinguish vagueness from ambiguity. Certainly, terms can be ambiguous *and* vague: 'bank' for example has two quite different main senses (concerning financial institutions or river edges), both of which are vague. But it is natural to suppose that 'tadpole' has a univocal sense, though that sense does not determine a sharp, well-defined extension. Certain theories, however, do

ticular, strictly no one is bald unless they have absolutely no hair (see e.g. Sperber and Wilson 1986). But even if this line is viable in some cases, it is hopeless for the majority of vague predicates. E.g. should someone count as 'tall' only if they are as tall as possible? How about 'quite tall'? Or 'very hairy'? And where is the strict boundary of 'chair'?

[3] There have, however, been some attempts at this type of solution to the sorites paradox using, for example, more elaborate notions of the context of a subject's judgement (see e.g. Raffman 1994).

attempt to close the gap between vagueness and a form of ambiguity (see chapter 7, §1).

2. TYPE OF VAGUE EXPRESSIONS

So far, I have focused on a single dimension of variation associated with each vague predicate, such as height for 'tall' and number of grains for 'heap'. But many vague predicates are *multi-dimensional*: several different dimensions of variation are involved in determining their applicability. The applicability of 'big', used to describe people, depends on both height and volume; and even whether something counts as a 'heap' depends not only on the number of grains but also on their arrangement. And with 'nice', for example, there is not even a clear-cut set of dimensions determining the applicability of the predicate: it is a vague matter which factors are relevant and the dimensions blend into one another.

The three central features of vague predicates are shared by multi-dimensional ones. There are, for example, borderline nice people: indeed, some are borderline *because* of the multi-dimensionality of 'nice', by scoring well in some relevant respects but not in others. Next consider whether multi-dimensional predicates may lack sharp boundaries. In the one-dimensional case, F has a sharp boundary (or sharp boundaries) if possible candidates for it can be ordered with a point (or points) marking the boundary of F's extension, so that everything that falls on one side of the point (or between the points) is F and nothing else is F. For a multi-dimensional predicate, there may be no uniquely appropriate ordering of possible candidates on which to place putative boundary-marking points. (For instance, there is no definite ordering of people where each is bigger than the previous one; in particular, if ordered by height, volume is ignored, and vice versa.) Rather, for a sharply bounded two-dimensional predicate the candidates would be more perspicuously set out in a two-dimensional space in which a boundary could be drawn, where the two-dimensional region enclosed by the boundary contains all and only instances of the predicate. With a *vague* two-dimensional predicate no such sharp boundary can be drawn. Similarly, for a sharply bounded predicate with a clear-cut set of n dimensions, the boundary would enclose an n-dimensional region containing all of its instances; and vague predicates will lack such a sharp boundary.[4] When there is no clear-cut set of dimensions – for 'nice', for example – this model of boundary-drawing is not so easily applied: it is then not possible to construct a suitable arrangement of candidates on which to try to draw a boundary of the required sort. But this, I claim, is distinctive of the vagueness of such predicates: they have no sharp boundary, but nor do they have a fuzzy boundary in the sense of a rough boundary-area of a representative space. 'Nice' is so vague that it cannot even be associated with a neat array of candidate dimensions, let alone pick out a precise area of such an array.

Finally, multi-dimensional vague predicates are susceptible to sorites paradoxes. We can construct a sorites series for 'heap' by focusing on the number of grains and minimising the difference in the arrangement of grains between consecutive members. And for 'nice' we could take generosity and consider a series of people differing gradually in this respect, starting with a very mean person and ending with a very generous one, where, for example, other features relevant to being nice are kept as constant as possible through the series.

Next, I shall argue that comparatives as well as monadic predicates can be vague. This has been insufficiently recognised and is sometimes denied. Cooper 1995, for example, seeks to give an account of vagueness by explaining how vague monadic predicates depend on comparatives, taking as a starting point the claim that 'classifiers in their grammatically positive form [e.g. "large"] are vague, while comparatives are not' (p. 246). With a precise comparative, 'F-er than', for any pair of things x and y, either x is F-er than y, y is F-er than x, or they are equally F. This will be the case if there is a determinate ordering of candidates for F-ness (allowing ties). For example, there is a one-dimensional ordering of the natural numbers relating to the comparative 'is a smaller number than', and there are no borderline cases of this comparative, which is paradigmatically precise. Since 'is a small number' is a vague predicate, this shows how vague positive forms can have precise comparatives. It may seem that

---

[4] Could there be a single, determinate way of balancing the various dimensions of a multi-dimensional predicate that *does* yield a unique ordering? Perhaps, but this will usually not be the case, and when it is, it may then be appropriate to treat the predicate as one-dimensional, even if the 'dimension' is not a natural one. Further discussion of this point would need a clearer definition of 'dimension', but this is not important for our purposes.

'older than' also gives rise to an ordering according to the single dimension of age, and hence that 'older than' must be precise. But, in fact, there could be borderline instances of the comparative due to indeterminacy over exactly what should count as the instant of someone's birth and so whether it is before or after the birth of someone else. And such instances illustrate that there is *not*, in fact, an unproblematic ordering of *people* for 'older than', even though there is a total ordering of *ages*, on which some people cannot be exactly placed. Similarly, though there is a single dimension of height, people cannot always be exactly placed on it and assigned an exact height. For what exactly should count as the top of one's head? Consequently there may also be borderline instances of 'taller than'.

Comparatives associated with multi-dimensional predicates – for example 'nicer than' and 'more intelligent than' – are typically vague. They have borderline cases: pairs of people about whom there is no fact of the matter about who is nicer/more intelligent, or whether they are equally nice/intelligent. This is particularly common when comparing people who are nice/intelligent in different ways. There are, however, still clear cases of the comparative in addition to borderline cases – it is not that people are *never* comparable in respect to niceness – thus the vague 'nicer than', like 'nice' itself, has clear positive, clear negative and borderline cases.

Can comparatives also lack sharp boundaries? Talk of boundaries, whether sharp or fuzzy, is much less natural for comparatives than for monadic predicates. But we might envisage precise comparatives for which we could systematically set out ordered pairs of things, $\langle x, y \rangle$ and draw a sharp boundary around those for which it is true that x is F-er than y. For example, if F has a single dimension then we could set out pairs in a two-dimensional array, where the x co-ordinate of a pair is determined by the location along the dimension of the first of the pair, and the y co-ordinate by that of the second. The boundary line could then be drawn along the diagonal at $x = y$, where pairs falling beneath the diagonal are definitely true instances of the comparative 'x is F-er than y', and those on or above are definitely false. But for many comparatives, including 'nicer than', there could not be such an arrangement and this gives a sense in which those comparatives lack sharp boundaries.

Another possible sense in which comparatives may lack sharp boundaries is the following. Take the comparative 'redder than' and choose a purplish-red patch of colour, a. Then consider a series of orangeish-red patches, x_i, where x_{i+1} is redder than x_i. It could be definitely true that a is redder than x_0 (which is nearly orange), definitely not true that a is redder than x_{100}, where not only are there borderline cases of 'a is redder than x_i' between them, but there is no point along the series of x_i at which it suddenly stops being the case that a is redder than x_i. So, certain comparatives have borderline cases and exhibit several features akin to the lack of sharp boundaries: they should certainly be classified as vague.

Having discussed vague monadic predicates and vague comparatives, I shall briefly mention some other kinds of vague expressions. First, there can be other vague dyadic relational expressions. For example, 'is a friend of' has pairs that are borderline cases. Adverbs like 'quickly', quantifiers like 'many' and modifiers like 'very' are also vague. And, just as comparatives can be vague, particularly when related to a multi-dimensional positive, so can superlatives. 'Nicest' and 'most intelligent' have vague conditions of application: among a group of people it may be a vague matter, or indeterminate, who is the nicest or the most intelligent. And vague superlatives provide one way in which to construct vague singular terms such as 'the nicest man' or 'the grandest mountain in Scotland', where there is no fact of the matter as to which man or mountain the terms pick out. Terms with plural reference like 'the high mountains of Scotland' can equally be vague.

A theory of vagueness should have the resources to accommodate all the different types of vague expression. And, for example, we should reject an account of vagueness that was obliged to deny the above illustrated features of certain comparatives in order to construct its own account of vague monadic predicates. (See chapter 5, §2 about this constraint in connection with degree theories.) The typical focus on monadic predicates need not be mistaken, however. Perhaps, as Fine suggests, all vagueness is reducible to predicate vagueness (1975, p. 267), though such a claim needs supporting arguments. Alternatively, vagueness might manifest itself in different ways in different kinds of expression, and this could require taking those different expression-types in turn and having different criteria of vagueness for comparatives and monadic predicates. Another possibility is to treat complete sentences as the primary bearers of vagueness, perhaps in their possession of a non-classical truth-value.

This approach would avoid certain tricky questions about whether the vagueness of a particular sentence is 'due to' a given expression. For example, in a case where it is indeterminate exactly what moment *a* was born and whether it was before the birth of *b*, we would avoid the question whether this shows 'older than' to be vague, or whether the indeterminacy should be put down to vagueness in *a* itself. Provided one can still make sense of a typical attribution of vagueness to some element of a sentence in the uncontroversial cases, I suggest that this strategy is an appealing one.

3. VAGUENESS IN THE WORLD?

Is it only linguistic items – words or phrases – that can be vague? Surely not: thoughts and beliefs are among the mental items which share the central characteristics of vagueness; other controversial cases include perceptions. What about the world itself: could the world be vague as well as our descriptions of it? Can there be vague objects? Or vague properties (the ontic correlates of predicates)? Consider Ben Nevis: any sharp spatio-temporal boundaries drawn around the mountain would be arbitrarily placed, and would not reflect a natural boundary. So it may seem that Ben Nevis has fuzzy boundaries, and so, given the common view that a vague object is an object with fuzzy, spatio-temporal boundaries, that it is a vague object. (See e.g. Parsons 1987, Tye 1990 and Zemach 1991 for arguments that there are vague objects.) But there are, of course, other contending descriptions of the situation here. For example, perhaps the only objects we should admit into our ontology are precise/sharp although we fail to pick out a single one of them with our (vague) name 'Ben Nevis'. It would then be at the level of our representations of the world that vagueness came in. (See chapter 7, §1 on an indeterminate reference view.)[5]

My concern is with linguistic vagueness and I shall generally ignore ontic vagueness. This would be a mistake if a theory of linguistic vagueness had to rely on ontic vagueness. But that would be surprising since it seems at least possible to have vague language in a non-vague world. In particular, even if all objects, properties and

---

[5] The most discussed strand of the ontic vagueness debate focuses on Evans's formal argument which aims to establish a negative answer to his question 'Can there be vague objects?' (1978; see Keefe and Smith 1997b, §5 for an overview of the debate).

facts were precise, we would still have reason, for everyday purposes, to use a vague expression such as 'tall', which would still have borderline cases (even if those cases could also be described in non-vague terms involving precise heights etc.). Similarly, in a precise world we would still use vague singular terms, perhaps to pick out various large collections of precise fundamental particulars (e.g. as clouds or mountains) where the boundaries of those collections are left fuzzy. So it seems that language could still be vague if the concrete world were precise.[6]

The theories of vagueness of this book are theories of linguistic vagueness and in the next section I briefly introduce them.

4. THEORIES OF VAGUENESS

The candidate theories of vagueness can be systematically surveyed by considering how they address two central tasks. The first is to identify the logic and semantics for a vague language – a task bound up with providing an account of borderline cases and of fuzzy boundaries. The second task is that of addressing the sorites paradox.

(i) The logic and semantics of vagueness

The simplest approach is to retain classical logic and semantics. Borderline case predications *are* either true or false after all, though we do not and cannot know which. Similarly, despite appearances, vague predicates have well-defined extensions: there is a sharp boundary between the tall people and the rest, and between the red shades of the spectrum and the other colours. As chapter 3 will describe, the *epistemic view* takes this line and accounts for vagueness in terms of our ignorance – for example, ignorance of where the sharp boundaries to our vague predicates lie. And a *pragmatic account* of vagueness also seeks to avoid challenging classical logic and semantics, but this time by accounting for vagueness in terms of pragmatic relations between speakers and their language: see chapter 6.

---

[6] These are only *prima facie* reasons for not approaching linguistic vagueness via ontic vagueness: a tighter case would require clarification of what vagueness in the world would be. They also do not seem to bear on the question whether there can be vague *sets*, which might also be counted as a form of ontic vagueness. Tye, for example, believes that there are vague sets and maintains that they are crucial to his own theory of the linguistic phenomena (see Tye 1990).

If we do not retain classical logic and semantics, we can say instead that when *a* is a borderline case of *F*, the truth-value of '*a* is *F*' is, as Machina puts it, 'in some way peculiar, or indeterminate or lacking entirely' (1976, p. 48). This generates a number of non-classical options.

Note that a borderline case of the predicate *F* is equally a borderline case of not-*F*: it is unclear *whether or not* the candidate is *F*. This symmetry prevents us from simply counting a borderline *F* as not-*F*. But there are several ways of respecting this symmetry. Some take the line that a predication in a borderline case is both true *and* false: there is a truth-value glut. This can be formalised within the context of a paraconsistent logic – a logic that admits true contradictions (see Hyde 1997 and chapter 7, §7 for discussion of that view).

A more popular position is to admit truth-value *gaps*: borderline predications are neither true nor false. One elegant development is *supervaluationism*. The basic idea is that a proposition involving the vague predicate 'tall', for example, is true (false) if it comes out true (false) on all the ways in which we can make 'tall' precise (ways, that is, which preserve the truth-values of uncontentiously true or false cases of '*a* is tall'). A borderline case, 'Tek is tall', will be neither true nor false, for it is true on some ways of making 'tall' precise and false on others. But a classical tautology like 'either Tek is tall or he is not tall' *will* still come out true because wherever a sharp boundary for 'tall' is drawn, that compound sentence will come out true. In this way, the supervaluationist adopts a non-classical *semantics* while aiming to minimise divergence from classical *logic*. A theory of this type will be defended in chapters 7 and 8.

Rather than holding that predications in borderline cases lack a truth-value, another option is to hold that they have a third value – 'neutral', 'indeterminate' or 'indefinite' – leading to a three-valued logic (see chapter 4). Alternatively, *degree theories* countenance degrees of truth, introducing a whole spectrum of truth-values from 0 to 1, with complete falsity as degree 0 and complete truth as degree 1. Borderline cases each take some value between 0 and 1, with '*x* is red' gradually increasing in truth-value as we move along the colour spectrum from orange to red. This calls for an infinite-valued logic or a so-called 'fuzzy logic', and there have been a variety of different versions (see chapter 4).

So far the sketched positions at least agree that there is *some* positive account to be given of the logic and semantics of vagueness. Other writers have taken a more pessimistic line. In particular, Russell claims that logic assumes precision, and since natural language is not precise it cannot be in the province of logic at all (1923, pp. 88–9). If such a 'no logic' thesis requires wholesale rejection of reasoning with vague predicates – and hence of most reasoning in natural language – it is absurdly extreme. And arguments involving vague predicates are clearly not all on a par. For example, 'anyone with less than 500 hairs on his head is bald; Fred has less than 500 hairs on his head; therefore Fred is bald' is an unproblematically good argument (from Cargile 1969, pp. 196–7). And, similarly, there are other ways of arguing with vague predicates that should certainly be rejected. Some account is needed of inferences that are acceptable and others that fail, and to search for systematic principles capturing this is to seek elements of a logic of vague language. So, I take the pessimism of the no-logic approach to be a very last resort, and in this book I concentrate on more positive approaches.

Focusing on the question how borderline case predication should be classified, we seem to have exhausted the possibilities. They may be true or false, or have no truth value at all (in particular, being neither true nor false), or be both true and false, or have a non-classical value from some range of values. When it comes to surveying solutions to the sorites paradox, however, there may additionally be alternatives that do not provide a theory of vagueness and perhaps do not answer the question how borderline cases are to be classified. I concentrate on those which do fit into a theory of vagueness.

(ii) *The sorites paradox*

A paradigm sorites set-up for the predicate F is a sequence of objects x_i, such that the two premises

(1) Fx_1
(2) For all i, if Fx_i then Fx_{i+1}

both appear true, but, for some suitably large n, the putative conclusion

(3) Fx_n

seems false. For example, in the case of 'tall', the x_i might be the series of men described earlier, each a hundredth of an inch shorter than the previous one and where x_1 is seven feet tall. (1) 'x_1 is tall' is then true; and so, it seems, is the inductive premise, (2) 'for all i, if x_i is tall, so is x_{i+1}'. But it is surely false that (3) x_{3000} – who is only 4 feet 6 inches – is tall.

A second form of sorites paradox can be constructed when, instead of the quantified inductive premise (2), we start with a collection of particular conditional premises, (2C$_i$), each of the form 'if Fx_i then Fx_{i+1}'. For example,

(2C$_1$) if x_1 is tall, so is x_2
(2C$_2$) if x_2 is tall, so is x_3

and so on. And the use of conditionals is not essential: we can take a sequence of premises of the form $\neg(Fx_i \ \& \ \neg Fx_{i+1})$ – a formulation that goes back at least to Diogenes Laertius (see Long and Sedley 1987, p. 222). Alternatively, (2) could be replaced by a quantification over the negated conjunctions of that form.

As well as needing to solve the paradox, we must assess that general form of argument because it is used both in philosophical arguments outside the discussion of vagueness (e.g. with the story of the ship of Theseus) and in various more everyday debates (the slippery slope arguments mentioned in §1).[7]

Responses to a sorites paradox can be divided into four types. We can:

(a) deny the validity of the argument, refusing to grant that the conclusion follows from the given premises; or

(b) question the strict truth of the general inductive premise (2) or of at least one of the conditionals (2C$_i$); or

(c) accept the validity of the argument and the truth of its inductive premise (or of all the conditional premises) but contest the supposed truth of premise (1) or the supposed falsity of the conclusion (3); or

(d) grant that there are compelling reasons both to take the

---

[7] As a further example of the former, consider Kirk 1986 (pp. 217ff). Regarding Quine's thesis about the indeterminacy of translation, Kirk uses an argument with the form of the quantificational version of the paradox to argue that there can be no indeterminacy of translation because, first, there would be no indeterminacy in translating between the languages of infants each of whom is at an early stage of language-acquisition and, second, if there is no indeterminacy at one step of acquisition then there is none at the next. He presents his argument as using mathematical induction but does not ask whether its employment of vague predicates casts doubt on that mode of argument.

argument form as valid, and to accept the premises and deny the conclusion, concluding that this demonstrates the incoherence of the predicate in question.

I shall briefly survey these in turn, ignoring here the question whether we should expect a uniform solution to all sorites paradoxes whatever their form and whatever predicate is involved. (Wright 1987 argues that different responses could be required depending on the reasons that support the inductive premise.) Any response must explain away apparent difficulties with accepting the selected solution; for example, if the main premise is denied, it must be explained why that premise is so plausible. More generally, a theory should account for the persuasiveness of the paradox as a paradox and should explain how this is compatible with the fact that we are never, or very rarely, actually led into contradiction.

(a) Denying the validity of the sorites argument seems to require giving up absolutely fundamental rules of inference. This can be seen most clearly when the argument takes the second form involving a series of conditionals, the $(2C_i)$. The only rule of inference needed for this argument is modus ponens. Dummett argues that this rule cannot be given up, as it is constitutive of the meaning of 'if' that modus ponens is valid (1975, p. 306). To derive the conclusion in the first form of sorites, we only need universal instantiation in addition to modus ponens; but, as Dummett again argues, universal instantiation seems too central to the meaning of 'all' to be reasonably challenged (1975, p. 306). I agree on both points and shall not pursue the matter further here.

There is, however, a different way of rejecting the validity of the many-conditionals form of the sorites. It might be suggested that even though each step is acceptable on its own, chaining too many steps does not guarantee the preservation of truth if what counts as preserving truth is itself a vague matter. (And then the first form of sorites could perhaps be rejected on the grounds that it is in effect short hand for a multi-conditional argument.) As Dummett again notes, this is to deny the transitivity of validity, which would be another drastic move, given that chaining inferences is normally taken to be essential to the very enterprise of proof.[8]

---

[8] But see Parikh 1983. In my chapter 4, §7 the possibility is briefly entertained.

Rather than questioning particular inference rules or the ways they can be combined, Russell's global rejection of logic for vague natural language leads him to dismiss 'the old puzzle about the man who went bald', simply on the grounds that 'bald' is vague (1923, p. 85). The sorites arguments, on his view, cannot be valid because, containing vague expressions, they are just not the kind of thing that can be valid or invalid.

(b) If we take a formulation of the paradox that uses negated conjunctions (or assume that 'if' is captured by the material conditional), then within a classical framework denying the quantified inductive premise or one of its instances commits us to there being an i such that 'Fx_i and not-Fx_{i+1}' is true. This implies the existence of sharp boundaries and the epistemic theorist, who takes this line, will explain why vague predicates appear not to draw sharp boundaries by reference to our ignorance (see chapter 3).

In a non-classical framework there is a wide variety of ways of developing option (b), and it is not clear or uncontroversial which of these entail a commitment to sharp boundaries. For example, the supervaluationist holds that the generalised premise (2) 'for all i, if Fx_i then Fx_{i+1}' is false: for each $F^\star$ which constitutes a way of making F precise, there will be *some* x_i or other which is the last $F^\star$ and is followed by an x_{i+1} which is not-$F^\star$. But since there is no particular i for which 'Fx_i and not-Fx_{i+1}' is true – i.e. true however F is made precise – supervaluationists claim that their denial of (2) does not mean accepting that F is sharply bounded (see chapter 7). And other non-classical frameworks may allow that (2) is not true, while not accepting that it is *false*. Tye 1994, for example, maintains that the inductive premise and its negation both take his intermediate truth-value, 'indefinite'.

Degree theorists offer another non-classical version of option (b): they can deny that the premises are strictly true while maintaining that they are *nearly* true. The essence of their account is to hold that the predications Fx_i take degrees of truth that encompass a gradually decreasing series from complete truth (degree 1) to complete falsity (degree 0). There is never a substantial drop in degree of truth between consecutive Fx_i; so, given a natural interpretation of the conditional, the particular premises 'if Fx_i then Fx_{i+1}' can each come out at least very nearly true, though some are not completely true. If the sorites argument based on many conditionals is to count as strictly valid, then an account of validity is needed that allows a valid argument to have nearly true premises but a false conclusion. But with some degree-theoretic accounts of validity, the sorites fails to be valid – thus a degree theorist can combine responses (a) and (b) (see chapter 4, §7).

Intuitionistic logic opens up the possibility of another non-classical position that can respond to the sorites by denying the inductive premise (2), while not accepting the classical equivalent of this denial, $(\exists x_i)(Fx_i \ \& \ \neg Fx_{i+1})$, which is the unwanted assertion of sharp boundaries. Putnam 1983 suggests this strategy. But critics have shown that with various reasonable additional assumptions, other versions of sorites arguments still lead to paradox. In particular, if, as might be expected, you adopt intuitionistic semantics as well as intuitionistic logic, paradoxes recur (see Read and Wright 1985). And Williamson 1996 shows that combining Putnam's approach to vagueness with his epistemological conception of truth still faces paradox. (See also Chambers 1998, who argues that, given Putnam's own view on what would make for vagueness, paradox again emerges.) The bulk of the criticisms point to the conclusion that there is no sustainable account of vagueness that emerges from rejecting classical logic in favour of intuitionistic logic.

(c) Take the sorites (H+) with the premises 'one grain of sand is not a heap' and 'adding a single grain to a non-heap will not turn it into a heap'. If we accept these premises and the validity of the argument, it follows that we will never get a heap, no matter how many grains are piled up: so there are no heaps. Similarly, sorites paradoxes for 'bald', 'tall' and 'person' could be taken to show that there are no bald people, no tall people and indeed no people at all. Unger bites the bullet and takes this nihilistic line, summarised in the title of one of his papers: 'There are no ordinary things' (Unger 1979; see also Wheeler 1975, 1979 and Heller 1988).

The thesis, put in linguistic terms, is that all vague predicates lack serious application, i.e. they apply either to nothing ('is a heap') or to everything ('is not a heap'). Classical logic can be retained in its entirety, but sharp boundaries are avoided by denying that vague predicates succeed in drawing *any* boundaries, fuzzy or otherwise. There will be no borderline cases: for any vague F, everything is F or everything is not-F, and thus nothing is borderline F.[9]

---

[9] See Williamson 1994, chapter 6, for a sustained attack on various forms of nihilism. For example, he shows how the nihilist cannot state or argue for his own position on

The response of accepting the conclusion of every sorites paradox cannot be consistently sustained. For in addition to (H+), there is the argument (H−) with the premises 'ten thousand grains make a heap' and 'removing one grain from a heap still leaves a heap', leading to the conclusion that a single grain of sand is a heap, which is incompatible with the conclusion of (H+). Such reversibility is typical; given a sorites series of items, the argument can be run either way through them. Unger's response to (H−) would be to deny the initial premise: there are no heaps − as (H+) supposedly shows us − so it is not true that ten thousand grains make a heap. Systematic grounds would then be needed to enable us to decide which of a pair of sorites paradoxes is sound (e.g. why there are no heaps rather than everything being a heap).

Unger is driven to such an extreme position by the strength of the arguments in support of the inductive premises of sorites paradoxes. If our words determined sharp boundaries, Unger claims, our understanding of them would be a miracle of conceptual comprehension (1979, p. 126). The inductive premise, guaranteeing this lack of sharp boundaries, reflects a semantic rule central to the meaning of the vague *F*. But, we should ask Unger, can the tolerance principle expressed in the inductive premise for 'tall' really be more certain than the truth of the simple predication of 'tall' to a seven-foot man? Is it plausible to suppose that the expression 'tall' is meaningful and consistent but that there could not be anything tall, when learning the term typically involves ostension and hence confrontation with alleged examples? A different miracle of conceptual comprehension would be needed then to explain how we can understand that meaning and, in general, how we can use such empty predicates successfully to communicate anything at all. It may be more plausible to suppose that if there are any rules governing the application of 'tall', then, in addition to tolerance rules, there are ones dictating that 'tall' applies to various paradigmatic cases and does not apply to various paradigmatically short people. Sorites paradoxes could then demonstrate the inconsistency of such a set of rules, and this is option (d).

Responses (c) and (d) are not always clearly distinguished. Writers

his own terms (e.g. the expressions he tries to use must count as incoherent). My discussion of methodological matters in chapter 2 will suggest that a swifter rejection of the position is warranted anyway.

like Unger are primarily concerned with drawing ontological conclusions. It is enough for them to emphasise the tolerance of a predicate like 'tall' which already guarantees, they claim, that the world contains nothing that strictly answers to that description: they are not so concerned to examine what further rules might govern the predicate and perhaps render it incoherent. But other writers, for example Dummett, explore these conceptual questions.

(d) Having argued in detail against alternative responses to the paradox, Dummett 1975 maintains that there is no choice but to accept that a sorites paradox for F exemplifies an undeniably valid form of argument from what the semantic rules for F dictate to be true premises to what they dictate to be a false conclusion. The paradoxes thus reveal the incoherence of the rules governing vague terms: by simply following those rules, speakers could be led to contradict themselves. This inconsistency means that there can be no coherent logic governing vague language.[10]

Once (d)-theorists have concluded that vague predicates are incoherent, they may agree with Russell that such predicates cannot appear in valid arguments. So option (d) can be developed in such a way that makes it compatible with option (a), though this route to the denial of validity is very different from Russell's. (Being outside the scope of logic need not make for incoherence.)

The acceptance of such pervasive inconsistency is highly undesirable and such pessimism is premature; and it is even by Dummett's own lights a pessimistic response to the paradox, adopted as a last resort rather than as a positive treatment of the paradox that stands as competitor to any other promising alternatives. Communication using vague language is overwhelmingly successful and we are never in practice driven to incoherence (a point stressed by Wright, e.g. 1987, p. 236). And even when shown the sorites paradox, we are rarely inclined to revise our initial judgement of the last member of the series. It looks unlikely that the success and coherence in our practice is owed to our grasp of inconsistent rules. A defence of some version of option (a) or (b) would provide an attractive way of

---

[10] See also Rolf 1981, 1984. Horgan 1994, 1998 advocates a different type of the inconsistency view. He agrees that sorites paradoxes (and other related arguments) demonstrate logical incoherence, but considers that incoherence to be *tempered* or *insulated*, so that it does not infect the whole language and allows us to use the language successfully despite the incoherence (see chapter 8, §2).

escaping the charge of inconsistency and avoiding the extreme, pessimistic strategies of options (c) and (d).

Rather like the liar paradox ('this sentence is false'), where supposed solutions are often undermined by the more resilient 'strengthened liar paradox' (e.g. 'this sentence is false or X' when the response to the original liar is to call it X), a solution to the original sorites paradox can leave untackled other persistent forms of the sorites, or other arguments of a very similar nature. First, consider the phenomenon of higher-order vagueness noted in §1: not only are there no sharp boundaries between the tall and the not-tall, there are no sharp boundaries between the tall and the borderline tall either (see §6). Like the former lack of sharp boundaries, the latter can also be reflected in a sorites premise, e.g. 'growing one thousandth of an inch cannot turn a borderline tall person into a tall one'. Such higher-order paradoxes must also be addressed.

There are also related metalinguistic paradoxes which threaten any theory of vagueness that introduces extra categories for borderline cases assuming they can thereby classify every predication of a given vague predicate in some way or other. In particular, Sainsbury's 'transition question' (1992) and Horgan's 'forced march sorites paradox' (1994) raise similar issues, both emphasising the need to avoid commitment to a sharp boundary between any two types of semantic classification. Horgan instructs us to take, in turn, successive pairs of a sorites series (x_1 and x_2, x_2 and x_3 etc.) and report whether they have the same semantic status. If the answer is 'no' for some particular pair then a sharp boundary is drawn between them, contrary to the vague nature of the predicate, but if the answer is always 'yes', all cases will be absurdly classified the same (e.g. the four-foot man will count as tall). And, as Horgan stresses, if a theory commits us to assigning some semantic category to every predication in turn then, assuming they are not all classified the same way, the theory will be stuck on the first horn of his dilemma and committed to sharp boundaries. This emphasises how theorists need to avoid solutions to the original sorites which are still committed to sharp boundaries between semantic categories.

To finish this section I shall briefly mention that there are approaches to the sorites paradox that, I claim, fail to tackle the primary issues those paradoxes raise. These discussions of the paradox do not slot conveniently into my classification of possible responses, or at least they are not presented as so doing. Unlike most the solutions I have been outlining in (a) to (d), these treatments are not situated in the context of a theory of vagueness more generally. Some, I suggest, may be better seen as tackling a somewhat different issue. For example, sometimes the approach seems to be more of a psychological study of how we respond to successive members of a sorites series and of how our classificatory mechanisms might work such as to prevent us from applying the predicate right through the series. Stories of these kinds do not settle the normative issues of how we *should* classify using vague predicates, what truth-values the problem ascriptions take and what logic governs the language, the very issues I have identified as central to the project in question.[11]

5. THE 'DEFINITELY' OPERATOR

When we construct an account of vagueness, in addition to considering the truth-values of borderline predications, we may seek to *express* the fact that a given predication is or is not of borderline status. Informally, our statement of the fact has relied on semantic ascent – e.g. talking about truth-values of predications. But we may hope to express it without that device. To do so we can introduce into the object language the sentence operators D and I such that Dp holds when p is determinately or definitely true, and Ip (equivalent to $\neg Dp$ & $\neg D\neg p$) holds when p is indeterminate or borderline. (The terms 'determinately' and 'definitely' are both used in the literature, but

---

[11] Though I will not argue it here, I consider the treatment in, for example, Raffman 1994 to be of the described type. Among other non-solutions are discussions which give some remedy through which we can avoid actually being driven to paradox (as if it wasn't already clear how this could be done). For example, Shapiro 1998 distinguishes serial processes from parallel ones and attributes the paradox to the use of a serial process that assigns values to predications on the basis of the assignment to the previous member of the ordered sorites series. Such a procedure is wrong because it yields absurd results, Shapiro argues, but he gives no indication of why it is plausible nonetheless (and reliable in other contexts), or what the consequences are regarding sharp boundaries. Moreover, in treating something like the inductive premise of the sorites as an instruction for applying the predicate given certain other members of its extension, Shapiro appears to ignore the fact that it can be treated as a plausible generalisation about the members of the series. On this typical interpretation the paradox persists in abstraction from contexts of running through the sorites sequence via some chosen procedure.

marking no agreed distinction.[12]) This is comparable to the introduction of the sentence operators $\Box$ and $\Diamond$ in modal logics: these
operators allow an object-language reflection of the meta-linguistic
device employed when we report on whether a sentence is possibly
or necessarily true. And just as $\Box$ and $\Diamond$ can be straightforwardly
iterated to express, for example, that necessarily possibly p, the D and
I operators can be iterated, where this iteration could perhaps be
employed to express higher-order vagueness. For, just as we want to
admit borderline cases of F, where $\neg DFx$ & $\neg D\neg Fx$, we may want to
allow borderline cases of 'definitely F', where we will have $\neg DDFx$
& $\neg D\neg DFx$. So one motivation for introducing the D operator is for
the treatment of higher-order vagueness, the issue to which I turn in
§6.

We may hold that no sentence can be true without being
determinately true. For how can a be F without being determinately
F? Dp and p will then be true in exactly the same situations. But the
operator is not thereby redundant: for example, $\neg Dp$ will be true in a
borderline case, when $\neg p$ is indeterminate. When there is some
deviation from classical logic and semantics, the fact that p and Dp
coincide in the way described does not guarantee that they are
equivalent in the embedded contexts generated by negating them.
(According to the epistemic view, which allows no deviation from
classical logic, p *can* be true without Dp being true, namely when p is
borderline and not known to be true. For the D operator must, on
that account, be an epistemic operator.)

The degree theorist can say that Dp is true if p true to degree 1
and is false if p is true to any lesser degree. A supervaluationist, on the
other hand, will say that Dp is true just in case p is true on all ways of
making it precise and is false otherwise (so if p is borderline, p itself
will be neither true nor false, but Dp will be false). Ways of making
the whole language precise each yield a model of the language, and
definite truth, as truth on all models, may be expected to share
structural and logical features with *necessary* truth construed as truth in
all worlds.[13] Alternatively the D operator could perhaps be taken as

---

[12] Some authors use Δ and ∇ in place of D and I, others use *Def* or *Det* for D; and some
chose an operator for 'definite *whether*' (i.e. $Dp \lor D\neg p$ in my terms).

[13] See chapter 8, §3. Note that it is not only on the supervaluationist scheme that the
comparison with modal logics is appropriate. Williamson, for example, explains its
applicability within an epistemic view of vagueness (see especially his 1999).

primitive, in the sense that there is no account of it that is derivative from other resources used in a theory of vagueness.

Wright claims that 'when dealing with vague expressions, it is essential to have the expressive resources afforded by an operator expressing *definiteness* or *determinacy*' (1987, p. 262). I take this to imply that we will fail to fulfil the central tasks of a theory of vagueness unless we introduce the D operator. It is only when we have that operator that we can state that borderline cases occupy a gap between definite truth and definite falsity without committing ourselves to a gap between truth and falsity (Wright 1995, p. 142). And, Wright also maintains, we need to use the D operator to say what it is for a predicate to lack sharp boundaries. Consider a series of objects x_i forming a suitable sorites series for F (e.g. our line of men of decreasing heights for 'tall'). Wright proposes (1987, p. 262)

(W) F is not sharply bounded when there is no i for which DFx_i & $D\neg Fx_{i+1}$.

This can be contrasted with the suggestion that a predicate lacks sharp boundaries when there is no i such that Fx_i & $\neg Fx_{i+1}$. This latter condition gives rise to paradox; but lacking sharp boundaries in the sense of (W) does *not* lead straight to paradox. In particular, suppose that there are some indefinitely F cases between the definitely F cases and the definitely not-F cases. Then, as (W) requires, there will be no immediate leap from DFx_i to $D\neg Fx_{i+1}$ (see also Campbell 1974 and my chapter 7, §5).

Suppose someone were to take Wright's claim about the importance of D to show that a theory of vagueness should proceed by introducing a primitive D operator and focusing on its logic and semantics. They would, I argue, be pursuing the wrong approach. Having a primitive D operator will not enable us to fulfil the tasks facing a theory of vagueness. In particular, replacing statements naturally used to express our intuitions about borderline cases and the lack of sharp boundaries with *different* (but similar) statements involving the D operator does not provide an excuse to ignore the very questions that are, and should be, at the centre of the debate, namely ones about the original intuitions.

For example, suppose the claim is that we are confusing the standard premise with something else which does not lead to paradox, namely the claim that there is no successive pair in the series of which the first is definitely *F* and the second is definitely not-*F*. We need still to ask how we should classify the original premise itself. If we say that premise is true, as it seems to be, the paradox remains untouched. But can we be content to call it false and hence accept that there is a last patch of a sorites series that is red and an adjacent pair in the series of which one is *F* and the other is not-*F*? Wright suggests that the inductive premises of some (but not all) sorites paradoxes may be of indeterminate status (1987, p. 267). But how are we to understand this claim? At the least it seems to imply that attaching a 'definitely' operator to the front of the premise-statement would result in a statement that was not true. But what should we say when we do *not* attach that operator? If regarding that premise as having indeterminate status is to be taken as ascribing it a non-classical truth-value (or just not ascribing a classical value), then a non-classical logic and semantics of vagueness needs to be provided to fill out the picture. But then surely providing such a system should be the central task, rather than concentrating on the logic and semantics of the *D* operator, which would then be an optional extra. Similarly for the claim that our intuition that a borderline predication is neither true nor false should be accounted for by the fact that it is actually neither *definitely* true nor *definitely* false. For are we then to say that it *is* either true or false, and if so, how are we to avoid the unwanted consequences of bivalence? And if, instead, it is said to be of indeterminate status, again we will need a logic that can accommodate such a non-classical truth-value status.[14]

In summary, how can it help to add a *D* operator to the language – creating new sentences that may be shown to be unproblematically true or false – when the task is to illuminate the semantics of the old statements which do not contain this operator? Using a *D* operator may allow us to say that it is not definitely the case that *a* is red, but how can this illuminate the semantics of the vague '*a* is red' itself?

It might be suggested that even if introducing the *D* operator does not provide the *key* to a theory of vagueness, such a theory must at least accommodate and give a plausible semantics for the operator.

---

[14] Could there be a coherent theory that retains bivalence but still maintains that some sentences are of indeterminate status? This would imply that there could be sentences that were both true and indeterminate, which goes against the earlier assumption that no sentence can be true without being determinately true. Williamson 1995 argues that such a theory is not possible unless the indeterminacy is taken to be epistemic.

For, in describing the semantics of our language we should acknowledge that expressions such as 'borderline' and 'definitely' are part of it. Moreover, the D operator enables us to make assertions about candidates for F-ness (e.g. borderline cases) as assertions about the things themselves, whereas without the operator we are strangely limited to judgements about the *language* if we are to say anything like what we want to say. But though I agree that there is a pre-theoretic notion of 'definitely', we should be wary of constructing an account of D via one's theory and assuming that it corresponds exactly to a pre-theoretic notion (even if the theory appropriately captures vague language without that operator). The ordinary use and apprehension of 'definitely' may well not straightforwardly conform to the kind of formal theory of the D operator that theorists seek. Intuitions about the operator may be inconsistent (just like those leading to sorites paradoxes). And, anyway, the consequences of the theory of D will outstrip the consequences we would expect given only our intuitions about 'definitely'. We should beware unargued theoretical assumptions that, for example, D can be used to capture the vagueness of *any* expression, including 'D' itself.[15]

It is thus reasonable, and perhaps necessary, to give 'definitely' a technical sense that depends on and is dictated by the theory of vagueness offered for the D-free part of language. And the theory may dictate that there is some departure from uniformity between the treatment of sentences with the operator and that of those without. For example, according to supervaluationism, though the logic of the D-free language is classical, the logical behaviour of the D operator has to be non-classical (see chapter 7, §4). So, although an account of the D operator may provide further details of a theory of vagueness, it forms the second and less central stage of such a theory. My prime concern is with the first stage: discussion of the second stage needs to be built on my account of the logic and semantics of D-free language.

I now turn to higher-order vagueness, in relation to which the D operator remains highly relevant.

---

[15] Wright offers principles governing the D operator, but these are insufficiently defended and are disputed in Sainsbury 1991, Edgington 1993, and Heck 1993. Evans's celebrated argument concerning indeterminate identity uses a determinately operator (frequently taken to be 'determinate whether') and again employs unjustified assumptions about its logic (1978).

6. HIGHER-ORDER VAGUENESS

Imagine – if we can – a predicate G that has a sharply bounded set of clear positive cases, a sharply bounded set of clear negative cases, and a sharply bounded set of cases falling in between. Although G is stipulated to have borderline cases in the sense of instances which are neither clearly G nor clearly not-G, it still has sharp boundaries – one between the Gs and the borderline cases and another between the borderline cases and the not-Gs. Our ordinary vague predicates such as 'tall', 'red' and 'chair' surely do not yield a three-fold sharp classification of this sort, with two sharp boundaries around the borderline cases. The familiar arguments that there is no sharp boundary between the positive and negative extensions of 'tall' would equally count against any suggestion that there is a sharp boundary between the positive extension and the borderline cases (consider the typical arguments for tolerance discussed in Wright 1976). For example, one hundredth of an inch should not make the difference as to whether someone counts as borderline tall. And a sharp boundary to the borderline cases of F would mean that there could be two things that are indiscriminable by those who use that word but yet that differ over whether F applies. More generally, just as the meaning of a vague predicate does not determine a sharp boundary between the positive and negative extensions, nor does it determine sharp boundaries to the borderline cases or other sharp boundaries. (On the epistemic view the requirement would need to be formulated differently, but parallel issues arise; see chapter 3, §1.) With the D operator, the lack of sharp boundaries to the borderline cases of F can be expressed as the lack of abrupt transition between the DFx cases and the $\neg DFx$ cases (and between the $D\neg Fx$ cases and the $\neg D\neg Fx$ cases), or the lack of a last x in a sorites series for which DFx is true (and the lack of a first x in a sorites series for which $D\neg Fx$ is true).

It is widely recognised in the literature from Russell onwards (1923, p. 87) that the borderline cases of a vague predicate are not sharply bounded. There is disagreement over whether or not a predicate with sharply bounded borderline cases should count as vague (for example, Sainsbury suggests not, 1991, p. 173, in contrast with Fine, 1975, p. 266). But however that question is settled, our ordinary vague predicates typically have borderline cases that are not sharply bounded, so that phenomenon needs to be examined.

31

Closely related to the lack of sharp boundaries to the borderline cases is the phenomenon of having possible borderline borderline cases (also known as second-order borderline cases), where borderline borderline cases of F are values of x for which 'Fx is borderline' is itself borderline. Suppose we accept that the borderline cases of H are not sharply bounded. We can infer that H has possible second-order borderline cases given a widely held assumption:

> (A_1) The lack of sharp boundaries between the Fs and the Gs shows that there are possible values of x for which 'x is borderline F' and 'x is borderline G' both hold.

For the lack of a sharp boundary between the definite Hs and the borderline Hs will then imply that there are possible cases between them which are borderline borderline cases of H as well as borderline cases of 'definitely H'. (And there will be a second variety of possible borderline borderline cases arising from the lack of a sharp boundary between the borderline cases and the definitely false predications.)

This argument for second-order borderline cases looks as though it should now iterate: if H is to be genuinely vague there should be no sharp boundaries to the borderline borderline Hs either, and this, in turn, will yield possible borderline borderline borderline Hs; and so on. If there is no order of borderline case which we are willing to acknowledge as having sharp boundaries, the iteration will continue indefinitely, resulting in an unlimited hierarchy of possible borderline cases of different orders; we can call this unlimited higher-order vagueness.

The term 'higher-order vagueness' has been used for several phenomena which we may wish to keep apart. In particular, sometimes it amounts to having borderline cases of any order above the first; sometimes the term is used to refer to the lack of sharp boundaries to the borderline cases; and occasionally it is used to mean the same as my 'unlimited higher-order vagueness'. When it is not important to make these distinctions, I shall use 'higher-order vagueness' for this cluster of phenomena, though elsewhere it will be preferable to use descriptions without this potential ambiguity (such as 'the lack of sharp boundaries to the borderline cases').[16]

---

[16] Williamson 1999 defends a different characterisation of the hierarchy of orders of vagueness such that there can be third-order vagueness in his sense without third-order borderline cases in the above sense. The dispute does not matter for our current

Another argument for unlimited higher-order vagueness can be constructed as follows. When F is vague, typically the predicate 'is a borderline case of F' is also vague. Given the assumption that if a predicate is vague, then it has possible borderline cases – call it (A_2) – it follows from the vagueness of H that there are possible borderline borderline cases of H, since the borderline cases of 'is borderline H' are themselves borderline borderline cases of H. And accepting 'if F is vague then "is a borderline F" is also vague' would guarantee that if a predicate is vague at all, it has possible borderline cases of all orders. Moreover, since the first-order borderline cases of one predicate coincide exactly with the second-order borderline cases of another, this suggests another (plausible) requirement, namely that higher-order borderline cases be given the same treatment as first-order ones: there should be consistency and uniformity in the treatment of different orders of vagueness.

Should we accept the commitment to an unlimited hierarchy of orders of borderline case associated with each of our typical everyday predicates?[17] It might be thought an extravagant and unrealistic commitment. Moreover, the hierarchy of borderline cases may still fail to capture the complete lack of sharp boundaries for F if there is a sharp boundary between those cases which are borderline cases of some order and those that are, as we might say, absolutely definitely F. (See e.g. Sainsbury 1990, p. 11.) And, relatedly, the hierarchy will be of limited benefit if it is such as to pin every candidate for being F into exactly one of the orders of borderline case, since again this seems to impose a determinacy where there is none.

(A_1) and (A_2), the principles used above in generating the hierarchy, both reflect the common emphasis on borderline cases, which seems reasonable at the first level, but may be less compelling once they are seen to draw us into the hierarchy. (A_2) amounts to the standard criterion of vagueness in terms of borderline cases (a criterion

purposes. Also relevant to a detailed discussion of the various related phenomena would be Williamson's argument that if F is second-order vague, it must be vague at all orders.

17 Burgess argues against unlimited higher-order vagueness, maintaining that higher-order vagueness terminates at a 'rather low finite level' (1990, p. 431), at least for secondary-quality predicates. He does this via a proposed analysis of one of the relevant notions, each of the elements of which, he argues, is only vague to a finite level. The strength of his arguments must rest in their detail – for instance they must avoid the objection that precision is simply assumed at some key stage of the account (see Williamson 1994, p. 296).

that can be found in Peirce 1902). It is particularly amenable to an iterative structure. To test whether a predicate F is vague, ask whether it has borderline cases. If so, this yields a set of cases (those borderline cases) and with regard to them we can apply the same test and ask whether they too have borderline cases (which, if so, will give second-order borderline cases of F). And so on through the progressive sets of higher-order borderline cases. An alternative criterion that takes vague predicates to be those lacking sharp boundaries would not have the same scope for the generation of a hierarchy of levels. (Testing whether the borderline cases themselves have borderline cases is no longer iterating the test for vagueness at the first level with this new criterion.) For the fact that there are no sharp boundaries to the positive extension is not a feature susceptible to iteration, just as precision, interpreted as the existence of a sharp boundary, leaves no scope for a notion of higher-order precision. Sainsbury 1990, claiming that there is no such thing as an unsharp boundary, identifies the defining feature of vagueness as 'boundary-lessness'. He argues that recognising the feature of boundarylessness is essential for a genuine understanding of vagueness and an account of its semantics. At the very least, we should say that it is more important to capture the lack of sharp boundaries to the borderline cases than to focus on the hierarchy of borderline cases, and this may mean not taking borderline cases as the centre of the debate.

A key issue here concerns vagueness in the metalanguage – the language in which we frame our theory and report the borderline status of some predications. If the metalanguage contains the object-language, so that sentences of the object-language are also sentences of the metalanguage, then the metalanguage will be vague given that the object-language is vague. The interesting issues concern whether the proper part of the metalanguage which is not also part of the object-language is also vague. This part will contain all truth-value predicates, plus expressions for the consequence relation etc. Or if the metalanguage is the same language as the object-language, then we can still ask about the cited elements of the language (they are still called upon to talk *about* the language). If these elements were all precise, then the (precise) metalinguistic predicate applicable to all and only those sentences of borderline case status would pick out a sharply bounded set of cases. But this would guarantee that, for all F, the borderline cases of F themselves had sharp boundaries. So accommodating the lack of such sharp boundaries requires a vague metalanguage. And the existence of higher-order borderline cases would impose the same requirement. For if x is a borderline borderline case of F, the metalinguistic report that Fx is borderline will itself be of borderline status, so the metalinguistic predicate it uses must have borderline cases. Whether and how to accommodate vague metalanguages is a question for any theory of vagueness, and the need for a vague metalanguage is emphasised in Sainsbury 1990, Tye 1990 and Williamson 1994. And Horgan's forced march paradox described in §4 bears on this issue, for with a non-vague metalanguage we can assume that some semantic status or other will be assigned to each object-language sentence, and, as Horgan argues, this will mean sharp boundaries along the relevant series.

There are difficulties, however, facing the idea of vague metalanguages. In chapter 4, §9 I shall argue that certain theories cannot be consistently defended on the supposition that their metalanguages are vague. But even if the metalanguage for some theory could be vague, the following question arises: can we can succeed in illuminating the vagueness of our language if we need to draw on a metalanguage that itself exhibits vagueness? There is at least a suspicion of circularity or triviality here, which has been alluded to in the literature. And Fine suggests that in constructing and assessing theories of vagueness, we might 'require that the meta-language not be vague, or, at least, not so vague in its proper part as the object-language' (1975, p. 297). This tension between needing and resisting vague metalanguages will be explored in later chapters in the context of specific theories.

If we approach higher-order vagueness by using the D operator within the object language, can we ignore the vagueness or otherwise of the metalanguage? I think not. With the statement (BB) $\neg DDp$ & $\neg DIp$, we may be able to express the fact that p is a second-order borderline case that is not definitely definitely true and not definitely borderline. And (BB) can be unproblematically assigned the value 'true' in a non-vague metalanguage. But when we come to assign truth-values to *all* statements of the object language, we will *still* be required to assess the truth-value of p itself. Being a second-order borderline case, p is appropriately called neither 'true' nor 'borderline', so even if the metalanguage has an expression for borderline status, that will not be enough unless that expression is itself vague. So a precise metalanguage cannot capture the truth-value status of a second-order borderline case, and it is not to the point to note that by using D and I we can still express the fact that p is a second-order borderline case.

In summary, I maintain that any putative theory of vagueness must accommodate the apparent lack of sharp boundaries to the borderline cases, and address the issue of higher-order vagueness. And, relatedly, it must answer the question whether the metalanguage for the theory is vague, while tackling the difficulties facing the chosen answer.

2

How to theorise about vagueness

In this chapter I shall examine in more detail the project of constructing a theory of vagueness. The apparent simplicity of its central question, 'what are the logic and semantics of a vague language?', masks considerable unclarity in the nature of the project and what would count as success. I shall discuss matters of methodology, the aims and constraints of the project and the standards by which we should judge candidate theories. And in §3 I shall investigate an important distinction between two attitudes to elements of a theory.

I. ESTABLISHING A REFLECTIVE EQUILIBRIUM

A theory of vagueness deals with the semantic structure of vague languages and the logical relations that hold between their sentences. It must specify the range of truth-values, or any alternative truth-value status, that a sentence can have. And it should capture the distribution of them among borderline cases, in particular through a sorites series. But, as we saw in chapter 1, §4, it may not be theoretically possible to assign some determinate truth-value status to each member of the series in turn – for that would commit us to sharp boundaries between any two semantic categories. The best description of the distribution of truth-values may have to be of some other form, where, for example, we take a step back from describing assignments case by case and describe the general structure of truth-values (see chapter 8, §1). Similarly, if we require of a theory of vagueness that it specifies truth-conditions for vague sentences, then we must allow such conditions to be stated in vague terms in such a way as not to settle a truth-value status for every sentence.

The theory is also concerned with the logical principles governing our language – with, for example, specifying how the truth-value of a complex sentence is determined by, or otherwise related to, its

37

component sentences (e.g. by giving recursive truth-clauses for the logical connectives). More specifically, it must identify any special logical features that arise owing to vagueness. Other obvious tasks for a theory include solving the sorites paradox and giving an account of higher-order vagueness.

The methodology by which theories of vagueness should be, and generally are, assessed is best seen in terms of establishing a 'reflective equilibrium'. Theorists should aim to find the best balance between preserving as many as possible of our judgements or opinions of various different kinds (some intuitive and pre-philosophical, others more theoretical) and meeting such requirements on theories as simplicity. And when counter-intuitive consequences do follow, the theorist needs to be able to explain *why* we are inclined to make those judgements that their theory regards as erroneous.

This is a familiar strategy in philosophical theorising. Aristotle aimed to produce theories which preserve 'the truth of all the reputable opinions, . . . or, failing this, of the greater number' (*Nicomachean Ethics* VII. 1 1145b5–6). And Rawls (1971, p. 20) uses the phrase 'reflective equilibrium' to describe 'the process of mutual adjustment of principles and considered judgements'. Closer to our topic is Goodman's pioneering discussion of the justification of deduction and of induction, which he shows to proceed in the manner described (Goodman 1954, pp. 63–4). And Lewis emphasises the central role of such a method within much current philosophy; see his 1983b, p. x, where the strategy is explicitly outlined and endorsed for application in a range of different areas, in particular metaphysics.

It is a holistic method: we assess a theory as a whole, by its overall success, allowing counter-intuitive consequences in one part of the theory for the sake of saved intuitions in another part. I do not assume that the best is good enough: it may be that no extant theory of the relevant phenomenon preserves enough intuitions to be acceptable, though I shall not now enter into the difficult question of how good is good enough.

In §2 I shall elaborate on the body of our intuitions, opinions and judgements that are relevant to the construction of theories of vagueness. That body certainly includes the classification of particular cases with respect to a vague predicate (e.g. we all agree that at 6 feet 8 inches someone is tall). Other elements of our linguistic practice are relevant, in particular our reasoning: we do not, for example, carry on applying a vague predicate right through its sorites series, and a theory should accommodate that fact. And it is too quick to assume that because we do not assent to p, the theory should count p as false. It may be, for example, that we all agree that q and that q implies p; or we may accept propositions relevantly like p as true. Or maybe p can only be denied in a framework which fails to respect many more things we say or which fails to respect the way we reason. And there may be pragmatic explanations of the unassertability of p. Similarly, the opinions of speakers and their commitment to a given claim may sometimes be better tested indirectly by, for example, checking their response to an argument rather than directly asking them whether they believe it: we are not always the best judges of what our own judgements are.

Not all the relevant judgements are appropriately called 'pre-philosophical' (e.g. the opinion that classical logic should not be revised unnecessarily; see §2iii). And various theoretical virtues should also be part of the equation: we may be prepared to deny occasional intuitive judgements for the sake of theoretical benefits such as simplicity. There is no sharp division between 'common-sense' opinions and those that are part of our general philosophical views, but no such division is needed since both should be taken into account in producing a theory. (Compare Lewis 1983b, p. x: 'they are all opinions, and a reasonable goal for a philosopher is to bring them into equilibrium'.) Relatedly, consider the distinction between 'wide' and 'narrow' reflective equilibrium: in relation to an ethical theory, for example, narrow equilibrium takes into account only our moral opinions (i.e. those directly concerning the subject matter in question), while wide reflective equilibrium also brings into the equation opinions and theories about other matters, e.g. psychological or empirical facts, which might bear on the moral judgements we make. Insofar as such a distinction is applicable here (and the distinction is certainly not clear-cut), it is wide reflective equilibrium that I am recommending: there is no restriction on the types of judgements entering into the equation.

Some of our judgements and opinions will need to be given up and counted as wrong despite initial appearances. The sorites paradox brings out the incompatibility of our intuitive judgements that each of its premises is true, its conclusion false, its inference valid, and yet its predicate coherent. More generally, our intuitions conflict with one another and are not reliable enough in the problematic cases: there will be no suitable system that accommodates all of them. This also answers the objection that my methodology should (absurdly) count as the ideal 'theory' that account generated by simply listing off the relevant opinions: such a list would not be consistent. It also would not constitute a theory of vagueness because it would not answer questions as to the status of borderline cases and the logic etc., for these questions are not settled by the list of our opinions and require some theorising to be employed.

Theorists should be most reluctant to deny very widely held judgements or those held among the experts thought most appropriate to judge the matter in question. (Compare Aristotle's regard for judgements 'accepted by everyone or by the majority or by the wise', *Topics* I. 1 100b21.) And they should have a similar regard for those most deeply held, i.e. that we are least prepared to revise. There will also be intuitions and judgements that are particularly important in the context, namely when giving a theory of vagueness. Certain opinions which could be ignored in another context are crucial because to ignore them would be to ignore a key factor bound up with vagueness. For example, the issue of higher-order vagueness is paramount: any account that fails to accommodate it is likely merely to push the untreated problems of vagueness elsewhere. That is unacceptable even if our intuitions about the higher-order matters seem to be less strongly held because they are of less everyday interest and concern.

Given the described methodology, there is unlikely to be any theory which can be conclusively defended: the strategy invites different equilibria reached by choosing to retain different judgements and justifying the sacrifices by emphasising different gains. And apart from by showing a theory to be inconsistent, there will be no test which will refute a theory by showing its incompatibility with certain apparent truths – any apparent truth on which such a test would need to rest may be denied if this is compensated for by those retained and by other virtues the theory can boast. In assessing some given theory, we should determine the extent and range of our judgements which it is forced to deny to reach its equilibrium. Controversy over the success of different theories can then arise in at least three related ways.

First, there can be disputes about what is in the relevant body of opinions – whether some given opinion is really one that we must attempt to save. It may take a (carefully formulated) questionnaire to discover what the opinions of the folk really are. (And it must not be assumed that the corrupted views of the theorising philosopher reflect the common view.) Then, in some cases, two theorists can agree that there is some relevant judgement that we should try to preserve, but disagree over exactly what its content is. One theorist's presentation of an intuitive judgement can be seen by another as prejudiced by the theory advocated. Take, for example, our intuitions about borderline cases. It might be said that we judge the predications to be semantically indeterminate, and so neither true nor false. But epistemic theorists can object that, as Wright puts it (1995, p. 134), 'the ordinary idea of genuine semantic indeterminacy is not itself a datum, but a proto-*theory* of data', and they will maintain that it is enough for the theory to reflect our ignorance in those cases. Another disagreement over what it takes to preserve an opinion arises when non-classical values are admitted. To capture our intuition that *p*, must *p* count as completely true or is it enough for it to be non-false or perhaps more than 0.5 degrees true?

Second, even if there were agreement over what judgements should be preserved, there could be disagreement concerning some particular theory over which of those judgements it does and does not preserve. Determining the counter-intuitive consequences of a theory is always a major part of its assessment. And we must be cautious of theories that appear to save the, or some of the, high-profile intuitions (e.g. regarding the law of excluded middle) but that do so in a way that requires the denial of a range of other lower profile, but equally important, intuitions.

Third, if we were to have some theories in front of us, along with a list of their counter-intuitive consequences, there could still be considerable disagreement over which of those theories provides the best fit for our body of opinions and intuitions. For it needs to be settled what costs are incurred by denying particular judgements and what would count as adequate compensation for denying them. Different parties to the debate will inevitably value different opinions differently and the methodology does not solve those disagreements.

In chapters 3 to 6 below I reject a series of theories. In most cases I am considering viable accounts which, for the reasons given above, are unlikely to be defeated by a single fatal blow. I thus build up, in each case, a powerful string of objections which taken together reveal the theory as an unattractive package in poor agreement with the crucial opinions. This is the most common strategy found in detailed discussions of vagueness. My defence of supervaluationism is in a large part a matter of answering a range of objections that opponents stack up, and making a case for its being in substantially better agreement with pre-theoretical opinion.

The method of reflective equilibrium is primarily a method of evaluating theories. It can, to a minimal extent, also figure in the methodology of constructing theories of vagueness – Goodman, for example, considered the deliberative process of mutual adjustments between rules and accepted inferences. But reflective equilibrium does allow theorists to come up with their theory however they like. (Though the merits of a methodology of construction can only be judged by the success according to the reflective equilibrium criteria of the resulting theories.)

There is, I suggest, no possible alternative methodology. Theorists may not be open about their search for a reflective equilibrium of the kind described, but this merely results in them privileging certain intuitions, opinions or considerations and ignoring others; it does not reveal that they have some better methodology to hand or any way of justifying their selection of the constraints that cannot be violated. The methodology I describe recommends assessing the theory on all of the evidence available. All we have to go on, apart from equally inconclusive theoretical considerations already factored in, is linguistic practice in the form of what we (speakers) say and believe and how we reason. My described methodology cannot ensure that theorists take account of all relevant information, but stressing the absence of a unique, small set of over-riding constraints could encourage better practice.[1]

2. THE CONSTRAINTS

In this section I shall discuss some intuitions, judgements and opinions that a theory of vagueness should seek to preserve. I refer to these as 'constraints' on the theory and many are found explicitly or implicitly

[1] For arguments that reflective equilibrium is the only rational methodology of philosophical inquiry in general see e.g. DePaul 1998.

in current theorising about vagueness. Recall that those constraints should in general be regarded as defeasible: each could be denied if this were to result in sufficient benefits. My discussion will also illustrate the lack of consensus over appropriate constraints: many debates about them are largely, as Machina describes one of them, just 'a battle of raw intuitions' (1976, p. 51).

(i) Classification of sentences and arguments

The first type of constraint concerns genuinely pre-philosophical judgements about what claims made in our vague language are true or are false. For example, there would be universal agreement that 'Todd is a tadpole' is true when Todd has just been born (even though he will later become a frog) and that 'one grain of sand makes a heap' is false. A theory is obliged to respect such judgements. Giving up one or two such judgements would not be unreasonable given that some judgements need to be denied. But no systematic theory of vagueness could be constructed by giving up just a moderate number of such intuitions. The only extant theory that systematically denies them is Unger's nihilism, which is forced to reject as false a huge range of intuitive judgements made in observational vocabulary, in particular everything of the form 'x is F' with atomic, vague F and any x.

When the applicability of non-observational predicates is in question, it might be necessary to deny judgements commanding widespread assent – fool's gold should not count as gold just because a large number of fools think it is gold. But it is another of our intuitions that there is a difference between these cases, even if the distinction between observational and non-observational vocabulary is not easily or precisely drawn. Similarly, though with observational terms there may still be some systematic errors of judgement (e.g. of someone who looks deceptively tall), a theory should and will be able to explain in intuitive terms the discrepancy in such cases (once people know the nature of the case, they would no longer concur with the original casual judgement).

As well as respecting our strong, agreed opinions about the truth or falsity of particular claims, we might demand that a theory similarly reflects those cases where we hesitate in judging either way or deny both judgements or disagree with each other or change our mind over time. Borderline case predications are typically like that. The theory may call them neither true nor false, or it may characterise them in some other way which helps explain our behaviour.

In addition to simple predications there will be complex sentences about which we have intuitions. Generalisations such as 'anyone taller than a tall man is also tall' are surely true, for example. Relatedly, there are Fine's penumbral connections which reflect logical relations between indefinite sentences. He claims that, regarding a borderline red–pink blob, we are obliged to respect the truth of 'if the blob is to be red then it is not to be pink'. And similarly 'if sociology is to be a science then so is psychology' is to count as a penumbral truth (1975, p. 276). Such cases constrain the relations between the component sentences (e.g. between the values of 'the blob is red' and 'the blob is pink'), and also the account of 'if'. And the accounts of other connectives will be constrained by other cases. For example 'sociology is a science and psychology is not' must be false. Fine's supervaluationary account meets these challenges and respects such penumbral truths, though inevitably, opponents query whether such supposed truths are really truths at all (e.g. Machina 1976, p. 77, Forbes 1983, p. 244). Somewhat more contrived cases of compelling complex sentences include 'the extension of "tall" does not have sharp boundaries' and 'the borderline cases of "tall" are not sharply bounded' (the latter raising issues of higher-order vagueness).

We should also consider the sentences that a theory declares *logically* true or logically false, comparing them with the typical opinions about such classifications. A logician's notion of logical truth may not be part of everyday vocabulary, in which case again such opinions will not count as 'pre-philosophical'. But, first, they will be closely related to common-sense judgements about what could not possibly be false/true. And, second, theories can also be constrained to reflect philosophically informed judgements about logical truth. Relatedly, a theory must make explicit what it takes a logical truth to be. Some of the constraints concerning logical truth will arise from judgements that the standard classification of some given sentence as logically true or logically false should not be challenged by the recognition of vagueness, while others concern features distinctive of vagueness that *are* thought to demand logical revision.

44

So what sentences should be classified as logically true? One case that is frequently cited is the law of non-contradiction stating that $\neg(p \ \& \ \neg p)$ is true for all p. It is said that this should be a principle within the portion of classical logic that goes unchallenged by vagueness (see e.g. Fine 1975, p. 270). Proponents of certain truth-functional many-valued theories acknowledge that this law fails according to their account, noting that its instances are, at least, never completely false. Sometimes they reply – unpersuasively, it seems to me – that this failure is, in fact, a consequence of distinctively vague aspects of language. On the other hand, the failure of the law of excluded middle is often seen as a distinctive characteristic of a language containing vague predicates. It is typically only when we take F to be precise that we are willing to affirm that, for every individual x, either Fx or not-Fx. So some theorists take as a starting point the requirement that a satisfactory theory of vagueness must not classify the classical law of excluded middle as logically true. But again, this is highly controversial, and defenders of the epistemic view and supervaluationism typically offer arguments for maintaining the logical truth of this law (e.g. Fine 1975, pp. 284–6).

Other candidate constraints on a theory of vagueness rest on the classification of particular arguments or types of argument, for there are many intuitive judgements that particular arguments are valid or invalid. A wide range of classically valid arguments seem entirely unthreatened by the recognition of vagueness; for example, why should vagueness threaten the rule of and-elimination? The validity of certain other types of argument is more controversial. For example, Frege noted that contraposition can fail in the presence of vagueness (Frege 1903, p. 65): one case where it looks suspect is in deducing the unacceptable statement 'if a is a borderline F then a is not F' from the apparently acceptable 'if a is F then a is not a borderline F'. Machina and others have shown how certain classical inferential rules (e.g. reductio ad absurdum) fail to be generally valid on the supervaluationist theory (see chapter 7, §4 below for discussion).

We have other intuitions that particular arguments are good or bad in a sense less precise than 'valid' and 'invalid'. In particular, the sorites paradox would be excluded from the list of good arguments (though, as Machina remarks, 1976, p. 75, 'the common man' is convinced that '"slippery slope" arguments are fine if they're not carried too far'). Additionally, a theory must provide a plausible definition of validity in terms of the truth-values (and possible truth-values) of premises and conclusions: theories that admit non-classical values or truth-value gaps may need to generalise the classical definition of validity. The classical definition can be expressed in a number of forms which, though classically equivalent, need not coincide in a non-classical framework. An argument is classically valid iff every valuation that makes the premises true also makes the conclusion true, which is equivalent to saying that there is no valuation in which all the premises are true and the conclusion false and also to saying that in any valuation in which none of the premises are false, the conclusion is also not false. With degree theories, for example, each of these conditions will yield different consequence relations, even once the other features of any given system are fixed (see chapter 4, §7). Again, the decision between alternative definitions will require consideration both of the individual arguments that each definition deems good or bad and of general principles and apparent truths. For example, must validity be preservation of *truth* even when the account is non-classical?

(ii) Some theoretical constraints concerning language-use

We can construct a very general and abstract restriction on theories of vagueness arising from an idea such as 'meaning and use are closely related'. In particular, an expression has the meaning it does partly because it is used as it is: use helps to determine, and maybe entirely determines, meaning. No theory of vague language should confer meanings on vague expressions that cannot be reconciled with this strong connection. (See chapter 3 for discussion of such a constraint in relation to the epistemic view.) Similarly, speakers clearly understand vague languages, and no theory of vagueness should imply otherwise. We can require, very loosely, that the theory does not make it seem impossible or extremely unlikely that we would have come to understand vague predicates with the features that theory attributes to them. And we use vague language very successfully: a theory of vagueness must not rule out the possibility of an explanation of how we manage this. Take, for example, Wright's objection that Dummett's view of vague predicates as incoherent makes our successful use of vague predicates inexplicable. And Unger complains that if there were sharp boundaries to our vague predicates, our understanding of them would be a 'miracle of conceptual comprehension', which he takes to be a challenge for those theories committed to such boundaries. But, as I argued in chapter 1, Unger's own claim that our vague predicates have no positive instances at all seems incompatible with our understanding of them and the fact that we use them successfully to communicate.

A theory of vagueness must be compatible with facts about how vague words come to have the meaning that they have and how those meanings sometimes change. This may involve considerations about the gradual evolution of our language with individual vague words sometimes being added to the vocabulary, and words that are initially very vague sometimes acquiring a less vague sense. And it must allow for the fact that words can be coined, where this process can and often will create a vague expression. For example, Tappenden 1995 envisages a situation in which the US Supreme Court coins the phrase 'brownrate' to mean 'with all deliberate speed' intending to avoid specifying an exact required speed: such a practice of incomplete stipulation would have the advantage of allowing the extension to become progressively more complete as new circumstances come to light, rather than requiring an exhaustive classification to be fixed at the outset. We can ask of a theory whether it allows for the coinage of vague predicates. Some critics of the epistemic view argue that it fails this test since it must say that if you coin a meaningful word then sharp boundaries are inevitably fixed and no areas of indefiniteness remain (see Tappenden 1995 and Sainsbury 1995b; for a response see Williamson 1997a).

(iii) The extent of departure from classical logic

How should the construction of a theory of vagueness be influenced by the idea that classical logic should not be revised, or at least that no such revision should be taken lightly? Williamson writes, 'Classical logic and semantics are vastly superior to the alternatives in simplicity, power, past success, and integration with theories in other domains' (1992b, p. 162). But classical logic should not be seen as unrevisable in this realm – the applicability of classical logic is just one more factor whose preservation is desirable, but it has to be balanced against the judgements that it forces us to deny (e.g. the failure of bivalence in borderline cases and the lack of sharp boundaries to vague predicates). And there can be no consensus over how high we should put the cost of revising classical logic.

First, what exactly is this 'standard logic' (as Williamson 1994, p. xi calls it) that we must respect so highly? It would be misleading to suggest that there is a complete system of logic that is appropriate and uncontroversial in the absence of vagueness. We might ask, for example, whether the logic should be free, whether it should be a relevantist logic and what is to be said about liar sentences or sentences involving category mistakes. Such questions may be currently unsettled, but theories of vagueness need not answer them. One way in which such a theory might avoid them entirely would be to provide rules that will modify *any* system of logic and semantics (whether free, relevantist or intuitionistic etc.) into one which can accommodate vagueness. This would permit independence from other logical questions, since, using the rules specified by the theory, a logical system for a vague language could be constructed from any logic that otherwise recommends itself. But this is not the standard form of a theory of vagueness, nor is it clear to what extent it is viable. In general, theorists avoid questions seemingly irrelevant to vagueness by assuming that by 'classical logic' we mean first-order predicate calculus with identity and without non-denoting expressions. I shall follow this usage.

Even if we allow that classical logic might be revised, we can still impose the constraint that any departure from classical logic must be well motivated and kept to a minimum. Such a constraint is widely adopted: see for example Fine 1975, p. 286, and Simons (1996, p. 326) states a closely related requirement that we need to 'rescue what can be rescued of classical logic'. Vagueness should not prompt us to alter logic and semantics any more than is necessary.

One common idea is that situations in which features distinctive of vagueness are absent should display none of the distinctive logical traits introduced to accommodate vagueness, and in those situations there should be no deviation from classical logic. The form of this requirement could differ for different theories. It is perhaps most clear in connection with a theory that introduces an additional non-classical value or values to be assigned to borderline case predications. The constraint then rules that sentences of determinate truth-value status (i.e. taking classical values) must behave classically and stand in classical relations of entailment etc. to other classically valued sentences. And if a compound sentence has component sentences that are each either completely true or completely false, then the value of the compound must coincide with the value it would receive in the classical framework given the same distribution of values among the component sentences. A constraint of this type is sometimes called a 'normality' or 'fidelity' constraint, since it requires that in certain special cases, the logic and semantics should be 'normal' or 'faithful' to the classical norm. For example Machina (1976, p. 55) writes 'vague propositions sometimes take the classical truth-values . . . and when they do, the usual classical treatment will be just as acceptable for them as it is for precise propositions'.[2]

3. MODELS AND ARTEFACTS

In this section, I describe two ways of regarding elements of a theory of vagueness, the realist and the modelling way. The distinction between them cuts across the usual classification of theories of vagueness – the same theory could be defended with either approach. And they are both compatible with the methodology of reflective equilibrium. But my distinction marks a crucial contrast between attitudes to theories that are found in the literature; it is particularly important in relation to degree theories. Making the contrast explicit should also give us a better grasp on the substance of the claim that some logical system is the logic of vagueness and it will have consequences for what count as appropriate ways of assessing proposed theories.

---

[2] The normality constraint is rarely justified in any detail and should be taken as no more than a defeasible constraint: a theory violating it should not be ruled out. For it constrains truth-values even for *vague* sentences when they take classical values. And could it not be the case, for example, that a vague sub-sentential element of a sentence (a vague predicate, for example) affects the logical behaviour of that whole sentence even if that sentence happens to be classically valued? Enforcing the normality requirement would also prematurely exclude the possibility of a theory that declared true the premises of a sorites, while denying that the conclusion was true (i.e. a theory that gives those sentences the values that they *seem* to take). For if the premises are (classically valued and) true, then the normality condition rules that they must stand in the usual classical relations, hence (given the classical validity of the sorites argument) that the conclusion is also true.

(i) The distinction

Suppose a theory of vagueness provides a detailed model of the truth-value status of borderline cases and the inferential features of our vague language. The question arises how much of the model we should take seriously, or take at face value. Regarding a given aspect of the theory, the realist approach takes it at face value, where it is taken to correspond to an aspect of the phenomenon with which the theory is concerned. By contrast, the modeller will take it less seriously and allow that there is nothing corresponding to it. They typically remark of their theory that 'it's only a model' and they use this claim to escape commitments. For example, they might deny that the assignment of truth-values in borderline cases should be viewed in a realist way. You can, of course, be realist about some aspect of the theory and a modeller about others. (I will sometimes talk about the approaches without specifying the elements towards which they are taken, for often either it will be clear which elements are in question, or the context will be such that the modellers fail themselves to specify.)

The realist conception is so called because the descriptions of the language that the theory provides, or commits us to, are intended to describe real features of that language. An epistemic theorist such as Williamson seems to be working with this conception of the project (1992b, 1994). He claims that, together with the facts, the meaning of a sentence (itself determined by its use, or the use of its components) suffices to determine whether it is true or false: all sentences are determined as having one of these two values and the logic governing them is classical.

By contrast, modellers emphasise that giving a theory of vagueness is a matter of modelling our vague language, where there may be elements of the model not corresponding to elements of reality. So, for example, a logical system that works as a model of our language might be committed to certain statements that appear to be descriptive of our language but which should not, in fact, be taken at face value as describing real features of it. According to the modelling approach, accepting a theory with such commitments can be justified if the theory as a whole is successful. For example, a modeller may not take seriously the truth-value ascriptions made in some borderline case predications, while maintaining that treating the language as if all sentences have some (unique) truth-value from their specified range enables us to draw conclusions about our vague language that we *should* take seriously and at face value. And some of those conclusions drawn (e.g. concerning matters of validity) will illuminate the features of the language distinctive of vagueness, and provide a solution to the sorites paradox. By contrast, for the realist such truth-value ascriptions are to be taken seriously and are to be seen as themselves illuminating vagueness as well as being involved in deriving further informative statements that do so.

Talk of a modelling approach suggests a comparison between the task of producing a theory of vagueness and the enterprise of scientific modelling. Goguen, for example, describes the task as parallel to providing typical mathematical models of empirical phenomena, even taking a theory of vagueness to play comparable predictive roles and to be 'subject to the process of experimental verification and subsequent modification usual in scientific research' (1969, p. 326). But note that it is compatible with the realist conception as well as the modelling approach to regard theories of vagueness as akin to scientific theories construed in terms of models. On the former, we can still see the theory as providing a model; the difference arises over how the model relates to the modelled phenomenon. Realists about *science* are characterised by van Fraassen as seeking a theory for which they can claim 'to have a model which is a faithful replica, in all detail, of our world' (1980, pp. 68–9). For the envisaged realist conception of theories of vagueness, substitute 'language' for 'world' in the quote. What is distinctive of the modelling approach is the fact that replication in every detail is neither expected nor demanded.

I suggest that many degree theorists, in particular, are best seen as adopting the modelling approach towards a number of features of their theories. Goguen, for example, dismisses the belief in 'some Platonic ideal "concepts" or logic embodying their essence' (1969, p. 325), and he emphasises instead that we are constructing models. And degree theorists often treat their intermediate truth-values as values that it is *useful* for us to ascribe to sentences, not as values that the meaning of a sentence (together with the facts) determines to be applicable to that sentence in the circumstances. They typically do not accept that there *is* a unique, exact value applicable to each sentence (in the actual world). Goguen claims (1969, p. 331) that 'any not identically zero function which is continuous decreasing and asymptotic to zero' would be appropriate for the representation of 'short', implying that there is not a unique function assigning values of shortness that is given by the meaning of 'short', but rather that we can profitably associate any of a range of functions with that predicate. Edgington also writes 'the numbers are to be taken with a pinch of salt . . . But the numbers afford us the luxury of addition, multiplication etc., in exhibiting a model of the structure of . . . reasoning' (Edgington 1992, p. 203; see also her 1997, p. 308, 'there are no exactly correct numbers to assign'). And Machina indicates similar sympathies in claiming that 'fortunately, the assignment of exact values usually doesn't matter much for deciding on logical relations between vague propositions' (Machina 1976, p. 61).

It would, however, also be possible for someone to see a degree theory as uncovering the true structure of our language in accordance with the realist stance and to insist that our sentences *do* each have one, and just one, of an infinite range of numerical degrees of truth. Equally, a proponent of classical logic could try to adopt the modelling approach and argue that it is not that our language has an underlying structure which is classical (as I portrayed Williamson's position), but rather that classical logic is the best, or perhaps the only, satisfactory way to model language. The position which Cargile labels 'nominalistic' may be of this form, and his distinction between this and his 'realistic' position seems to be a special case of my distinction between the modelling and realist approaches. His realistic line takes it to be true that in turning from a tadpole into a frog, a creature, Amphibius, ceases to be a tadpole at some precise instant: 'that is how logic requires that change must be, and so it must (logically) be' (Cargile 1969, p. 200). This is contrasted with his nominalistic alternative according to which 'if we are making use of logic, we may be forced to choose some instant arbitrarily to be the instant at which Amphibius ceases to be a tadpole, in much the same way that we have to assume, in applying the differential calculus to a physical problem, that matter is infinitely divisible'. The chosen instant will be singled out in the model, but it will be denied that this corresponds to a feature that is privileged in reality. How much sense we can make of that sketchy proposal is unclear: I would argue that to make a genuine theory out of it, the best option is to adopt a supervaluationist account. We would not be led far astray by choosing an arbitrary instant – at least all our inferences not referring to that instant would be reliable. But to commit ourselves only to truths not resting on the specific choice made, we should quantify over the range of acceptable models, as supervaluationism instructs.

The modelling approach can be pursued in a range of different ways and so a global verdict on them all could be inappropriate. Nonetheless I shall argue that taking that approach all too often amounts to leaving unanswered what seem to be (and what the realist often takes to be) the key questions to be addressed by a theory of vagueness.

(ii) Artefacts of a model

We can distinguish between the genuinely representational features of a model which we should take as capturing or revealing aspects of the modelled phenomenon, and those which are mere *artefacts* of the model, not representing anything in the phenomenon itself. The major difference between the realist and the modelling approaches can then be described in terms of the features of a model that are taken to be mere artefacts – the realist approach to a given feature is to take it as representational while the modeller regards it as a mere artefact of the model.

Consider an analogy with the debate in the philosophy of science between van Fraassen's constructive empiricism and his realist opponents (see e.g. van Fraassen 1980). Roughly sketched, the difference between these positions concerns whether descriptions of unobservables (or of relations between observables and unobservables) should be taken at face value as providing true descriptions of features of the world, or whether we should only believe the predictions and descriptions of behaviour at the observable level, though acknowledging that a model involving unobservables can aid understanding and predictions involving observables. The realist about unobservable entities takes the former line and maintains that there are unobservable entities and objective truths about them, while van Fraassen defends the latter line and does not share the belief that there are unobservable entities. He can be regarded as taking statements about unobservable entities to be artefacts of the model which may not correspond to elements of reality, while the realist maintains that they do directly correspond to aspects of reality.

Taking the modelling approach to any type of theory of vagueness will, I suggest, involve taking truth-value assignments in at least some borderline case predications to be mere artefacts. We have seen that this attitude is common among degree theorists. Consider again the modelling approach towards classical logic. The important contrast with the attitude of the realist who defends classical logic is displayed in the modellers' denial that we need to take sharp boundaries seriously. But if they were to take seriously the truth-value ascriptions in all borderline cases around that boundary, then they would be committed to a realist attitude to the boundaries themselves, whose existence would be guaranteed by those truth-values. So truth-value ascriptions in at least some borderline cases must be regarded as artefacts. A question such as 'what truth-values, if any, are taken by borderline case predications?' – earlier presented as a central question for theories of vagueness – must then be seen by the modeller as sometimes inappropriate. Though values may be assigned, this can only be interpreted instrumentally, which is not to say that they have no truth-value, for that would be to place them, equally mistakenly, in a truth-value gap. But then we need an explanation of why it is not a reasonable question. The modeller talks instead about what values it is useful for us to apply to them in a non-realistically construed theory, but that only raises the questions why such a theory is useful and what features of the modelled phenomena guarantee the utility of a non-realistic model.

Suppose there is information in the model which it is implausible or otherwise undesirable to assume corresponds to elements of the real modelled phenomenon; by adopting the modelling approach, a theorist seems able simply to deny that there is any such correspondence, without this threatening the use of the model. The modeller then avoids a range of objections that the realist must face. For example, first, in discussing the epistemic view in chapter 3, I shall raise a question about what could possibly determine the classical values taken by certain sentences or the sharp boundaries that the epistemic theorist claims the extensions of our vague predicates have. A theory advocating classical logic within the modelling approach need not face these questions: according to such a view the values are simply usefully assigned rather than picking up on elements of reality. Similarly with the demand for the epistemic theorist to explain why we do not know facts in borderline cases and about where sharp boundaries lie: on the realist conception the demand is reasonable, while on the modelling approach an advocate of classical logic and semantics may hope to deny that there *are* such facts of which we are ignorant. A second example: there is a natural worry about the fact that the degree theorist's model makes assignments of exact numerical values to all sentences, for this seems to impose fine detail and apparent precision that is altogether inappropriate for the modelled vague phenomenon (see chapter 4, §9). By adopting the modelling approach and not taking those assignments seriously, many degree theorists hope to avoid such worries. Similarly, there may be sharp boundaries imposed by a degree theory (e.g. between sentences of degree 1 and those of degree less than 1). The realist would be forced to take them seriously, while on the modelling approach it might be argued that they are mere artefacts of the model.

But unwanted commitments cannot be avoided so easily. It is not acceptable simply to provide a theory and deny that we have to take all of it seriously without explicitly stating what we *are* supposed to take seriously. To justify both defending a model and regarding some of its features as mere artefacts, we need to know what a theory of vagueness is supposedly modelling and what features of the model are genuinely representational. But typically proponents of the modelling approach do not confront this crucial issue: they simply offer a model and choose at will which aspects of it to take seriously, hoping to avoid worries about the other elements by casually remarking that it is 'only a model'. If this is all they do, they are at very best merely gesturing at a theory of vagueness without really providing one. What is needed is an explicit, systematic account of how the model corresponds to or applies to natural language, stating which aspects of the model are representational, and justifying the treatment of others as mere artefacts. It is far from clear how this could be done.

To emphasise this point, I return to the comparison with scientific modelling. We can regard the model itself as an abstract structure (e.g. the mathematical structure defined by the laws of Newtonian mechanics). A scientific theory typically identifies that structure and specifies how it corresponds to the aspect of the world that is being modelled, stating what features of the model reflect the world, or in what respects the model is similar to the world and to what degree. This correspondence is specified by 'application rules' or 'theoretical hypotheses'; for example that 'the positions and velocities of the earth and moon in the earth-moon system are very close to those of a two-particle Newtonian model with an inverse square central force' (Giere 1988, p. 81). In these terms, my criticism of current theorists within the modelling approach to vagueness is that they offer no application rules, or any indication of an alternative device fulfilling the same crucial role. Realists are not open to a similar objection: in assigning truth-values to sentences and describing logical relations that hold between them, such theorists aim to capture the truth-values that those sentences actually have and the logical relations that they stand in. The ascriptions and descriptions are not a surrogate for capturing some other (unspecified) features of the language; they are to be taken at face value.

To summarise, I object to modellers who attempt to avoid commitments that their models force on them, when, as is usually the case, they state only that their model is not to be taken realistically and not how it *is* to be taken.

There is one way that modellers who are degree theorists might respond in relation to their refusal to take seriously the numerical truth-value assignments. They could maintain that the instantiation of truth-values by sentences forms an ordinal structure, where it is only the ordering of values that counts. Such a structure is legitimately represented numerically, but when we consider that representation we should not take it entirely seriously, since there will be features of the numerical structure (corresponding, e.g., to ratios or intervals between values) with no parallel in the purely ordinal scale. In chapter 5 I shall examine the viability of an account of this type and assess whether it meets worries about the objectionable precision involved in assigning exact values.

But if viable at all, this type of response is only available to a degree theorist. Consider, for example, a theorist who seeks to defend a classical logic theory of vagueness while seeing the resulting models in terms of the modelling approach. With just two truth-values, there is no room for a discrepancy with the structure of the system representing the instantiation of those values in the way that there is in the infinite-valued case, and there will be no non-representational features in the model of the instantiation of those values, in the way that there would be in the numerical representation of an ordinal scale. Similarly for theories committed to exactly three values. Modellers employing these theories would have to deny that truth-value ascriptions in borderline cases should be taken seriously at all, not just that we should take care with regards to the chosen representation of them. This more extreme type of modelling approach could also be adopted with a degree theory or any other type of theory; the objections I raised above are particularly pressing for such an account. Nonetheless, in the rest of this chapter I shall continue to examine the modelling approach in general, comparing it with the realist approach and considering it in the light of the methodological theses of §§1–2.

(iii) Models as idealisations

The modelling approach is frequently combined with the view that theories of vagueness have to be idealisations. Some theorists emphasise that their theory gives a precise model of an imprecise phenomenon, but that this must not be seen as undermining the theory. Rather, they imply, models and systems of logic *must* be precise, so this form of idealisation is unavoidable. Goguen, for example, writes (1969, p. 327), 'our models are typical purely exact constructions, and we use ordinary exact logic and set theory freely in their development . . . It is hard to see how we can study our subject at all rigorously without such assumptions.' And Edgington describes her own account as 'a precise mathematical model of an imprecise phenomenon', but claims that nonetheless 'it gives, modulo that imprecision, the structure of the phenomenon. The demand for an exact account of a vague phenomenon is unrealistic. The demand for an account which is precise enough to exhibit its important and puzzling features is not' (Edgington 1997, p. 305; see also her 1993, p. 200). Thus such modellers maintain that theories of vagueness must be idealisations in virtue of the very nature of the modelled phenomenon, namely vagueness. (Note that the analogy between the modelling approach and instrumentalism in science breaks down here, if not before, but this does not undermine the original comparison since this issue is a matter of the *motivation* for the approach.)

The position of these modellers is thus that we can, at best, produce an idealised model of vague language because all logical systems are precise. But, first, we need to be told why a model must be precise. Is a mathematical model precise simply in virtue of being a *mathematical* structure? Zadeh would say not, since he describes his own system of fuzzy logic (which uses fuzzy truth-values) as 'an imprecise logical system' (1975, p. 407). Alternatively, we might deny that a model is precise in the case where the metalanguage in which it is framed is itself vague. For if the theory must be formulated within a vague language, then the suggestion that the description is of something precise would surely be misplaced and there may be no need for idealisation.

Even if we were to acknowledge the precision of typical models, the modeller's position on idealisation needs to assume that the logic of vague language cannot be given by a precise system. Machina appears not to share this assumption when he writes, 'This is not to say that in order to fulfil its mission to handle vague propositions logic itself must become vague. (The study of dead civilizations need not itself be dead.)' (1976, pp. 47–8). Moreover, some people maintain that being vague is a matter of coming in degrees, and this feature of predicates *can* be captured within a mathematical model. So there may be room for a position which provides a theory of vagueness employing a precise system without yielding to the criticism that it imposes that precision on the phenomenon itself. The claims both that logical systems must be precise and that a precise system is inadequate for an account of vagueness are, at best, too hastily made.

It is correct, though, that if idealisation were necessary in theories of vagueness, we would have to take the modelling approach. From the realist standpoint, an account of an imprecise phenomenon that rendered it precise would be an account that fails, whereas on the modelling approach it is viewed as a reasonable device in modelling a phenomenon. So, if idealisation is unavoidable, we must take the modelling approach if we are to succeed in producing a theory of vagueness at all; and proponents of the modelling approach might be seen as taking as their starting point the inevitable failure to produce a realist account. But adoption of that starting point is unwarranted unless further argument is provided. And it should be a last resort anyway. Compare idealisation in science: if we are interested in movement of objects on a particular real surface, then an idealisation treating it as frictionless may be fine for practical purposes and useful because of its simplicity, but it will never accurately describe actual movement on that surface. Similarly, an idealised model of a language may help for some purposes but it gives the wrong answer to some questions about the real features of language and in particular to ones bound up with vagueness. Moreover, surely we can still ask about the real phenomenon. There may indeed be a tension between the vagueness of language we are hoping to capture and the use of logical models that have at least an appearance of precision. But to respond by declaring the model to be merely an idealisation is to give up on the task in hand. The way forward is to admit that the metalanguage is itself vague: an accurate account of vagueness may then be given in terms that are themselves vague.

(iv) Uniqueness

The two approaches I have been comparing may also differ with respect to the question whether there is a uniquely correct theory of vagueness. Some philosophers imply that there must be a unique system of logic and semantics for vague language when they talk of providing *the* system of logic and semantics (e.g. Fine 1975, p. 297). But might not several systems be equally appropriate? A claim of uniqueness needs to be carefully stated to allow for different non-conflicting systems, such as a propositional logic and a compatible predicate logic, or a system of predicate logic with identity and one without. We can say, at best, that there is a uniquely correct system for a chosen level of generality and stock of logical constants, e.g. a unique propositional logic for vague language.

The realist view that theories uncover aspects of the language strongly suggests, at the very least, restrictions on the range of different systems that could count as giving the logic and semantics of a vague language, and it may ensure there must be a uniquely correct system. In particular, no two theories that disagree over the range of truth-values available for sentences could both be acceptable. And on the assumption that definitions of (at least some of) the connectives are intended to capture natural language connectives, there could not be two acceptable theories that agree on admitting infinitely many values but disagree over the definitions of those connectives and hence over what relations hold between complex sentences and their components.

If we adopt the modelling approach, there are no such immediate reasons to expect a uniquely acceptable logic and semantics for vague language (even for a chosen level of generality). For why think it would not be possible to construct different models for vague languages that are equally successful? (As Goguen 1969, p. 326, writes: 'we do not assume there is some unique best theory'.) There is nothing in the conception of the project itself that suggests that uniqueness should be expected, or even desired, even when it comes to deciding the range of truth-values assigned. If the target for a theory is, at least in part, its utility in illuminating the phenomenon without directly corresponding to it, uniqueness should not be assumed – perhaps different ways of modelling vagueness are useful for different purposes and none is ideal for all. The extent of flexibility depends, however, on what aspects of their model the modeller does regard as corresponding to reality. For example, could we be so permissive as to admit that there is no best choice between degree theories and supervaluationism, despite their radically different consequence relations? No theorists seem prepared to accept that.

Moreover, the same considerations implying that uniqueness need not be expected among theories when they are seen as mere modelling devices also suggest that regarding some given theory in that way could be compatible with there being a different theory meeting realist standards. For the correctness of the latter theory does not prevent some other theory from suitably illuminating the phenomenon of vagueness in a different way. This observation bears on my earlier criticisms of certain versions of the modelling approach, namely that they leave unanswered certain key questions (e.g. about real truth-values as opposed to what it is simply useful to treat as truth-values). It is the search for a theory meeting realist standards that really counts, and if we are to settle for a modeller's offering we need reasons to believe that no realist theory is possible and an explanation of why the questions it confronts are unanswerable.

In §1 I suggested that the holistic method described there encourages the thought that we could reach different equilibria that balance our intuitions in different ways but that seem equally plausible and where each theory counts as best according to slightly different (but equally valid) standards of judging the 'best balance'. Is there thus a tension between advocating the methodology of reflective equilibrium while urging a preference for the realist conception of theories (at least when these views are combined with an optimism rather than a scepticism about the possibility of success in theorising)? Certainly the methodology is compatible with the modelling approach. And this combination of views could reduce the need for the tricky task of adjudicating between two good competitors which preserve different intuitions, since they could both be declared successful models (and perhaps appropriate for different purposes). It might then be suggested that the reflective equilibrium process can only provide a way of choosing theories on pragmatic grounds or according to subjective preference, and that it thus cannot be a route to the underlying truth behind the phenomena. So, the argument could continue, if we advocate that methodology we should also believe that there is no fact of the matter about one theory being objectively correct and we should thus take an anti-realist line. But there is nothing in the nature of the method of reflective equilibrium that commits us to such anti-realism. Compare the situation with inference to the best explanation. Someone might similarly argue that deciding on the best explanation can at best be a decision made on pragmatic and subjective grounds and cannot be guaranteed to deliver the correct explanation: there is no fact of the matter that one explanation is uniquely right. But such an anti-realism is not forced upon advocates of inference to the best explanation either: they can see their method as the way to reach the objectively and uniquely correct explanation.

If it turned out that there were ties for the best theory, as judged by §1 standards – two or more theories that were both sufficiently good to be judged successful theories of vagueness – then I might be obliged to rethink my commitment to reflective equilibrium plus realism plus a lack of scepticism. But we will be lucky if there is one adequate theory, let alone more than one. And if there is an outright winner, as I maintain, my combination of views is reasonable.[3]

In the next chapter I turn to the epistemic view – a theory offered as a realist account and defended as uniquely correct.

---

[3] There is, perhaps, an analogy between my response here and an attitude taken by Lewis (1994, p. 479). He considers the objection to his best-system account of laws that the standards of simplicity and strength (by which the best system is decided) are psychological, opening up the position to an undesirable idealist claim that what laws there are is up to us. He replies that if 'nature is kind' – a reasonable hope, he suggests – the best system will be robustly best, coming out first under any standards of simplicity and strength and balance. If nature is unkind, we would need to choose between a number of different (less appealing) responses; but he recommends that 'we not cross these bridges unless we come to them'.

3

The epistemic view of vagueness

I. THE THEORY

Epistemic theorists retain classical logic in its entirety. This commits them to sharp boundaries to the extensions of our predicates: there will be a unique precise point at which a growing boy suddenly becomes tall, and a precise boundary between red and orange in a colour chart showing continuous variation between red and orange. The solution to the sorites paradox is then clear. In the version with a quantified premise, that premise will be false: growing one tenth of an inch *can* make the difference between not being tall and being tall.

The Stoics supposedly held a version of the epistemic view, and the position is associated in particular with Chrysippus.[1] The view has recently been revived by Cargile (1969), Campbell (1974) and Sorensen (e.g. in his 1988).[2] But by far the most detailed and sophisticated defence of the epistemic view is to be found in Williamson's book, *Vagueness* (1994, based on his earlier papers 1992a and 1992b), and it is Williamson's version that I shall primarily take as my target.

The epistemic view does not deny that vagueness is a real and ubiquitous phenomenon: the claim that predicates have sharply bounded classical extensions must not be taken to preclude vagueness by definition. According to the epistemic view, vagueness is a type of ignorance. The feature loosely described as having a fuzzy boundary is to be characterised in terms of our ignorance about

[1] Chrysippus' own writings on the topic do not survive, though he is reported, for example, in Cicero (see Long and Sedley 1987, pp. 224–5). Williamson 1994, chapter 1, provides a speculative reconstruction of the Stoic position.

[2] Campbell is reluctant to call the uncertainty distinctive of vagueness *epistemic*, since there is nothing we could find out that would allow us to have knowledge of the matter; instead he calls it 'semantic uncertainty'. But he still acknowledges a commitment to sharp boundaries, accepts the falsity of the sorites inductive premise etc.

where the limits of a predicate's extension fall. Similarly the view admits borderline cases, characterising them epistemically. Although there *is* a fact of the matter about whether borderline Tek is tall – bivalence holds, so either he is tall, or he is not tall – we do not, and perhaps cannot, know which. Cargile suggests that it is 'absurd to make an effort to find out' the fact in such a case (1969, p. 200). Certainly, we would still be ignorant about whether borderline Tek is tall even if we had all the evidence about his exact height and the heights of everyone else in the world. Thus, at least in this natural sense, it seems that we *could not* know the cut-off points of vague predicates (Sorensen 1988 describes borderline case predications as unknowable 'blindspots').

By appealing to the vagueness of predicates such as 'knows that' and 'is knowable' the epistemic view can also explain higher-order vagueness in terms of ignorance. The boundaries to the borderline cases of *F* appear fuzzy because of our ignorance of the exact boundary to the cases in which we are ignorant whether *F* applies. (See Williamson 1999 for a detailed discussion of higher-order vagueness.) There is then uniformity in the treatment of different orders of vagueness at least to the extent that all orders of vagueness are treated as a matter of ignorance with classical logic applicable at every stage.[3]

Much of the support for the epistemic view comes from emphasising problems facing the non-classical alternatives. For example, Cargile 1969 shows how much of classical logic would have to be abandoned to cope with sorites paradoxes if the epistemic view were rejected: it would not be enough to modify or drop just one or two disputable principles. And Williamson 1994 and Sorensen 1988 in particular provide detailed reasons for rejecting a range of non-classical theories.[4]

---

[3] Contrast this with Campbell's approach to higher-order vagueness: borderline cases are those over which there is 'semantic uncertainty' about whether the predicate applies; but rather than allowing cases for which it is semantically uncertain whether the case is one of semantic uncertainty, he introduces *degrees* of semantic uncertainty about *Fx* determined by the proportions of (competent) people assenting to the proposition that *Fx* (Campbell 1974, pp. 187–9).

[4] In this chapter I will not examine Williamson's argument that bivalence cannot be denied (1992b). In chapter 8 I shall argue that in the light of vagueness we need to revise the Tarski (T) and (F) schemata on which Williamson's argument rests.

But the epistemic view is often met by an incredulous stare. Many consider, or have considered, the thesis that our vague predicates have sharp boundaries to be unworthy of serious consideration, judging it absurd to think that there is a precise point on the spectrum where red turns to orange, or that the loss of a single hair can turn Fred bald, or that I can be not tall at one height and then suddenly tall when less than one hundredth of a millimetre taller. Defenders of the epistemic view are sensitive to the charge of implausibility and they have sought to make the approach more palatable and to answer articulations of the implied criticisms. In this chapter I shall illustrate and reject the most important of these attempts (mainly Williamson's). Although this does not rule out alternative epistemicist responses to the major objections, along the way I indicate why the search for such alternatives looks futile. I am left, I claim, with sufficient grounds on which to reject the theory.

2. THE IGNORANCE CHARACTERISTIC OF VAGUENESS

Why are we ignorant of the facts about where the boundaries of vague predicates lie and about the correct classification of borderline cases? This is a natural and reasonable question to ask epistemic theorists.

Some defenders of the epistemic view (e.g. Sorensen 1988, pp. 245–6) have suggested that opponents who pursue an objection to unknowable sharp boundaries betray a residual verificationist antipathy to unknowable facts in general. It may also be suggested that ignorance is our default state and that lack of knowledge does not stand in need of explanation. Such very general responses, however, will strike many as unsatisfactory. Williamson, by contrast, offers a specific explanation of the source of our ignorance using his notions of inexact knowledge and 'margin for error' principles (see especially his 1994, chapter 8). As it is by far the best offered, I concentrate on this explanation.

(i) Inexact knowledge

We can introduce the phenomenon of inexact knowledge through examples which have nothing to do with vagueness. A typical instance is my knowledge of the number of words in Williamson's book. I know that there are at least 20,000 and at most 200,000 but I do not know the exact number. This is inexact knowledge. Or take a tree which I have just casually observed. I could locate its height in inches within a range of heights, but not at a specific number of inches. Knowledge from perceptual sources will typically be inexact in this way.

Williamson proposes that when there is inexact knowledge, there is a margin for error principle at work. If your true belief that p is to count as knowledge, it should not be true just by luck. But if p would have been false in situations that you could not discriminate in the relevant respects from the actual case, then you are lucky if your belief happens to be true. So, for your belief to count as knowledge, p should also be true in cases – call them similar cases – falling within a 'margin for error'. Margin for error principles can thus be expressed in the form (1994, p. 227):

(M) 'A' is true in all cases similar to cases in which 'It is known that A' is true.

Sainsbury (1997) chooses to explain the proposal captured by the principles in terms of a 'reliability conditional' – if you know something, then you couldn't easily have been wrong, where the 'easy possibilities' in which you must not be wrong correspond to the similar cases in Williamson's margin for error.

To illustrate, suppose that, on the basis merely of a rough estimate, you come to believe that there are at least n words in Williamson's book. And suppose that there are exactly n words in the book, so your belief is in fact true. Applying the same error-prone method of estimation, you could still have reached the same belief even if there had been a dozen fewer words there; your belief would then have been false. This prevents your actual true belief counting as knowledge, for the way you formed it does not allow the necessary margin for error; in Sainsbury's terms, you could easily have been wrong. Similarly, if the tree is m inches high, an appropriate margin for error principle implies that I will not know, on the basis of casual inspection, that it is m inches, nor will I know that it is not $m+1$ inches (the situation in which it is $m+1$ inches high is a similar situation within the margin). Because my perceptual apparatus has limited sensitivity and is not capable of complete accuracy, such margins for error are required if I am to have knowledge. If I *measured* the tree rather than just looking at it casually, the margin for error would be narrower, but there would still be a margin due to the limited accuracy of the measurement. More generally, what counts as the 'similar cases' in (M) will differ according to the proposition p and the source of putative knowledge.

Before turning to the explanation of vagueness-related ignorance, I shall explore the nature of inexact knowledge a little further. Williamson describes inexact knowledge as an 'easily recognised cognitive phenomenon' (1994, p. 227), but though his examples are of familiar sorts of situations, this does not settle exactly what the term 'inexact knowledge' denotes. What knowledge is it that is inexact in the tree case? Clearly, it cannot be knowledge that the tree is 12 feet 0 inches, say, because that is a fact of which I am ignorant. And my knowledge that the tree is not exactly 2 feet or that it is between 8 feet and 20 feet is not threatened by the margin for error principle and would be inappropriately called inexact.

I suggest that the phenomenon of inexact knowledge is better captured by reference to a cluster of instances of ignorance of certain facts and knowledge of others, along with the role of a margin for error in explaining the former. So inexact knowledge is not straightforwardly expressed in the form 'S knows that p', but is a type of knowledge best expressed as 'knowledge *about* the height of the tree', or 'knowledge *of* the height of the tree'. In such cases there will typically be specific exact facts of which we are ignorant (e.g. the actual height of the tree), and there will be related less specific facts (e.g. that the tree is more than 8 feet, or that it is not 20 feet) which we know. The cluster will contain those facts that can be cited in answer to the key question 'how high is the tree?', where possible answers can vary in specificity (e.g. giving a single height or a range). Similarly, for inexact knowledge of the number of words in Williamson's book, the corresponding question will be 'how many words are there in the book?', which again admits answers of varying specificity.

If talk of inexact knowledge is to illuminate cases relevant to vagueness, we can ask exactly what the inexact knowledge is in those cases. Williamson says that when TW is a borderline case of thinness, our 'knowledge of his thinness' is inexact (1994, p. 230). But how does this fit the structure of other cases? The relevant question could be expected to be 'is TW thin?', but this is not a question that allows a range of answers as in the other cases of inexact knowledge: it is a yes/no question – at least according to the epistemic view – and we are simply ignorant of its answer. Our knowledge of the size of his waist is likely to be inexact, but although such knowledge is clearly relevant to knowledge whether he is thin, this does not render the knowledge of whether he is thin inexact, and it would not be a matter of vagueness if it did. Thus the analogy between unproblematic cases of inexact knowledge and the supposed cases surrounding the phenomena of vagueness may be somewhat strained. In fact, despite the presentation via inexact knowledge, that notion could be dropped for Williamson's purposes. What matters are the margin for error principles and the ignorance and explanation of it. Indeed, vagueness is to be characterised via borderline cases where 'the mark of a borderline case is a distinctive kind of obstacle to knowledge' (1997b, p. 945).

(ii) Margin for error principles and vagueness

Consider the predicate 'tall', whose extension has a sharp boundary according to the epistemic view. And suppose that Tek is a borderline case of tallness who *is* tall, but who is only *just* on that side of the supposed sharp boundary. Williamson claims that knowledge whether Tek is tall would be inexact and that a margin for error principle is in play. A first attempt at filling out these claims – not Williamson's own choice – could run as follows. Even if you believe Tek to be tall, this will not count as knowledge, for if he had been marginally shorter (on the other side of the boundary and so no longer tall) you would still have formed the same belief, though it would then have been false. So the requirement that you leave a margin for error would prevent your original belief about the borderline case counting as knowledge. Drawing on his supposedly ubiquitous margin for error principles in this way, Williamson could explain why predicating a vague predicate to its borderline cases yields sentences that are unknowably true or false.

But there are at least two related problems with this *prima facie* attractive explanation. First, in calling upon a possible situation in which Tek is a different height, it renders us ignorant for the wrong reason, namely that we do not know enough about the thing to which we are predicating the vague predicate. It is then comparable to my ignorance of whether Tek is 5 feet 10 inches to the nearest inch when I have only casually glanced at him. But we can suppose we have access to all the relevant information about Tek's measurements, and we would *still* fail to know whether he was tall. If a vague predicate does have a determinate extension as Williamson claims, it is our ignorance of the requirements for falling into that extension which is relevant, not ignorance about the things which may or may not fall into it.

This leads on to our second potential problem – an issue which Williamson particularly emphasises. The above explanation involves the knowledge whether a given person is tall. When we come to consider general propositions such as that anyone of a certain height is tall, or that n grains is enough to make a heap, an explanation of the same kind cannot be used. For the truths in these cases are necessary truths, or at least are true in all similar worlds. To say that being a heap just is being composed of at least n grains (optimally arranged) is to say something that does not depend on contingencies of the world. Williamson himself is committed to the necessary truth of the generalisation (G) 'n grains (optimally arranged) form a heap', because of his thesis that 'vague facts *supervene* on precise facts' (1994, p. 202). For example, being a heap supervenes on the number and arrangement of grains, since whether something counts as a heap depends only on these (precise) matters. In other words, if two collections of grains (in the same or different worlds) have exactly the same number and arrangement of grains, then either both or neither count as heaps. This ensures that a generalisation such as (G) about collections with a certain constitution of grains is true in all worlds if actually true. So if true, (G) could not be false no matter how circumstances were altered, and in particular it would be true in all similar situations, so no margin for error principle adverting to similar situations in which (G) is false can provide an obstacle to our knowledge.

Williamson's response is to draw on a new kind of margin for error principle where the different situations in the margin differ over *how the relevant predicate is used*, rather than over the putative members of its extension. Were 'heap' to have been used differently, it could have had a different meaning and extension (e.g. perhaps using it with stricter standards for its application would have set the boundary at a larger number of grains). And, Williamson maintains, in a very similar case to the actual one where the predicate is used just slightly differently, it would not have been correct to call an arrangement of *n* grains a 'heap': in general meanings are very sensitive to differences in use. Some expressions may latch onto natural boundaries in the world, and this can ensure a stability in their extensions across worlds despite some variation in use. But Williamson claims that when there are no such natural boundaries, as is typically the case for vague predicates, even slight differences in use can alter meaning, and when small enough, those differences in use would be undetectable by us.

So although it is the case that if *n* grains make a heap then *n* grains also make a heap in close worlds, in some of those worlds *n* grains may not count as 'a heap' by the meaning the predicate would have in that world. And, Williamson maintains, if you are to know that *n* grains form a heap, then those grains must count as a 'heap' in situations involving undetectable (or very small) differences in the linguistic usage of 'heap'. So we do not know the necessary truth '*n* grains make a heap'. Similar arguments about the use and meaning of 'tall' explain why we cannot know propositions like 'anyone of height *h* is tall' (where *h* is the height of borderline Tek). And take the sentence, which is actually true according to the epistemic theorist, and which locates the boundary of a vague predicate *F*. To make a statement using the same words in certain counterfactual circumstances would be to make a different but false statement. The different uses of *F* in those circumstances would yield a different boundary to its extension, so we cannot know the actual boundary of *F*.

The postulated sensitivity of meaning to use is also relevant to the question of our understanding of vague predicates. An initial thought might be that if we do not know where the boundary lies, surely we do not know its meaning and thus have an incomplete understanding of it. And one might back this up with a margin for error principle, (U) if I know that *u* says that *p*, then *u* says that *p* in relevantly similar circumstances, for the fact that *u* does *not* say that *p* in relevantly similar circumstances seems to guarantee that I do not know that *u* says that *p*.[5] But the assumption that (U) is the appropriate margin for error principle will be denied by Williamson. The falsity of '*u* says

---

[5] Tye 1997 raises an objection of this type.

that *p*' in a similar situation is not enough to undermine my knowledge if in that situation I would not still have had that false belief. In the relevant counterfactual situation where *u* does not say that *p* I would not believe that *u* says that *p*, for the meanings of my words is determined by the community's use of them and if that use shifted enough to change the meaning of *u*, my belief about its meaning would similarly shift. (As Williamson says, 1994, p. 209: 'what determines what the utterance says is the same as what determines what I think the utterance says'.) In Sainsbury's terms we can say that it is not an easy possibility that I falsely believe *u* means that *p* when in fact it means that *p**. To capture this we might choose the margin for error principle (U*) if my belief that *u* says that *p* counts as knowledge, then the same belief is true in all relevantly similar circumstances. (But on the notion of 'same belief' required here, see below.)

The semantic externalism required by this explanation – the way in which the meanings of my words depend on matters independent of me – would be rejected by many philosophers. For example, it yields what might be thought to be a surprising dependence of my thoughts on other people (even when those thoughts do not, for example, involve concepts for which we defer to experts). For the pattern of other people's assertions could stop me being able to have a belief with a given content. Entering into the debate surrounding semantic externalism would, however, take us too far afield. I merely note the commitment and the possibility of further objections to Williamson's epistemic view that involve these issues in the philosophy of mind.

(iii) Not knowing and not believing

Before assessing the details of the explanation of ignorance that Williamson offers, we should stand back to consider the strategy used and ask how far such an explanation, if successful, would help the defence of the epistemic view. With Williamson's appeal to margin for error principles, we take a belief in (or assertion of) a given proposition and show that it cannot constitute (or express) knowledge since the subject would be lucky to have a correct belief (or to have made a correct assertion). No such belief can constitute knowledge and no such assertion express knowledge, we are to conclude, and so we cannot know that proposition. Now, a person S can lack knowledge that p either by having a belief that p (perhaps prompting the assertion that p) which fails to count as knowledge (for example, if it is not acquired by a reliable enough method) or by *not* believing that p (whether by believing that not-p or simply by having no opinion whether p). Williamson's explanation of the lack of knowledge draws on the first of these scenarios. But usually people do not, in fact, form beliefs or make assertions about the location of the sharp boundary to a vague predicate, or that Fa or not-Fa when a is a borderline F. After all, people are usually convinced that there *are* no sharp boundaries and that there is no fact of the matter in borderline cases.

It may be that Williamson is more interested in explaining why we *cannot* know rather than why we happen not to know. And if we cannot have a belief that constitutes knowledge (and we cannot have knowledge without belief), we cannot know. But where does that leave us with the explanation of our ignorance? It cannot be assumed that our not knowing is appropriately explained by our inability to know. In general, an explanation of why we cannot ϕ does not provide the right explanation of why we *do* not ϕ. For if we do not take the required first step towards ϕ-ing – trying to ϕ as it might be – to explain why we do not ϕ we should ask why we do not take that step, not what would happen if we did. It might be that we do not try to ϕ because we know we will not succeed – perhaps because we have internalised the explanation offered of why we cannot ϕ. But that is only one possible explanation and it will be implausible in certain cases. For the situation in question the equivalent of the first step towards knowing that p (e.g. that a is F when a is a borderline F) would be believing that p. The reason why we do not believe that p might be that we (rightly) believe that such a belief could not constitute knowledge. But Williamson cannot have it that we recognise *his* explanation of why we cannot know (in his 1994, p. 234, he assumes, reasonably, that we do not recognise it) and so it remains to be answered why we believe we cannot know the fact of the matter in borderline cases or the location of sharp boundaries. The explanation of our ignorance that a is F, for example, should not pass over the explanation of why we lack any belief about whether a is F.[6]

---

[6] Horwich 1997 notes the 'paralysis of judgement' typically witnessed in borderline cases and uses this to criticise and propose a replacement for Williamson's characterisation of vagueness in terms of ignorance. In reply (1997b), Williamson imagines an

Consider in the light of the chapter 2 methodology the demand for explanations of our ignorance. The most common and entrenched intuitions relevant here are intuitions that there are no sharp boundaries, that the sorites inductive premise is true and even that there is no fact of the matter in borderline cases. Williamson indicates how he hopes to explain away these intuitions using his explanation of ignorance (1994, p. 234). He envisages us taking our inability to find sharp boundaries 'as evidence of their non-existence' because we have not seen the point that if there are sharp boundaries we will not be able to find them: without seeing that point 'one might naturally suppose that if they exist then we should be able to find them'. But that is an implausible and uncharitable explanation of our strongly held beliefs. We do not generally believe something does not exist just because we cannot find it. Our reasons for believing that there are no sharp boundaries include, for example, the thought that nothing could determine particular sharp boundaries (see §3 below).[7] At the very least there is a further task for the epistemicist to complete. Even if Williamson has managed to 'explain the ignorance postulated by the epistemic view', he has *not*, contrary to his claims, explained 'the apparent intuitions that run counter to that view' (1994, p. 234).

So the main issue should not be that of explaining why hypothetical beliefs locating sharp boundaries are not knowledge, but of explaining why we do not form those beliefs at all and believe instead that our predicates lack sharp boundaries. Williamson's explanation invoking margins for error provides no such account and thus he gives no explanation of the way in which we do in fact lack knowledge, nor, more importantly, does he explain away our intuitions.

'opinionated macho community' where there is no hesitation over assertions about borderline cases, but the pattern of use of the words shows them to be vague: he concludes that the paralysis of judgement is not necessary for vagueness. For my purposes here, the *possibility* of a community where borderline case predications are never left unresolved is not to the point, given that *typically* we exhibit such indecision.

7   In Williamson's discussion of imagination and vagueness (1997a) he suggests a further (related) explanation of our intuition that there are no sharp boundaries. For 'our intuitions depend on our imagination' (p. 221) and we cannot imagine a sharp boundary to 'heap', where this inability is explained by the epistemic view via the explanation of our inability to *recognise* the boundary in experience which supposedly shows that we could not recognise it when *imagining* the experience either. But again it is too quick to assume that our inability to recognise in imagination that any particular point is the boundary leads us to suppose there *is* no boundary.

(iv) Williamson's margin for error principles

Leaving aside the objections from the previous section and the issue of what the epistemic theorist should be trying to explain, I will examine some details of Williamson's explanation and bring out further commitments with which it is saddled. I start with the margin for error principles themselves.

According to the margin for error principles that Williamson requires, we are prevented from knowing a given fact, not because that fact would not have obtained in suitably similar cases, but because the sentence we actually use to describe the fact would have been false in circumstances in which it would have slightly shifted in sense. The focus is on questions about what the sentence would have said rather than what would have been the case. Should we allow this change of focus from the original examples?

Williamson defends the margin for error principle by considering an assertion of *p* and asking whether it would have been a false assertion in the counterfactual circumstances in the margin. He claims of someone who asserts '*n* grains make a heap' that 'although he could not have asserted the proposition that he actually asserted without speaking truly, he could very easily have asserted a different and necessarily false proposition with the same words' (1994, p. 230). So an assertion that *p* cannot express a piece of knowledge if, in a similar situation and using the same words, a false assertion would have been made: for the speaker would then, given the choice of words, have been lucky to be right. As Williamson recognises, we need here a notion of 'same word' for which 'words are not individuated by their meanings' (1994, p. 303; see also 1995, p. 184) as opposed to a legitimate sense of 'same word' requiring the same meaning; and correspondingly for 'same assertion', understood as 'assertion made with the same words'.

Now, we also need to assess whether my belief is knowledge when I do not assert that belief and perhaps when it is not an occurrent belief either. Williamson takes a similar line with beliefs and the concepts involved in them, thereby committing himself to the highly non-individualistic view of concepts mentioned above (1994, pp. 231–2). The content of one of our concepts, he claims, depends on the pattern of our uses of it (where the 'use' of a concept seems to amount to having a propositional attitude involving that concept);

but we are not perfectly sensitive to those uses (for example, we cannot survey them at once), and so we are not entirely sensitive to its content either. As a result, certain beliefs involving those concepts will not count as knowledge, since our concept could have had a different content without our recognising this, and with that content the belief would have been false.

Corresponding to the ambiguities over 'same word' and 'same assertion' there will need to be ambiguities over 'same concept' and 'same belief'. The senses that Williamson requires are ones for which concepts and beliefs are not individuated by their contents. Are these viable notions of 'same concept' and 'same belief'? Can we allow that the same belief may have different contents? And how would beliefs be individuated if not by content? Williamson's informal justification for his required notion of 'same word' is that it is the sense needed when we report that a word has changed its meaning since 1600 (1994, p. 303). But the corresponding justification for concepts is not available: we would not claim 'I have kept the same beliefs, they have just changed in content'. Williamson's appeal to the same belief having a different content in the counterfactual circumstances is equally problematic.

Perhaps the reference to 'same belief' could be dropped: whether it counts as the *same* belief in the counterfactual circumstance may not matter, just whether the corresponding belief you would have had would have been false. In Sainsbury's terms, easy possibilities can involve the having of a different belief. The problem then becomes how to pick out *which* belief is the relevant one in the counterfactual situation. Sainsbury calls upon the 'belief-forming mechanism' (1997, §6): it is the belief yielded by the same mechanism. In some kinds of cases, this mechanism will be relatively easily identified and re-identified in the counterfactual circumstances. For example, Sainsbury considers the situation where you guess at the sum of two large numbers and we can imagine the counterfactual circumstance where you guess that some other number is the sum. But in the type of cases concerning our beliefs about the application of vague concepts, there may not be a single discrete and relevant belief-forming episode to consider. There may be no perceptual or similar episode triggering the belief and it may be that however we came to believe it, what matters to its being warranted is rather how and why we *keep* the belief. For example, if my reasons for believing p have shifted, the actual belief-forming process then seems irrelevant. That point aside, the question relevant to whether I would have formed a false belief in situations in the margin for error would concern what mechanism(s) of belief-formation are involved in my forming the belief that *a* is *F* when *a* is borderline *F*. But remember, as noted above, that we do not actually have the beliefs in question, so we cannot even be directed to counterfactual situations similar to the actual one. At best, the relevant situation must be twice removed – one similar to the situation we would be in if we *had* had a belief about the truth or falsity of '*a* is *F*'.

(v) The sensitivity of meaning to use

Next, suppose that the relevant margin for error principles hold, so that if my assertion expresses knowledge, my assertion would have been true in similar situations within the margin for error. The explanation of ignorance drawing on those principles still depends on Williamson's views on the relation between meaning and use. We must accept that a tiny difference in the use of a word (e.g. marginal increase in someone's disposition to describe a 5-foot 11-inch man as 'tall') would yield a different extension: this makes for an *extreme* sensitivity of meaning to use. An objector may agree that use bears a significant relation to meaning without agreeing that meaning is typically altered by such tiny differences in use. Meaning may be less sensitive to use than Williamson claims.

In his 1997b (in reply to Horwich 1997), Williamson admits that the required correspondence between small shifts in use and small shifts in reference, 'although simple, natural and plausible, is not indubitable'. But he criticises what he presents as the only alternative to his postulated correspondence of gradual shifts in reference with gradual shifts in use, namely the hypothesis that reference is insensitive to most small shifts in use, but occasionally exhibits jerky shifts for some key shifts of use. For, he argues, this would implausibly commit us to natural boundaries (at the points of the jerky shifts). And he invokes inference to the best explanation: his own explanation of our ignorance appeals to the postulated correspondence between meaning and use, so the success of the explanation would give us reason to believe the assumptions to which it is committed (p. 948). But *is* it the best explanation? It may be better than alternatives such as Horwich's within the framework of classical logic and semantics (perhaps postulating the jerky shifts in meaning), but without such classical restrictions, there is the straightforward explanation that we are ignorant of where sharp boundaries lie because there are no such boundaries, so no fact of the matter for us to know.[8]

Questioning the sensitivity of meaning to use does not commit us to a general principle that 'meaning can *never* be altered by very slight changes in use' – we should be wary of *this* principle since it threatens to yield a sorites paradox in which we are forced to conclude that meaning could not be altered by huge differences in use (e.g. where 'tall' is used as 'short' is actually used). But how we respond to this difference-in-meaning sorites will depend on our response to sorites paradoxes in general. And, outside the classical framework, we may maintain that there is sometimes indeterminacy about whether a given range of changes in use is sufficient to alter meaning.

Without the thesis that the boundaries of vague predicates are so very sensitive to use, Williamson's margin for error principles would not prevent us from knowing those boundaries. So the strong thesis – for which we have been given no independent grounds – must be acknowledged as a further cost incurred by the proposed explanation of our ignorance and hence by the most promising version of the epistemic view.

Before becoming a committed epistemic theorist himself, Williamson was worried by two 'mysteries': *how* our words such as 'heap' have acquired their determinate extensions and *why* we cannot know what those extensions are (see Williamson 1990). I have challenged his treatment of the second of these questions and in the next section I shall argue that his answer to the first question also fails.

3. HOW EXTENSIONS ARE DETERMINED

It is a natural line of criticism of the epistemic view to point out that while there may be natural boundaries that fix the extensions of some

---

[8] He considers his explanation to be available to views other than the epistemic view, but if proponents of such theories were to adopt his explanation they too would be committed to the thesis regarding the sensitivity of the meaning–use relation; and they are likely to prefer the simpler form of explanation given in the text.

terms, for example natural kind terms, there are no such natural boundaries for vague expressions. Nature does not privilege a particular sharp division in the world for our expression 'tall' to latch onto, nor do thin people or heaps form natural kinds. Moreover, with vague expressions we do not *stipulate* where those boundaries lie either. What then draws the sharp line determining the well-defined extension of 'tall' to which the epistemic theorist is committed? There are many lines which would be equally appropriate (and equally inappropriate) should a precise divide be demanded – what chooses between them? The epistemic theorist needs to explain away the intuition that *nothing* does.

One tactic here is to deny the intuition and give an account of what determines the sharp boundaries. First, it may be claimed that the boundaries and extensions are largely determined by the world, and specifically by properties in the world (though it would be our use of the expressions that helped to fix which properties correspond to which predicates). This might narrow the gap between vague predicates and natural kind predicates, and may require maintaining that there are, after all, natural boundaries to our vague predicates. For example, Williamson suggests (1992b, pp. 155–7) that sometimes the sharply bounded property corresponding to a vague predicate may be singled out by the *causal* role it plays in producing our judgements. Any account on which (well-defined) extensions are determined by properties will need to understand properties as entities independent of language, such as universals or sets of tropes, and not as semantic entities (predicates or concepts). And note that drawing on properties will only be useful for the epistemic theorist if the properties in question are precise; we can assume here that they are.

With a theory of properties according to which there is a property for any set of possible entities (see e.g. Lewis 1983a), the sets that are postulated as the well-defined extensions of our vague predicates are then guaranteed to correspond to a property. But this only shifts the issue to the equally pressing question why our predicate should correspond to one particular such property rather than another with a very similar extension (since on this view there are properties for any possible extension), and what determines the one to which it corresponds. If the suggestion that the extensions of predicates are determined by properties is to help, we need to assume something like Lewis's thesis that there is an elite class of properties, the 'natural properties' (whether or not there are also the abundant properties corresponding to every set of possible entities). Lewis's natural properties are those that science aims to discover, and they are the properties that figure in laws and ground objective resemblances between individuals; he suggests that universals or equivalence classes of tropes may play the role of natural properties. But, as those theorising about properties often stress (see e.g. Armstrong 1978), it is highly implausible to suppose that each of our vague predicates corresponds to a precise natural property so understood. We may classify things as 'chairs' or people as 'computer nerds', but in so doing we are not reporting on a natural classification with any scientific role and the reason why not is not necessarily because of the vagueness of those predicates.

Perhaps vague predicates (or some of them) correspond not directly to a single natural property, but rather to a complex of such properties, such as a disjunction, or a disjunction of conjunctions. In what we may assume is a one-dimensional case, namely 'tall', the disjuncts could be determinate height properties, each of which (we may suppose) is a natural property. But the pressing question then arises: what could determine exactly which height-properties are disjuncts for 'tall'? Any precise selection of disjuncts will provide a precise extension, and a wide range of selections will be compatible with the majority of our uses of the predicate. Should *being 5 feet 11 inches* be among those properties, and where does the sharp boundary fall between the properties that are disjuncts and those that are not? Similarly, each different way in which something could be a chair might be equated with a conjunction of natural properties, so that by disjoining these conjunctions we could obtain a condition satisfied by all and only chairs. But what determines what the components of that complex property-construction are?

Williamson suggests that the property of F-ness is the conjunction of all those properties that are candidates for being the property which our (fallible) mechanism for recognising F-ness detects best (1994, p. 208). For 'tall', these candidate properties would be properties *taller than x*, for some height x. But the condition for satisfying the conjunction of these properties would then be the same as the condition for one of the properties, namely that specified by the highest value of x. The move to conjunctions does not remove the implausibility of identifying tallness with exactly one of the sharp properties, and it is unclear why the highest value of x should be privileged in this way. To summarise: the call on worldly properties and complexes of them is of no help for isolating unique sharply bounded extensions for our vague predicates.

So what does determine the sharp boundaries? Williamson's main reply – the only plausible one left – is that it is our use of the word in question which draws the lines determining meaning, though we are not conscious either that it does or how it does. He equates this with the claim that meaning supervenes on use. As discussed in §2, Williamson claims that meaning can differ when there are different patterns of use; the supervenience claim adds that an expression cannot have a different meaning in different circumstances *without* a difference in use.

The supervenience thesis gives no indication of *how* use determines meaning, and Williamson suggests that 'meaning may supervene on use in an unsurveyably chaotic way' (1994, p. 209): even if we could examine use in all its detail, this might not reveal the boundaries of meaning. We should not expect an algorithm by which meaning could be calculated from use. It would be an unlikely theory which required that a belongs to the extension of F iff at least 90 per cent of speakers would assent to 'a is F'. The chaotic supervenience allows that the assent of different proportions of speakers is required for 'red' than for 'green', say, and that 'table' may work in another, different way. Provided the same pattern of uses of our predicates would always draw the same boundary, the supervenience thesis is upheld.

Williamson uses his supervenience thesis to meet an objection about the relation between meaning and use. It is undeniable that meaning is intimately connected to use; Williamson claims that 'words mean what they do because we use them as we do' (1992b, p. 154). Now, in the case of a vague predicate, when neither natural boundaries nor stipulation determines a sharp boundary to its extension, its sharp boundary, if it has one, must be drawn entirely in virtue of how we use that predicate. But we do not use 'tall' as if one hundredth of an inch could make a difference to its applicability. More generally, we do not use vague predicates as if they are sharply bounded. Thus it might seem that a theory that maintains a commitment to sharp boundaries must sever the connection between meaning and use. In response, Williamson argues that the connection *can* be preserved by the supervenience thesis: the connection between meaning and use is not severed if the use of a predicate is always tied to its meaning in such a way that no other meaning could accompany that pattern of uses.

But the complaint that the epistemic view severs the connection between meaning and use must not be run together with my original issue, which centres on the lack of natural or stipulated boundaries which 'draw a line' around the extensions of our vague expressions, and asks *what* draws this line. It is this issue that poses the greater threat to the epistemic theory, and the supervenience thesis does not meet it, as I shall show.

Having presented such an objection in terms of 'drawing lines' around extensions, Williamson turns his attention entirely to the supervenience claim. This is justified thus: 'On the face of it, "drawing" is just a metaphor for "determining". To say that use determines meaning is just to say that meaning *supervenes* on use' (1994, p. 206). But, I shall argue, the sense of 'determining' that corresponds to 'drawing' lines is not the weak sense associated with a supervenience relation. So the move from questions of drawing lines to the supervenience issue does not provide a reasonable response to his objections.

First note that the supervenience thesis guarantees that *if* there are sharp boundaries then, being an aspect of meaning, they are determined by use. But this does not touch the implausibility of the claim that such lines *are* drawn. For the supervenience thesis could equally be maintained within non-classical frameworks ruling, for example, that if a sentence is neither true nor false, it will be neither true nor false unless there is a difference in the subvening base. Or within any other theory of vagueness it could be held that, without a difference in use, there is no difference in meaning, in that there is no difference in the clear cases of the extension of a vague predicate, or in the location of the *fuzzy* boundary.

Furthermore, the supervenience thesis does not answer the question how unique lines around extensions are singled out. The thesis is compatible with almost *any* meaning being paired with a given pattern of use. The only requirement is that such a pattern of use would *always* be coupled with that meaning – but that imposes little constraint. The fact that there can be no difference in meaning without a difference in use does not fix the boundaries of extensions any more than a pass–fail divide is fixed by the requirement that qualitatively identical exam scripts should receive the same mark. To say that the nature of the script determines what mark it receives in the weak sense that this supervenience requirement holds would do nothing to meet someone's worries that a sharp pass–fail divide has not been determined or drawn.

Even if we could rule out many possible pairings of meaning and use (just as we could rule out many possible pass–fail divides), that obviously is not enough. According to Williamson there is a – possibly chaotic – function that maps the uses of predicates to the sets which are their precise extensions. But now consider a different function that maps the same uses to sets that are in some cases slightly different – a function that differs only in being marginally more strict over the membership of one or two particular extensions. Call its values the extensions★ of the predicates in question. This function will determine sharp extensions★ and these too will supervene on use. Then the question is: why is it extensions rather than extensions★ that play the roles we associate with meanings in, for example, determining the truth-conditions of sentences? What could it possibly be that singles out the uniquely correct extension-determining function?

The sense (if there is one) in which use determines meaning is not a sense that will help answer the initial question of why, for example, the sharp boundary to the extension of 'tall' is drawn at one point rather than another. For a claim that the facts about A supervene on the facts about B is not always enough to answer the question *how* the facts about B determine what the facts about A are. Something needs to be said about the *way* in which the one set of facts determines the other – about the function which maps facts about B into facts about A. With other supposed cases of supervenience it might be laws which fill the missing explanatory role. For example, it might be that the mental supervenes on the physical and that psychophysical laws fix the mental facts given the physical facts. Given a specification of the laws, the supervenience claim would then answer questions about what determines which mental facts obtain and how it does so. In other instances of supervenience, the supervening facts might follow from the subvening ones plus meaning constraints: if it were built into the meaning of the relevant terms used in expressing facts about A just how they depended on the facts about B, this too would uniquely fix the facts about A given those about B (and if the meanings were vague, it might be appropriate for the facts to be fixed only vaguely). But in Williamson's account there is nothing to play the equivalent role.

Now, Williamson correctly observes 'every known recipe for extracting meaning from use breaks down even in cases to which vagueness is irrelevant. The inability of the epistemic view of vagueness to provide a successful recipe is an inability it shares with all its rivals' (1994, p. 207). But my objections have not required him to provide such a recipe, rather they have been dissecting his reply to what he acknowledges to be a reasonable question about line-drawing. Another indication that he should, by his own lights, take seriously my points is that he confronts a similar but more restricted line of attack. He envisages a case where there is perfect symmetry within the uses of a sentence *p* such that assertions and denials of *p* are balanced. He considers the objection that 'any assignment of truth or falsity would involve an implausible breaking of the symmetry in an arbitrarily chosen direction' (1994, p. 207; see also his 1997a where the case is of a similar symmetry in the stipulated meaning of a word). In such a case, he seems to be acknowledging that use is inadequate for choosing between the alternatives. His response is to uncover an asymmetry between truth and falsity, the details of which do not matter for us here. But if the call upon supervenience were good enough to explain what determines meaning and so truth-values in general, it should also serve here. The symmetry can be broken in either direction with the supervenience retained. If an explanation of 'why one extension rather than another' is needed in his case, why is it not needed in general? My cases are more complex: there is nothing to decide between a larger number of alternative extensions: the decision among them would again be arbitrary. Williamson should admit that something more than supervenience needs to be invoked if there are to be grounds for believing that the arbitrary choice is settled. The appeal to the asymmetry of truth and falsity is of no use in my more general case (even if it works in his own) and there are no comparable principles available to complete the task.

Williamson allows that meaning can be determined by several different factors (e.g. by natural boundaries or by stipulation), but maintains that if none of the other factors is good enough to fix a sharp extension, then our use does so. But we need a reason to suppose that *anything* succeeds in pinning down precise extensions when nothing appears to, in particular when there are no appropriate natural boundaries in the world. What is the guarantee that our practices *do* in fact determine precise meanings for all our words? Could it not be that our uses of words are simply not adequate to serve this purpose, so that, for example, 'tall' picks out only a rough region of the height scale? Compare Williamson's remark that 'To know what a word means is to be completely inducted into a practice *that does in fact determine a meaning*' (1994, p. 211; my italics), suggesting that practices might not do so. Williamson has simply not answered his hypothetical opponent who suggests that 'our use leaves not a line but a smear' (1994, p. 206). And, to summarise: appeal to the supervenience of meaning on use does not help either in establishing that there are sharp boundaries, or in answering the crucial question how such boundaries could possibly be determined: everything rests on the demands of classical logic and semantics.

In terms of the distinction between realism and the modelling approach (see chapter 2, §3), I take the epistemic view to be a form of realism – the (classical) truth-values assigned to sentences represent real (though sometimes unknown) features of those sentences in relation to the world, rather than just being artefacts of a model. That approach makes the objections of this section highly relevant: it is reasonable to ask about these real features and the sharp boundaries to which the theory is committed, and in particular how they are determined (see chapter 2, §3iv). And the arguments in this section can be adapted and used against certain other realist theories of vagueness that are committed to sharp boundaries of some sort: see §9 of the next chapter.

My arguments in this chapter have not, of course, shown the epistemic view to be untenable. I have not dwelt on the prime attraction of its adherence to classical logic and semantics. Williamson says of the methodology of the epistemic view that 'one holds one's logic fixed, to discipline one's philosophical thinking' (Williamson 1997a, p. 218). This is not mere stipulation, however, rather 'the epistemicist's hunch is that in the long run the results of discipline will be more satisfying from a philosophical as well as from a logical point of view'. That hunch has not been borne out. We should entertain the revision of classical logic and semantics and seek a theory that can respect more of our intuitions. By the end of this book I hope to have shown that there is a philosophically, logically and intuitively satisfying theory and so we are justified in rejecting the epistemic view as the overwhelmingly predominant initial reactions to it would have us do.

4

*Between truth and falsity:
many-valued logics*

I. INTRODUCTION

When *a* is a borderline case of *F*, it seems that, *pace* the epistemic view, '*a* is *F*' is neither true nor false. According to a natural interpretation such a predication takes some intermediate, non-classical truth-value. In this chapter I consider theories of vagueness that introduce one or more new truth-values and that adopt a many-valued logic. Such theories can vary along a number of dimensions, and to bring this out I shall focus on four central questions.

(i) How many values should we admit? And how are these values to be understood?

(ii) Are the sentential connectives truth-functional?

(iii) What is the detailed semantics of the connectives and quantifiers?

(iv) What is validity? How is the classical notion to be generalised?

'Many-valued' is often used to describe logics which have more than two truth-values and which are truth-functional in the sense that the value of a compound sentence is determined by the values of its components (the term 'value-functional' may be more appropriate, but I stick with the more familiar term). The answer to (ii) must then be 'yes' for any theory which is many-valued in this more specific sense. But this chapter will also deal with certain theories that admit more than two values within a non-truth-functional framework, and I shall use 'many-valued' to cover these logics as well.

Answers to the four questions will serve to fix most of the main features of any given theory and place it within the space of possible many-valued theories. To illustrate, I shall first outline the answers for Tye's three-valued logic (Tye 1990, 1994) and Machina's infinite-valued logic (Machina 1972, 1976), which I suggest are the best of the three-valued and infinite-valued treatments. In §§4–7, I examine a wider range of responses to questions (i) to (iv) and strategic issues bound up with answering them. This will serve to eliminate some possibilities altogether, thus narrowing the field of plausible candidate theories, and it will also raise some serious objections faced by the remaining options.

The variety of possible theories means that we should be wary of arguments that seek to reject *all* many-valued theories on the basis of some given feature, for that feature may not be essential to all many-valued theories. Thus, for example, counter-intuitive consequences need to be reckoned up separately for the different definitions of the connectives that may be chosen. I suggest, however, that all the options that succeed in reaching a reflective equilibrium have substantial costs (denied intuitions and opinions etc.) and I illustrate this by returning to Tye's theory in §8. In §9 I shall argue that issues surrounding higher-order vagueness and sharp boundaries pose insurmountable problems for all many-valued theories. Chapter 5 provides some further arguments that show degree theories to be untenable.

2. TYE'S THREE-VALUED LOGIC

How does Tye answer the four questions (i) to (iv)? (i) Tye employs three truth-values: true, false and indefinite, and thus he defends a three-valued logic governing sentences with these values.[1] (ii) According to his semantics, the logical connectives ¬, &, ∨, ⊃ and ≡ are truth-functional. (iii) Tye endorses the normality constraint (see chapter 2, §3iii above), according to which if a compound sentence has components that are all either true or false, then its value must coincide with the value it would receive in the classical framework. And he offers some further considerations regarding the specific connectives which, he claims, serve to isolate Kleene's three-valued tables as uniquely appropriate for capturing vagueness (Tye 1994, p. 194; Kleene 1952, pp. 332–40). For example, 'a conjunction is true if both its conjuncts are true and false if either conjunct is false. Otherwise it is indefinite.' The definitions are as follows:

---

[1] Strictly speaking 'indefinite' labels a truth-value gap rather than a third value. On this contrast see §4 below.

p	$\neg p$		p	q	$p \,\&\, q$	$p \vee q$	$p \supset q$	$p \equiv q$
T	F		T	T	T	T	T	T
I	I		T	I	I	T	I	I
F	T		T	F	F	T	F	F
			I	T	I	T	T	I
			I	I	I	I	I	I
			I	F	F	I	I	I
			F	T	F	T	T	F
			F	I	F	I	T	I
			F	F	F	F	T	T

Tye notes that his account yields no tautologies – i.e. no formulae which are always true. For example, the law of excluded middle is not a tautology since $p \vee \neg p$ is indefinite when p is indefinite. He observes, however, that this and other classical laws are at least never false and he coins the phrase 'quasi-tautology' for schemata satisfying this condition. The quantifiers are defined as follows: $(\exists x)Fx$ is true if Fx is true for some value of x, false if Fx is false for all values and indefinite otherwise; and $(\forall x)Fx$ is true if Fx is true for all values of x, false if Fx is false for some value and indefinite otherwise.[2]

To turn to point (iv): Tye endorses a notion of validity for which preservation of truth is of the essence (see e.g. 1994, p. 203, footnote 13). This allows him to treat the typical sorites argument as valid but to hold that the falsity of its conclusion indicates only that one of the premises is not true, i.e. is false or indefinite. He goes on to claim that the inductive premise of the argument is in fact indefinite (since on his truth-tables 'if Fx_i then Fx_{i+1}' will be indefinite when x_i and x_{i+1} are both borderline Fs).

3. MACHINA'S DEGREE THEORY

Much of the technical material used in degree theories relies on Zadeh's work on fuzzy logic and fuzzy set theory (e.g. Zadeh 1965, 1975). But Zadeh will not figure centrally in this chapter since his *philosophical* contribution is less significant. The best philosophical

---

[2] Horgan 1994 notes that his own account is very similar to Tye's, though in his presentation via a 'Tarski-style truth-characterisation' rather than truth-tables, there is no explicit mention of three values.

discussion is in Machina 1976, so I outline his position here in relation to questions (i) to (iv).

(i) Machina admits infinitely many truth-values corresponding to degrees of truth, represented by the set of real numbers in the interval [0, 1]. (ii) His chosen semantics is again truth-functional, or *degree-functional* as it is sometimes known when the truth-values are degrees of truth. And (iii) he defends the following truth-conditions for the connectives:

$|\neg p| = 1 - |p|$ (where $|p|$ denotes the value of p).
$|p \, \& \, q| = \min(|p|, |q|)$ [i.e. the minimum of the values of the conjuncts]
$|p \vee q| = \max(|p|, |q|)$ [i.e. the maximum of the values of the disjuncts]
$|p \supset q| = 1$ when $|p|$ is less than or equal to $|q|$
$\qquad\quad = 1 - |p| + |q|$ otherwise.
$|p \equiv q| = 1 - |p| + |q|$ if $|p| \le |q|$ and $1 - |q| + |p|$ if $|q| \le |p|$.

These are the same as in Łukasiewicz's family of many-valued systems (see Łukasiewicz and Tarski 1930). When given in the above general form, the same stipulations can be used in many-valued logics with different numbers of values, including a three-valued theory if we associate the intermediate value with 0.5 (the tables for $\&$, $\vee$ and $\neg$ then coincide with Tye's, but those for $\supset$ and $\equiv$ do not).

As well as the sentential connectives, we can ask about sub-sentential semantics. Given the standard connections between $\&$ and $\forall$ and between $\vee$ and $\exists$ – connections that are no less compelling in the presence of vagueness – the semantics of the universal and existential quantifiers will be fixed once we have decided the truth-definitions for $\&$ and $\vee$. Thus for finite domains the value of $(\forall x)Fx$ should coincide with the value of the conjunction of all the instances of Fx, and $(\exists x)Fx$ with their disjunction. So, given Machina's interpretation of conjunction, $(\forall x)Fx$ must take the value of the least true instance of Fx, or (to accommodate infinite domains) the greatest lower bound of the values of Fx. Similarly $(\exists x)Fx$ takes the least upper bound of those values.

What about the interpretation of predicates that come in degrees? According to Fregean semantics, a first-level predicate takes as its semantic value the function which maps the objects which satisfy the predicate to the truth-value T and all other objects to F. In the natural many-valued generalisation, predicates are assigned functions from objects into the new, larger set of truth-values. So on Machina's degree theory these will be functions from objects to real numbers in the interval [0, 1] – for example, 'red' is assigned the function which maps each object to the number representing the degree to which it is red. Such functions correspond to 'fuzzy sets', where an object o belongs to a fuzzy set to degree d if the defining function maps o onto the number d (see Zadeh 1965 on fuzzy set theory). In fact, Machina elaborates the basic account by allowing a predicate to be associated with several fuzzy sets (1976, pp. 66–8). This device can be used to capture the phenomenon that he labels 'conflict vagueness', where the application of F can be a vague matter because there are several relevant factors which are in conflict. But Machina's valuation function still ensures that any predication receives a single, final value from the original truth-value set (e.g. by balancing the contribution of the different factors).

As to (iv), Machina's preferred definition construes validity as preservation of degree of truth in the following way: an argument is valid iff the conclusion must be at least as true as the least true premise. Using this definition, we can assess the validity of the sorites paradox. Consider a version with a series of conditional premises of the form 'if Fx_i then Fx_{i+1}'. In borderline cases, the value of Fx_{i+1} will be lower than that of Fx_i. But for a decent sorites series with small enough differences between consecutive members, the difference in successive truth-values will always be small and so, given Machina's truth-definition for conditionals, 'if Fx_i then Fx_{i+1}' will be at least nearly true for each i. Thus, since the first premise of the form Fx_0 is true to degree 1, all premises will be (at least) nearly true. But, since the sorites takes us from nearly true premises to a conclusion Fx_n which is, we can assume, completely false, the argument is invalid.

4. THE TRUTH-VALUES

Tye and Machina represent the two most common positions on the range of truth-values for a many-valued theory of vagueness: i.e. most theorists either assign all borderline predications the same intermediate value and defend a three-valued logic or adopt an infinite-valued logic and interpret the values as degrees of truth. In this section I examine these choices and show that the alternatives can be more swiftly rejected. I shall also argue that no arguments show that we must admit a third value or that degrees of truth are required; the defence of either truth-value set must rest on more specific details of the theory.

Consider first three-valued logics. Are we warranted in introducing a third value at all? Proponents may argue that it is necessary since neither of the classical pair of values can be used to capture the status of borderline case predications. And unless we allow for the intermediate value, they continue, we will not be able to reveal the logical behaviour of a vague language. The acceptability of introducing a third value will then rest on the success of the attempt to capture the logic of vague terms and other phenomena bound up with vagueness. But the non-classical status of borderline cases is not alone enough to warrant the introduction of a third value. An alternative position such as supervaluationism agrees that borderline sentences do not take classical values, but it captures their logic without introducing a new value or new definitions of the connectives etc. Instead it admits truth-value gaps, while requiring only the logical principles that govern the classical values.

It seems, then, that we can either introduce a new value or admit a truth-value gap. But the assumption that there is a significant distinction between a third value and a gap may be challenged: consider Tye's remark that 'the third value here is, strictly speaking, not a truth-value at all but rather a truth-value gap' (1994, p. 194). In support of this gap-interpretation of the three-valued logic used for vagueness, it might be argued, for example, that there are no truth-values besides truth and falsity, it is just that some sentences take neither of these values, and that when we model the logical behaviour, we can do so with a three-valued logic where the third value is reserved for sentences that lack classical values. (This would be comparable to Kripke's treatment of truth and the liar paradox (1975): he admits truth-value gaps but claims that from outside the language the Kleene system can be used to capture logical relations.) In relation to many-valued theories of vagueness, the difference between viewing the intermediate truth-value status as a lack of value (i.e. a lack of classical value) and viewing it as a new intermediate value will not matter for our purposes. None of my criticisms relies on the latter view. Either way the aim is to describe the truth-value status of such predications and to give an account of their logical behaviour. The important issue will turn out to be not what we call the intermediate status but whether it plays a truth-functional role like truth and falsity, as on Tye's approach, or not, as supervaluationists claim.

Alternative accounts that admit some finite number of values greater than three are rarely defended for the purposes of a theory of vagueness. Any motivations for admitting non-classical values are either satisfied by having a single intermediate value or require the whole range of values which degree theorists accept. So I turn next to infinite-valued treatments of vagueness.

In addition to Machina, advocates of an infinite-valued account have included Goguen 1969, Lakoff 1973, Sanford 1975, King 1979 and Forbes 1983. The prime motivation for this choice of the set of truth-values is to allow a continuous range of values that reflect, for example, the continuity of heights determining degrees of tallness. We can then discriminate among borderline cases: there are pairs of borderline tall people, *a* and *b*, where *a* is taller than *b*, and this fact can be captured by assigning a higher value to '*a* is tall' than to '*b* is tall'. Machina, for example, argues that there could be a continuum of borderline cases, each differing from one another and such that for no two such cases does the predicate apply to the same degree. He concludes that this requires the introduction of infinitely many (indeed, continuum many) truth-values to capture degrees of truth (1976, p. 60). So borderline cases take intermediate values, and do not always take the same value. And the fuzzy boundary of 'tall' is supposedly accommodated by the gradual change in truth-value of predications as height gradually increases through the borderline cases. Such discriminations and gradual changes in truth-value cannot be marked within a three-valued theory.

But should we even admit that truth comes in degrees? I will confine myself to examining the notion specifically in connection with vagueness.[3] The major argument for degrees of truth stems from the initial motivation for a degree theory of vagueness, namely the supposed need to discriminate among borderline cases with respect to degrees of application. The argument is a common one, but is

---

[3] Haack 1980 argues that there are no compelling general reasons to admit degrees of truth, for example, given methodological, metaphysical and linguistic considerations. I am equally persuaded that there are no reasons to reject degrees of truth outright.

particularly clearly stated by Forbes (1983, pp. 241–2), on which I base my formulation.

Consider a pair of men, *a* and *b*, such that

(1) *a* is taller than *b*.

We can infer that

(2) *a* is tall to a greater degree than *b*; so
(3) *a* satisfies the predicate 'is tall' to a greater degree than *b*; and so
(4) '*a* is tall' has a higher degree of truth than '*b* is tall'.

It cannot be denied that there are pairs of things satisfying (1) and that this is typical of a vague predicate: standardly, for vague *F*, one thing can be more *F* than another. In chapter 5 I shall offer a sense of 'coming in degrees' that legitimises the move from (1) to (2), but *not* the inference from (2) to (3). Here I shall compress these steps and reject the inference from (1) to (3) (remaining neutral as to which intermediate step should be denied): we cannot always conclude from the fact that *a* is more *F* than *b* that *a* satisfies the predicate *F* to a greater degree than *b* does.

Suppose *a* is 6 feet 9 inches and *b* is 6 feet 8 inches. Though *a* is taller than *b*, so (1) holds, they are both unquestionably *tall* and satisfy 'is tall' completely, so that '*a* is tall' and '*b* is tall' both count as completely true, and (3) fails (Klein 1980, p. 6 and others have raised cases of this kind). The degree theorist might reply that Forbes's argument only works when *a* and *b* are borderline *F*s, and that it is only for borderline cases that comparatives track differences in degrees of truth. But then we will need a new argument for adopting this apparently ad hoc position. Why suppose the argument works at all when it fails in such a wide range of cases? At the best, it will not then be available as a reason for admitting degrees of truth. Alternatively, a degree theorist could maintain that comparative relations *do* always reveal differences in truth, but that no one is ever really tall to degree 1 and no collection of grains ever counts as a heap to degree 1. The numerical assignments for 'heap' would then be asymptotic to 1 for increasing size of the collection of grains (i.e. approaching nearer and nearer, but never reaching, 1). But the denial of degree 1 (or completely true) cases is unreasonable, and any account exhibiting this feature fails to give the semantics of the predicate as it actually is, according to which many collections of grains are definitely heaps. (Additionally, with a popular definition of validity as the preservation of complete truth – see §7 – the strategy of excluding degree 1 truths would render useless the corresponding account of inference for vague language.)

As a second counter-example, substitute 'acute' (as applied to angles) for 'tall' in (1)–(4): many instances of the equivalent of (1) are true, i.e. when *a* is more acute than *b*, but the corresponding conclusions (3) and (4) must be resisted, for being acute is an all-or-nothing matter, and calling an angle 'acute' is either completely true or completely false. (See Williamson 1994, p. 126 on the behaviour of 'acute'.) In short, even the degree theorist needs an account of one thing's being more *F* than another which does not commit us to calling one predication of *F* more true than another, and we could then use this account for all instances of the comparative without adopting a degree theory. The Forbes argument fails to show that the fact that one thing can be more *F* than another implies that predications of *F* can be true to different degrees.

Should we also object to the inference from (3) to (4)? Someone might object that this move is undermined by the suggestion that two-place predicates of the form 'is *F* to degree ...' could be used to report degrees of satisfaction of 'is *F*', for there would then be no need to invoke degrees of truth in connection with these two-place predicates.[4] More generally, they might object that even if a theory of vagueness uses the idea of degrees of application (degrees of redness etc.), it can do so without committing itself to degrees of truth. But the introduction of new two-place predicates does not remove the need to enquire about predications using the old one-place predicates, and it is *these* which require degrees of truth if *F*-ness comes in degrees. The degree theorist cannot do without degrees of truth in this way.

Though I deny that the Forbes argument shows that we need degrees of truth, I shall proceed by giving degree theorists the benefit of the doubt and allowing them to employ the notion of degrees of truth. If by making the assumption that there are degrees of truth the optimum theory of vagueness can be produced – a theory that

---

[4] Compare Haack on a number of other applications of many-valued logic: 'what looks on the face of it like the assignment of a non-standard value to a standard item may turn out to be best explicable as the assignment of a standard value to a non-standard item' (1978, p. 214).

performs all of the relevant tasks, respects more intuitions than other theories and boasts appropriate theoretical virtues – then I suggest that this gives enough reason to accept that assumption. A successful degree theory of vagueness may thus support the thesis that truth comes in degrees, even if other arguments to this end are inconclusive.

Granting the legitimacy of assignments from a range of infinitely many values, we can ask about the size and structure of that range. Degree theorists typically adopt a continuum of values rather than countably many – the values are represented by the real numbers in the interval [0, 1], and not, for example, the rational numbers in that interval. They often argue that we need a continuum to represent relevant differences between candidates because, for example, change in colour can be continuous (see Machina 1976, p. 60). And there is also a technical reason against choosing the rationals, due to the standard definitions of the quantifiers: the greatest lower bound of a set of rationals need not itself be a rational, and so, given the Łukasiewicz definition of the universal quantifier in terms of the greatest lowest bound of its instances, the reals are required (as noted by Williamson, 1994, p. 290). In chapter 5, however, I shall argue that the use of the real numbers in the interval [0, 1] misrepresents the phenomena of vagueness (as indeed would the use of the corresponding range of rationals).

There are other alternatives to the standard infinite set of values – alternatives that still permit continuity, but deny that the interval [0, 1] will suffice to represent all values. I shall discuss them only briefly because even if they are viable (which is doubtful) they would involve a huge increase in complexity without substantial gain over the more standard theories, and without providing any new response to the most serious criticisms of degree theories (in particular the objections I will raise in §9).

Goguen (1969) has suggested various generalisations of the basic degree-theoretic story. For example, for multi-dimensional predicates the truth-values may sometimes be better considered as n-tuples of real numbers, with a component for each dimension. Take 'big' (applied to people), which depends on both height and volume. If there were a uniquely correct way to weigh these dimensions so that it was clear how each factor contributes to counting as 'big', a single value could be assigned and for any two people, one or other will count as 'big' to at least as high a degree as the other. (Compare the way Machina's valuation determines a unique value to '*a* is *F*', despite the association of several different fuzzy sets with *F*; see §3.) But there is no such non-arbitrary balancing of the dimensions and the comparison between two borderline big people is sometimes made impossible because of differences along different dimensions. (In chapter 1, §2 I showed that multi-dimensional predicates typically have vague comparatives – the relevance of this to degree theories will be discussed in chapter 5.) An *n*-tuple may then provide a better semantic representation by taking account of all factors relevant to the application of the predicate without forcing them into an inappropriate regimentation. But even the use of *n*-tuples may not be sufficient for representing those multi-dimensional predicates where the dimensions are not themselves clear-cut and where there is no space of relevant dimensions in which candidates can be naturally placed – a feature that, in chapter 1 §2, I illustrated with 'nice'. Using an *n*-tuple in this type of case will be subject to the same misleading regimentations as using the unit interval in other multi-dimensional cases.

Introducing *n*-tuple values creates a very substantial increase in the complexity of the theory and it is not clear how we should understand the new set of values even if we could understand those of the standard theories. These complaints are even more pertinent when Goguen seeks to generalise further in such a way that he is not limited to *n*-tuples either. This discussion is conducted at such a high level of generality that, as Williamson objects (1994, p. 133), although elements of the structure of a theory are specified, Goguen does not actually provide a system that could be taken as the logic of our vague language and it is far from clear how one could be generated from his discussion.

Zadeh 1975 defends a different modification to the truth-value set and introduces fuzzy truth-values corresponding to vague expressions such as 'very true', 'quite false' etc. The new values are themselves fuzzy sets: sentences can be members of them to different degrees (e.g. a sentence that is true to degree *n* might be a member of the truth-value 'quite true' to degree *m* and a member of 'not very false' to some other degree). But these fuzzy truth-values are fixed on the basis of an assignment of numerical degrees of truth and their membership can only be artificially stipulated, so Zadeh's approach does not in fact depart very substantially or justifiably from other infinite-valued theories (see Haack 1979 for further criticisms of it).

Williamson summarises matters by saying 'semantic theories using non-numerical degrees are inchoate' (1994, p. 135). I shall continue my discussion of many-valued theories on the assumption that the only viable options have either three values or else a continuum of degrees of truth represented by [0, 1].

5. TRUTH-FUNCTIONALITY

Most of the proposed many-valued theories have been truth-functional, though detailed reasons for this choice are rarely given. Advocates might defend the assumption simply by claiming that a convincing truth-functional account of the connectives can be given so deviation from it is unwarranted, but the discussion of the next two sections will show this straightforward line to be over-optimistic. Alternatively, they could appeal to considerations of simplicity or claim that the resulting accounts generalise classical logic in the right sort of way. And it might be argued that truth-functionality is of the essence of at least some of the logical connectives in question – it is a feature that cannot be given up without distorting the meaning of the expressions themselves. (Special concerns about whether the conditional is really truth-functional should be set aside here as they are generally independent of the issue of vagueness.)

As critics, on the other hand, we can produce cases apparently showing that there is no satisfactory choice of many-valued truth-function for a connective that is truth-functional in two-valued logic. Suppose Tim is borderline tall (say, tall to degree 0.4) and Tek is taller (tall to degree 0.5), and assume negation reverses values so that 'Tek is not tall' is also true to degree 0.5. Then consider (a) 'Tim is tall and Tek is not tall' and (b) 'Tim is tall and Tek is tall'. Truth-functionality would imply that (a) and (b) must have the same value. But it seems that (a) must be false: if Tim is shorter than Tek, then it cannot be that Tim is tall and Tek is not. And (b) is surely *not* false for a degree-theorist, but is true to some positive degree. Though the theory was advertised as successfully modelling comparisons between borderline cases by assigning different values, it gets matters wrong when it comes to assigning values to complex sentences that should reflect those comparisons. This is also illustrated in examples with conditionals. With the same scenario consider, for example, (c) 'if Tim is tall, Tek is tall'– plausibly true – and (d) 'if Tim is tall, Tek is not tall' – surely false. These two sentences must each have the same value given the commitment to truth-functionality. Similarly, the same value must be given to (e) 'if Tek is tall then Tek is not tall' as to (f) 'if Tek is tall then Tek is tall' since the respective values of the antecedent and consequent of these two conditionals are the same. But (f) is intuitively true and (e) is not, so again no choice of value will capture our intuitions about both of these cases (for Tye both come out indefinite, while for Machina both are true).

Next, (g) 'Tek is tall and Tek is not tall' must be assigned the same value as (h) 'Tek is tall and Tek is tall'. Most theories achieve this by allowing the first sentence – a contradiction – to be less than completely false, and this is a common objection to such theories. Problems for defending the truth-functionality of disjunction arise if we accept that Fine's penumbral connections involving disjunction are also compelling. For example, for a blob on the borderline between red and pink (j) 'the blob is red or pink' is true but (k) 'it is red or red' is only as true as 'it is red', perhaps half true, though the respective components of (j) and (k) may be identically valued. (See chapter 7 for further discussion of penumbral connections.)

So a range of cases show that the price of truth-functionality is very high. With too many complex sentences, a many-valued theory is forced to assign inappropriate values in order to retain a uniformity with structurally similar sentences that it must treat in the same way despite our intuitions that they are crucially different. (See Fine 1975, pp. 269–70, Williamson 1994, pp. 135–8 and Edgington 1997, pp. 304–5 for a range of further examples.)

Could there, however, be pragmatic explanations for our tendency to judge problem cases in a different way from their valuation according to the systems in question? Grice (1975) has provided explanations for our reluctance, when following our intuitions, to declare 'if p, q' true just because p is false: in brief, that conditional is not assertable, being less informative than the assertable ¬p. Any attempt to provide such explanations in the context of a many-valued theory will be complicated by the fact that the relation between degrees of truth and assertability is unclear. (E.g. if something is half true, is it ideally half assertable, perhaps tentatively hedged, or is it unacceptable because we should assert only what is definitely true?)

Advocates of many-valued theories would, at best, face lengthy and complex tasks to get such explanations underway. And the prospects are not promising. Take $p \supset p$, for example: Tye must say that we *over*-estimate its value (judging it true when it is only half true). Normal problems with conditionals – to which Grice's strategy applies – are instances that are counted as true by the truth-definition despite not seeming true. (Similarly, it is usually acknowledged that the truth of $p \supset q$ at least captures a *necessary* condition for the truth of 'if p, q'.) But with $p \supset p$ we have a challenge in the other direction, since that sentence counts as not true despite seeming true. Similarly, Grice's treatment of conditionals would not help explain our alleged over-estimate of the value of 'if Tim is tall then Tek is tall' when Tek is taller than Tim (intuitively true, but indefinite according to Tye when Tim and Tek are borderline tall).

Degree theorists have not pursued such detailed explanations. They typically simply claim, without further discussion, that it is enough that an intuitively true sentence is non-false according to their theory, or perhaps that it takes a value greater than 0.5 (and similarly with an apparently false sentence – e.g. 'he's tall and not tall' – which the theory can show to be non-true or to have a value less than 0.5).[5] More generally, the degree theorist can insist that the counter-intuitive valuations are outweighed by the advantages of the resulting theory as a whole, including, perhaps, theoretical gains bound up with the simplicity and clarity of retaining truth-functionality. But how far retaining truth-functionality *should* be regarded as an advantage in itself largely depends on the viability of theories that deny truth-functionality. I shall argue in chapters 7 and 8 that supervaluationism, the paradigm such theory, provides a successful account of our language that comfortably accommodates those intuitions that degree theories deny. Truth-functionality should be abandoned.

Edgington's interesting proposal (1992, 1997) is to give up truth-functionality, except for keeping the standard definition of negation as $\mid \neg p \mid = 1 - \mid p \mid$. She pursues an analogy between assignments of

---

[5] Even this line will not work for all examples: 'if Tek is tall then he is not tall' is apparently false but counts as completely true on Machina's scheme when Tek is tall to 0.5 degrees, though the comparison with the truth in the classical system of 'if p, $\neg p$' for false p, suggests that some sort of Gricean explanation is available at least here.

probabilities and of 'verities' (her term for degrees of truth or, strictly, for 'degrees of closeness to clear truth'). Just as the probability of p & q is not determined by the probabilities of p and of q alone – it depends on other factors such as the logical relations between p and q – so the verity of p & q is not determined simply by the verities of p and of q. To define her non-truth-functional two-place connectives, she invokes the idea of conditional verity (an analogue of conditional probability), where the verity of q conditional on p is the verity which would be assigned to q if we were to decide to count p as definitely true. For example, suppose a and b are both borderline cases of redness, but b is redder than a: then deciding that a counts as red would commit us to accepting that b is red too, so the conditional verity of 'b is red' given 'a is red' is 1. On the other hand, the conditional verity of 'b is bald' given 'a is red' is equal to the verity of 'b is bald', since the decision to count a as red does not affect the judgement that 'b is bald'. The verities of conjunctions and disjunctions are calculated on the basis of such conditional verities by analogues of the familiar probabilistic formulae: for example, the verity of p & q is the conditional verity of q given p multiplied by the verity of p (see 1997, p. 306). And in her 1992 (p. 202) Edgington identifies the verity of the conditional 'if p, then q' with the conditional verity of q given p. (This is perhaps surprising given her insistence elsewhere that conditionals are not bearers of truth and falsity; see e.g. her 1986.)

But the idea of verity and in particular conditional verity – the value to be assigned to q if we were to decide that p is definitely true – is not as straightforward as Edgington implies. First, surely definite truth is not something we can just decide: if p, say Fa, is not definitely true we cannot just decide that it is. We *can* ask what value we would be obliged to assign to q if we were to *call* Fa definitely true or change the meaning of F such that a does qualify as definitely F. This, then, starts to resemble supervaluationism. Moreover, second, note the assumption of uniqueness in implying that deciding that a is definitely F fixes a specific value for any q, namely *the* verity of q if Fa counts as definitely true. Even if we accept the two initial illustrations, what can we say about the conditional verity of 'a is red' given 'b is red' (when, as before, a and b are both borderline cases of redness, but b is redder than a)? We might count b as red by drawing a boundary for redness between a and b so that a counts as not-red, or by drawing the boundary in such a way that both *a* and *b* count as red, or by reallocating verity values among the cases less red than *b* – and we could do this in many ways – so that '*a* is red' has a value higher than before the decision about *b*, but still less than 1. The notion of conditional verity explained as above does not settle which of these options is appropriate: the uniqueness assumption is unwarranted. The only plausible way to deal with this lack of uniqueness is in the way supervaluationism deals with the lack of a unique precisification, namely by quantifying over alternatives. But that would be to offer a radically different account, the details of which have not been given and could be developed in a number of different ways.

The most straightforward way to build on supervaluationist ideas to develop Edgington's degree theory would be to interpret non-truth-functional verities on the basis of a measure over admissible valuations; the conditional verity of *q* given *p* could then be calculated by taking the valuations in which *p* is true and measuring the proportion of these valuations in which *q* is also true. This account would then be a development of the Lewis–Kamp suggestion to be discussed in chapter 7, §3. Edgington suggests the supervaluational interpretation in her 1992, p. 201. In 1997, pp. 315-16, she also suggests it as a model, though she is reluctant to rely on it or to regard it as anything more than heuristic because of general doubts about the supervaluationist framework. Her doubts, however, are unfounded (see chapter 7, §6) and, as indicated, I think Edgington needs some version of a supervaluationary theory to make sense of conditional verities (unless they are merely epistemic: see §9v).

In the rest of this chapter the rejection of truth-functionality for Edgington's account will not be relevant. For example, her account of validity (§7) could be combined with a truth-functional account. And the objections I raise in §9 and chapter 5 concerning, for example, higher-order vagueness are applicable to all degree theories including Edgington's. First I return to the various truth-functional definitions of the connectives.

6. DETAILED SEMANTICS OF THE CONNECTIVES

In the last section I argued that truth-functional accounts deliver unacceptably large collections of counter-intuitive classifications of compound sentences. But the possibility of explaining away our intuitions about the sentences was not (and cannot be) ruled out. And if a persuasive case could be made for adopting a particular set of definitions of the connectives, this could help compensate for the disadvantages of truth-functionality. Presentations of many-valued theories often proceed by offering such a case. But when we take all such presentations together, it seems that each just offers a convenient package of considerations and ignores others, and no set of truth-functional definitions satisfies them all. In this section I survey some of the types of considerations that have been called upon to justify choices of definitions. And I shall illustrate the conflicts: by emphasising different pre-theoretical intuitions and theoretical considerations, various different sets of definitions can be reached. For example, Williamson (1994, pp. 115–17, in seeking the best possible many-valued theory, which he goes on to reject) provides a series of reasonable assumptions and shows in detail how they dictate the Łukasiewicz semantics summarised in §3. Tye and others seek to justify competing alternatives. In §8, in summarising unattractive features of Tye's theory, we will see a typical range of problems raised by that particular set of definitions of the connectives. Perhaps, there are several many-valued systems that are acceptable (and unacceptable) to the same extent. Such theories may tie as judged by the reflective equilibrium test, but, I claim, they fall well below theories which do not cleave to truth-functionality within a non-classical framework. Moreover, as I will show, many of the motivations described in this section would suit a supervaluationist framework much better; and many considerations that conflict in the context of the constraints of truth-functionality can be accommodated together in that alternative framework.

The truth-definition of negation, $|\neg p| = 1 - |p|$ (or the non-numerical equivalent of reversing values e.g. where the negation of an indefinite sentence is also indefinite), is universally agreed upon by many-valued theorists. There is, though, scope for having another type of negation as well (weak negation) which is (completely) true as long as the proposition is less than completely true, (i.e. defined as $|-p| = 0$ if $|p| = 1$ and $|-p| = 1$ otherwise). Horgan, for example, calls upon both types of negation. Then conditionals are defined for Horgan in terms of negation and disjunction, so they also come in two different varieties depending on which negation is involved.

The truth-functional treatment of conjunction and disjunction introduces more substantial variation, even if we assume that the number of truth-values has been fixed. And there is still more variation in the generalisation of the classical material conditional. For example, Goguen suggests deviation from the Łukasiewicz definitions of the connectives, such that $| p \& q |$ is taken to be the product of $| p |$ and $| q |$ and that $| p \supset q | = | q | / | p |$ when $| p | \geq | q |$ and $| p | > 0$ and $= 1$ otherwise.

I consider three related categories of the most common sorts of considerations appealed to when deciding between the various alternative truth-definitions. In addition to these, there are sometimes aspects of a theory that impose a general restriction on the definitions of all the connectives. For example, there are the widely supported normality conditions that are satisfied by all leading candidates.[6]

The first type of consideration is raised when a theorist insists on the inter-definability of several connectives. Tye, for example, reaches his definition of $\supset$ by stating that $p \supset q$ must be equivalent to $\neg p \lor q$, and he goes on to define $p \equiv q$ as $(p \supset q) \& (q \supset p)$ (Tye 1994, p. 194). Williamson, however, reaches a different pair of definitions by defining $p \supset q$ as $p \equiv (p \& q)$, having previously established a definition of $\equiv$ (using the thought that the connective reflects the extent of sameness of truth-value between component sentences; 1994, p. 116). Every many-valued theory gives up some of the classical inter-definability relations. How should we decide which of those relations should be retained? Machina warns against taking any given relation for granted once vagueness is recognised (1976, p. 62; he has to give up, for example, the relation between $p \supset q$ and $\neg p \lor q$). Privileging some particular ones, however, appears arbitrary. By contrast, the thought that all inter-definability relations should be preserved can be entirely respected by supervaluationism. And why, we might ask, should vagueness challenge those relations, especially when their defence is often presented in vague natural language?

---

[6] An example more specific to a particular framework arises within Körner's three-valued logic (1966). That logic is taken to be applicable merely at the provisional stage before the elimination of vagueness and neutrality by decisions on the classifications of atomic sentences. See Williamson 1994, pp. 109–11, who argues that Körner's requirements are better met by supervaluationism.

The second type of consideration generalises the previous one and specifies relations between the degrees to be assigned to various related sentences. For example, Williamson (1994, p. 115) makes the assumption that repeating a proposition in a conjunction should not lower the truth-value i.e. ($\&_1$) $| p \& p | \geq | p |$. Along with two other proposed assumptions, this dictates the Łukasiewicz definition of conjunction, whereby a conjunction takes the minimum value of its conjuncts. But Goguen (1969, p. 347) complains that this definition implies that a conjunction is never affected by the values of *both* conjuncts. As an example, we can consider again 'Tim is tall and Tek is not tall' when Tek is taller than Tim: asserting both conjuncts together is worse than asserting either. Goguen's alternative definition $- | p \& q | = | p | . | q | -$ requires denying Williamson's ($\&_1$) and accepting that repeating a proposition usually does lower the degree of truth of what is said. This is a good example of the conflict between the various intuitions affecting our choice of definitions. Again, both intuitions would be respected in a supervaluationist theory, for $p \& p$ always receives the same value as p, and yet the value of a conjunction does not *always* depend on just one conjunct – logical relations between it and another less than true conjunct can affect the value of the whole.

A third type of consideration affecting the choice of truth-definitions concerns the resulting logical truths and, relatedly, the valid formulae. We have already met the example of $p \supset p$. Machina rejects a candidate interpretation of 'if' because $p \supset p$ could then fail to be true (1976, p. 62): assuming $\supset$ is still to be a candidate for regimenting 'if', the logical truth of 'if p, then p' should not be brought into question just because p is vague. But this constraint would rule out Tye's system, according to which $p \supset p$ is indefinite when p is itself indefinite. Similarly, $\neg(p \& \neg p)$ is a popular example of a valid formula but on the Łukasiewicz definition of conjunction, it is not always true. Each many-valued theory must deny that some classical law that is intuitively unthreatened by vagueness can nonetheless be less than true. Supervaluationism retains all classical laws (see chapter 7, §4 for a defence of the law of excluded middle which many-valued theorists sometimes argue *should* fail in the presence of vagueness). Comparable considerations concern the validity of arguments: restrictions may be placed on definitions of the connectives that they allow certain selected classical arguments to remain valid.

Whether this restriction is satisfied, however, depends not only on the definition of the relevant connectives, but also on the account of validity in the new semantics. And the same applies if the case concerning $p \supset p$ is phrased in terms of its being a valid formula. Does it mean that the formula should be always true, or never false, or always take a value above some other given threshold? What is to count as validity was one of my original set of questions, and it is to it that I turn in the next section.

No set of truth-definitions can satisfy all the plausible constraints that proponents of many-valued theories place on them. There is no case for accepting the unpalatable consequences forced upon us when classical logic is abandoned but truth-functionality retained. The next section, on definitions of validity, is something of an aside in my overall rejection of many-valued theories. The discussion serves a number of functions. In particular, first, for purposes of clarification and exposition: no theory is complete without an account of validity and there are very different consequences for the different choices. Second, my discussion reveals further difficulties for some many-valued accounts. And matters of validity are crucial in relation to responses to the sorites paradox.

7. VALIDITY

A popular strategy for generalising the classical definition of validity to the many-valued case is to select certain 'truth-like' values as designated, and to equate validity with preservation of designated values, so that an argument is valid iff whenever the premises take designated values, so does the conclusion; and a formula is valid iff it takes a designated value whatever the interpretation of its schematic letters. With a three-valued logic, the designated values could be either truth alone (Tye's choice), or both truth and indefiniteness (when validity would be preservation of non-falsity; see e.g. Halldén 1949). And even given a fixed set of truth-definitions of the connectives, different choices of designated values will render different arguments valid or invalid. (For example, the same argument with true premises and an indefinite conclusion could be valid if there were two designated values but invalid if just truth were designated.) In the infinite-valued case, designated values could be just degree 1 or all values greater than some chosen threshold. Peacocke, for example, adopts a designated value approach, with complete truth as the only designated value (1981, p. 139).[7]

Although three-valued logics tend to be combined with a designated-value account, not all treatments of validity within a degree theory follow that simple approach. Some focus on preservation of degree of truth in a more general sense which does not privilege any particular values. For example, Machina deems an argument valid iff necessarily the conclusion is at least as true as the least true premise; and Forbes 1983 adopts the same definition. Edgington proposes that an argument is valid iff the degree of falsity of the conclusion (1 minus its degree of truth) cannot be greater than the sum of the degrees of falsity of the premises (1997, p. 302). It is then possible for the conclusion of a valid argument to acquire degrees of falsity from each of the premises.[8] These accounts differ over which arguments they count as valid (and, as we will see, the first labels as invalid certain intuitively valid arguments), but they both have more of a claim than a designated value approach to be taking degrees seriously throughout the theory and not just at the initial stage of assigning values.

The Machina–Forbes and Edgington accounts of validity have parallels for three-valued logics, which do not coincide with either of

---

[7] With a single designated value the validity of an argument provides no guarantee at all about the value of the conclusion of an argument if any of the premises are less than completely true. So you could take one true and one nearly true premise, follow a valid inference, and end up with a completely false conclusion. Declaring an argument valid may then vindicate its use in a disappointingly narrow range of circumstances. And, to be justified in employing a valid argument, you would have to be justified in thinking the premises were completely true, and that may be a tough demand. As Edgington puts it, such an account 'leaves us inferentially impotent in the presence of vagueness' (1997, p. 303).

[8] Edgington's proposal is not, in fact, presented as a *definition*, rather she claims she can derive it from the standard (usually classical) definition – an argument is valid if it is impossible for all the premises to be true and the conclusion false – where this is understood in terms of a notion of truth (plain truth) that she employs and which is not identified with verity 1. The derivation is questionable, however. It starts with the one premise case requiring the result that if A entails B then the verity of $A \leq$ verity of B. Her argument proceeds via the result that the verity of (A given B) must be 1 because 'hypothetically deciding that A is definitely true [i.e. has verity 1] . . . commits one to the definite truth of the logical consequences of A' (1997, p. 307). But deciding that A has verity 1 – not the same as deciding it is plain true – only commits you to some specific value for a logical consequence of A on the assumption that entailment constrains verities, the very thesis to be proved.

the designated value approaches (as before, the intermediate value is to be equated with value 0.5). We can illustrate the differences by considering what patterns of truth-values for the premises and conclusions of a valid two-premise argument are or are not ruled out by each definition of validity. I summarise the results in a table: the heading of each column indicates the values of the two premises followed by the conclusion, and each row represents a different account of validity. A tick means that on that account of validity it is possible to have a valid argument with premises and conclusions taking the cited truth-values, and a cross means that no such valid argument is possible. (On all plausible accounts, it is possible to have a valid argument with a false premise and a conclusion of any value; so I omit columns for the remaining permutations of values.) (1) is a designated-value approach with truth as the sole designated value, (2) designates both truth and indefinite, (3) is the three-valued analogue of the Machina–Forbes account and (4) is the analogue of Edgington's account.

	TTT	TTI	TTF	TIT	TII	TIF	IIT	III	IIF
(1)	✓	✗	✗	✓	✓	✓	✓	✓	✓
(2)	✓	✓	✗	✓	✓	✗	✓	✓	✗
(3)	✓	✗	✗	✓	✓	✗	✓	✓	✗
(4)	✓	✗	✗	✓	✓	✗	✓	✓	✓

Even given reasonable restrictions (e.g. the first, fourth and seventh columns could not contain a cross) there are still further possibilities; but it is unlikely that they could be plausibly motivated.

With an infinite-valued logic there is still more room for choice. Consider, for example, the question whether there could be a valid argument whose two premises were each true to degree 0.8 and whose conclusion was true to degree 0.7. This possibility would not be ruled out by designated-value approaches whose threshold is 0.7 or below, or by Edgington's account, but it would be ruled impossible on the Machina–Forbes account, and on a designated value approach with a threshold at 0.75.

On all the accounts so far discussed, validity is a sharp, all-or-nothing notion. But could validity itself be vague, allowing borderline cases of valid arguments and imposing no sharp boundaries between valid and invalid arguments? The suggestion that validity is vague may have been resisted because it would seem to preclude the possibility of an account of inference using the usual kind of logical systems which appear to be paradigmatically precise. But once vagueness is taken as a matter of coming in degrees which can be represented numerically, vague validity seems not to be ruled out. The natural development would introduce degrees of validity, where these could be determined by the extent to which degree of truth is preserved. I merely leave this possibility in play as another in the range of options.

How should we choose between the different candidate notions of validity? Our pre-theoretical notion of validity, and our intuitions about it, do not force a decision: they may rule that an argument with true premises and a false conclusion cannot be valid, but, as we have seen, much room for choice remains.

Consider the sorites paradox in a version with a series of conditional premises. Our conviction that the argument goes wrong somewhere allows for its regimentation as being invalid, or having an untrue premise, or both. But whatever option is chosen, the account must be reconciled with the fact that the argument is nonetheless persuasive in the sense that it *seems* as if the premises are true and the inference valid. Degree theorists typically explain the force of the argument by noting that some of the premises seem true because they are nearly (though not completely) true. But its persuasiveness also depends on matters of validity, and whether the sorites argument is declared valid depends again on the chosen account of validity. If validity is preservation of a single designated value, the argument can count as valid. The plausibility of the reasoning can then be explained: we are mistaken in taking the premises to be completely true, but if they had been true then the conclusion would have been true too. The argument is also valid on Edgington's account: since many of the conditional premises will be slightly less than completely true and the conclusion can inherit a little degree of falsity from each of them, the conclusion can be completely false even though the argument is valid.

According to other accounts of validity, however, the sorites is invalid. Take approaches designating more than a single value. We can ensure that all the premises have values above the chosen threshold of designation despite the false conclusion, so it cannot be a valid argument. And on the Machina–Forbes account modus ponens and the sorites argument are both invalid. For if $\mid p \mid = 0.5$, say, and

$| q | = 0$, then $| p \supset q | = 0.5$ and the step from p and $p \supset q$ to q takes us from half-truth to falsehood.

Edgington objects that 'to reject [modus ponens] as "invalid" in the presence of vagueness . . . is to lump it together with a bloomer like "Jones broke the law and anyone deserving a life sentence broke the law so Jones deserves a life sentence"' (1997, p. 303). But no definition of validity prohibits discrimination among invalid arguments – some invalid arguments may just be worse than others. And we might be able to use a notion of the *extent* to which an invalid argument preserves truth to explain that the argument seems valid because it is nearly valid. Machina, for example, explains how his notion of validity can be generalised so that arguments which fail to be valid in his sense can still be judged according to the extent to which they preserve degrees of truth – the smaller the possible drop in value between the least true premise and the conclusion, the more nearly valid the argument. But this does not help Machina and Forbes as regards the sorites paradox with a series of conditional premises, since for them, modus ponens is not even nearly valid, as shown by the case cited above which takes us from two half-true premises to a completely false conclusion.[9]

With a vague notion of validity, we could hope to maintain that the sorites argument is valid for the initial steps and invalid when the whole sequence of inferences is considered, but that there is no determinate point at which it ceases to be valid: its validity seeps away as the argument is carried through. This response could reflect the way in which our willingness to trust the argument decreases gradually as the number of steps increases.

As we have seen, if we were to specify, for a many-valued system, the number of values and the definitions of the connectives, there would still be room to consider several different properties of arguments corresponding to the different accounts of validity outlined

---

[9] The sorites argument using a series of negated conjunctions of the form $\neg(Fx_i \,\&\, \neg Fx_{i+1})$ is even more problematic. As Machina notes (1976, p. 74), in this case some of the premises are only slightly more than 0.5 degrees true (for example, when $| Fx_i |$ is around 0.5, then $| \neg Fx_{i+1} |$ and $| \neg(Fx_i \,\&\, \neg Fx_{i+1}) |$ will also be around 0.5). Wright (1987, pp. 251–2) accuses Peacocke's 1981 account and other truth-functional degree theories of being unable to treat sorites paradoxes with the premises in this conjunctive form in a way comparable to the version with conditionals. Machina attempts to defend the asymmetry.

above. Each such account yields some form of generalisation of the classical notion of validity and may be of particular interest for some reason (e.g. in explaining the apparent validity of an argument or in explaining how it can have a false conclusion). What matters in the account is the range of values that could be taken by the premises and conclusion of an argument of a given form, and that matter is settled by the features of the system already specified; which sorts of possible ranges we label 'valid' is a less substantial and perhaps purely verbal matter. I propose that, if we were to adopt a degree-theoretic approach to vagueness then we should take a *pluralist* attitude to the different candidate notions of validity, allowing several of them to give equally legitimate senses of 'valid'. In particular, there may be room for a strict account of validity as preservation of complete truth, a Machina-type preservation of degrees of truth account, and a vague notion of validity. There may be different contexts in which we want to rely on arguments with these different guarantees, and where the warranty in such cases is reasonably called validity. We need not then demand that one notion is singled out as the uniquely important property of arguments in a many-valued system. In defence of this approach, it might be claimed that our intuitions about validity are not clear enough to settle a unique account – there are several ways of regimenting the pre-theoretical notion (and it does need regimentation of some sort) and we should not assume that only one of the new notions is of interest. The possibility of this pluralist attitude to validity provides another slant on the questions of uniqueness of theory that I addressed in chapter 2, §3.

8. TYE'S THEORY ASSESSED

Before presenting a range of problems that faces all varieties of many-valued theories, I return to Tye's theory and summarise some of the negative features arising from issues discussed in the previous few sections. From the point of view of the reflective equilibrium that Tye needs to be striving for, my summary shows a substantial range of costs. Those costs need to be met with a stronger set of advantages than we have so far seen. A full defence of the theory should explain away those supposedly mistaken intuitions, but Tye's attempts on that score are unsatisfactory. Though I focus on Tye's theory here, the list of problems for other varieties of many-valued theories would be, if not exactly the same, at least equally bad. This is thus a case-study in the light of the previous sections.

First, penumbral connections are not respected. For example, 'Tim is tall and Tek is not tall' counts as indefinite (not false) when Tek is taller than Tim and both are borderline tall. Similarly 'If Tim is tall then Tek is tall' is indefinite (not true). Relatedly, there are highly compelling quantificational truths that get counted as only indefinite. 'Everyone taller than someone tall is also tall' has indefinite instances, and so it is not true. Similarly 'if x is tall and y is one hundredth of an inch *taller* then y is tall' is indefinite, showing that along with the supposedly attractive feature that the sorites inductive premise is indefinite, the theory is saddled with the indefiniteness of sentences of a comparable structure for which that classification is undesirable.

Intuitively, sentences of the form 'all F's are G' are true if all definitely F things are definitely G and all borderline F's are borderline G; but they will then fail to count as true on Tye's account because 'if Fx then Gx' will count as indefinite for those borderline cases. So 'all red socks are red' does not count as true, according to Tye's theory, because there are indefinitely red things (though 'all red socks are coloured' *is* true, since borderline red socks are definitely coloured). And there will be similar problems for compelling candidates for analytical truths when the vagueness of the corresponding terms is appropriately matched. Take, for example, 'all ambidextrous people are proficient with both hands' and 'all cygnets are young swans': for Tye these sentences can only be indefinite. And consider the (T) schema: even if p and 'p is true' are always valued the same, there will be instances of 'p iff p is true' that are merely indefinite.

The above cases arise because 'if p, q' and 'p iff q' both count as indefinite if both components are indefinite. As noted above, this also has the undesirable consequence that 'if p, p' can fail to be true as can 'p iff p' (the latter violating Williamson's condition (1994, p. 116) that if p and q have exactly the same value, $p \equiv q$ should be perfectly true). Relatedly, $p \ \& \ \neg p$ can be indefinite, rather than always false. Many of the standard inter-definability conditions for the connectives are satisfied in the sense that the equated compound sentences – e.g. $p \supset q$ and $\neg(p \ \& \ \neg q)$ – are always assigned the same values. But, first, one exception is the equivalence of $p \supset q$ and $p \equiv (p \ \& \ q)$, which fails when p is indefinite and q is true. And second, the equivalences that do hold cannot be stated using '$\equiv$' in the normal way: $(p \supset q) \equiv \neg(p \ \& \ \neg q)$ is not always true (being indefinite when p and q are each indefinite).

Next, I turn to standard inference-forms that can fail. First take conditional proof, also known as the deduction theorem, i.e. from $A \models C$, infer $\models (A \supset C)$. This fails for $A = C$, since every sentence entails itself but $A \supset A$ can be merely indefinite, as we have seen. Tye does note the failure of the deduction theorem (1994, p. 283, footnote 3), but he offers no explanation of why it is nonetheless an intuitively compelling inference pattern: this introduction rule for $\supset$ is arguably central to the very meaning of that connective; its rejection should be more than just noted. Similarly, Tye cannot allow the inference from the mutual entailment of A and C to $\models (A \equiv C)$. Reductio ad absurdum can fail too (though this is not surprising since contradictions need not be false). For example, inferring $\models \neg A$ from $A \models (C \ \& \ \neg C)$ fails for $A = (C \ \& \ \neg C)$ since A can sometimes be indefinite.[10]

Tye provides very few comments towards explaining why we make so many mistaken judgements with the kind of cases I have raised. The only remarks are those noting that, for example, $p \supset p$ may indeed be sometimes indefinite, but at least it is never false (he admits that the stronger outcome would undermine the theory). He coins the phrase 'quasi-tautology' for such a sentence which has no false substitution instances. Similarly $p \ \& \ \neg p$ may be sometimes indefinite, but it is, at least, a quasi-contradiction which is never true. He then reiterates the connections between these formulae and $p \lor \neg p$ whose truth, he claims, is reasonably denied for borderline p. But more needs to be said to justify responding in Tye's way rather than either accepting the law of excluded middle, or denying the relations between these various sentences. And the appeal to quasi-tautologies adds nothing: if earning this title is enough for his purposes, then the fact that $p \lor \neg p$ also earns it should be of concern. Moreover, what matters for validity does not relate to quasitautologies, and assertion depends on sentences being true not

---

[10] The failure on the supervaluationist theory of some such inference rules in certain contexts has been much more widely publicised. I take up the objection in chapter 7, §4, where I argue that the limit on the contexts in which it fails makes the result acceptable.

being either true or indefinite, so the role for the notion seems to be merely one of appeasement.

So Tye's theory falls down on a range of issues. Demonstrating my claim that the other many-valued alternatives fare no better would be too lengthy, so I turn instead to a range of issues that, I shall argue, undermine many-valued theories almost independently of the issues in this and previous sections.

9. HIGHER-ORDER VAGUENESS, SHARP BOUNDARIES AND EXACT VALUES

Difficulties arising in connection with higher-order vagueness are often seen as a major reason to move from a three-valued logic to an infinite-valued one. In particular, traditional three-valued theories cannot accommodate any of the hierarchy of borderline cases beyond the first order. A borderline borderline case – which ought to fall between the borderline cases and the others – cannot be slotted into a *three*-fold classification any more easily than borderline cases can within a classical *two*-fold classification. And the standard three-valued approach formulated with a precise metalanguage replaces the classical true/false sharp boundary by *two* sharp boundaries – one between the true and the indefinite cases, and one between the indefinite and the false cases. So there are still abrupt changes along the sorites series; for example, there would be a single hair whose removal makes the difference between being bald and being borderline bald. In chapter 1, §6, this commitment to sharp boundaries to the borderline cases was shown to be an unacceptable feature of a theory of vagueness. Moreover, we can adapt the objections to the epistemic view raised in chapter 3, §3, where I argued that there is nothing that determines unique sharp boundaries between the positive and negative extensions of our vague predicates: the same considerations count against the supposition that the borderline cases have sharp boundaries. For what could determine the exact location of sharp boundaries falling either side of the borderline cases? Admitting borderline cases that take an intermediate value only serves to shift the problem. And it is no help saying that 'indefinite' is not really a value but a truth-value gap: sharp boundaries between valued and non-valued cases are equally unacceptable.

These problems for a three-valued logic have parallels for any finite-valued logics: each will yield new sharp boundaries and abrupt changes in truth-value. For example, to capture first and second orders of vagueness, a five-valued logic might be adopted, where the two new truth-values correspond to the two varieties of borderline borderline cases (one intermediate between truth and borderline and the other between falsity and borderline). But five-valued logic will face just the same objections about sharp boundaries to the borderline borderline cases as three-valued logic did about sharp boundaries to the borderline cases. Continuity demands at least a dense, and hence infinite, set of truth-values.

But although degree theories allow continuous, gradual change between complete truth and complete falsity, they do not avoid all sharp boundaries. In particular, there remains a sharp divide between sentences taking truth-value 1 and those taking a value less than 1. Consequently, there is still, for example, a last man in the sorites series who counts as tall to degree 1, and no room for higher-order borderline cases between such men and the borderline tall. Generalising, there will be sharp boundaries to those qualifying as 'tall' to a degree greater than n, for all n. Objections to boundaries of this kind are raised in Wright 1976, Sanford 1976, Sainsbury 1990, and elsewhere. Degree theories, like three-valued theories, violate the constraints laid down in chapter 1, §6 about the need to avoid all sharp boundaries.

These problems might be traced to a more general one, namely the charge that the degree theorist's assignments impose precision in a form that is just as unacceptable as a classical true/false assignment. In so far as a degree theory avoids determinacy over whether a is F, the worry is that it does so by enforcing determinacy over the *degree* to which a is F. In particular, if the semantics for a many-valued logic is described using a precise metalanguage, then sentences will always be assigned exact values, since sentences of the metalanguage ascribing degrees of truth will themselves be true or false simpliciter. For example the metalinguistic claim ' "this coat is red" is true to degree x' will be (completely) true for a single value of x and (completely) false for all other values of x, and that single value will be the exact and uniquely correct value to assign to 'this coat is red'. And similarly all other predications of 'is red' will receive a unique, exact value. But it seems inappropriate to associate our vague predicate 'red' with any

113

particular exact function from objects to degrees of truth, as this requires.

For a start, what could determine which is the correct function, settling that my coat is red to degree 0.322 rather than 0.321? This, again, can be treated as parallel to the question asked of the epistemic view (chapter 3, §3) about what determines the valuations fixing sharp boundaries to the extensions of predicates. Both questions ask what determines the function into truth-values, differing only over what the respective theories take those truth-values to be.[11] Machina's claim (1976, p. 49) that 'there is no reason to suppose that meaningful predicates *must* have completely determinate extensions' suggests a generalisation: why should there be reason to suppose that predicates must have the kind of fuzzy extensions the degree theorists claim they have? To adapt another quote, why should we suppose that propositions relate to the facts of the world in a neat infinite-valued way any more than in 'a neat two-valued way' (Machina 1976, p. 49)? Objections to the exact values of many-valued theories have been raised elsewhere, but without an examination of possible responses such as that I give below.

To summarise, there is a cluster of questions facing all many-valued theories. Can the theory deal with higher-order vagueness? Are all sharp boundaries avoided? Is the assumption that all sentences take exact values acceptable? Is it necessary? These questions are often not

---

[11] Black (1937) employed a measure of degrees reflecting the proportion of speakers who assent to the sentence in question. In particular, the measure is given by the ratio of those (competent) speakers of the language who would assent to the predication to those who would dissent from it if they had to judge one way or the other. But, at best, this proposal is unacceptably crude in simply calculating semantic status on the basis of a head-count (and one that will not even reflect the immediate intuitions of speakers, since they are not given the option of refusing to classify either way). Consider, for example, the apparent possibility that x_i is taller than x_{i+1} though as it happens 'x_i is tall' commands *less* assent than 'x_{i+1} is tall', even among those speakers counting as competent by any reasonable standard. On Black's scheme 'x_i is tall' would have to be assigned a smaller number than 'x_{i+1} is tall', which severs the fundamental connection between being taller and counting as taller to a greater degree. See Hempel 1939 and Williamson 1994, pp. 73–83 for more detailed demonstrations of the failure of Black's account. Machina offers nothing so crude, but he does briefly suggest that a measure involving 'the common man's classifications' could be used in assigning truth-values to sentences, while not determining those values uniquely (1976, p. 61). He might thus hope to achieve a suitable balance between an empirical determination of values and the required abstraction from our fallible practices. But we are not given any indication of how this can be done.

directly confronted by degree theorists, but I shall examine five types of responses which have been defended, or at least alluded to, in the literature.

(i) Biting the bullet

First, we could claim that sentences do take unique exact values, that there are sharp boundaries to the completely true sentences, that there is no higher-order vagueness comparable to first-order vagueness, and that precise metalanguages are acceptable as they stand. (This response could be taken with three-valued logics or infinite-valued logics alike.) It could then be said that any apparent problem is simply due to the fact that we do not *know* what values sentences receive. The epistemological aspect of this response highlights its similarities to the epistemic view and suggests that if there is to be any sort of second-order vagueness, it must be a form of ignorance. Machina, who emphasises that we could not know exact assignments, indicates that he takes this to be an epistemic matter when, for example, he describes attempted assignments as having the character of an empirical hypothesis (1976, pp. 60–1).

But, first, this strategy would yield a heterogeneous account of borderline cases, since being a borderline case would be a matter of intermediate degrees of truth at the first-order level, but of ignorance at higher levels. Second, it calls for an answer to the question: what has been gained over the classical epistemic view? The best epistemic theorists offer detailed explanations of *why* we are ignorant in a borderline case (see chapter 3, §2); a degree theorist taking option (i) similarly owes us an explanation of the ignorance it postulates, but one that does not at the same time justify the epistemic theorist's position about first-order vagueness. It is far from clear that this can be done. Third, arguments that our predicates are higher-order vague, in the sense of having no sharp boundaries at all (see chapter 1, §6) would still need to be confronted and shown to be flawed. And questions about what determines the unique (though unknown) values would remain pressing.

Biting the bullet does nothing to meet the objections or answer the crucial questions raised, and the only resources available to fulfil the task are ones whose use is likely to undermine the original many-valued theory or the motivations for adopting it.

115

(ii) Assigning a range of values

Sanford recognises worries about the assignment of exact values to sentences and he seeks to produce a many-valued theory that is not committed to the principle of multi-valence (i.e. the principle that every meaningful sentence has a value from the specified range). He suggests that instead of assigning a single value to each sentence, a *range* of truth-values should be assigned (e.g. 1976, p. 201 and 1979, pp. 179–80).

But the truth-definitions of the connectives normally give rules for calculating a value for a complex sentence given the values of each of its components (e.g. that $\mid p \mathbin{\&} q \mid$ receives the minimum of the values of p and q – Sanford does not defend that logical system, but the idea behind his own definitions are the same in the relevant respects). How can such definitions be used if the component sentences have, not a single value to be substituted into the calculation, but a range of values such as 0.25–0.75?

The only viable reply to this question would be that when p is assigned a range of values then any truth-value in that range is *admissible* and the admissible values of $p \mathbin{\&} q$, for example, are those calculated according to the definition of conjunction for every combination of admissible values of p and q. This amounts to an infinite-valued version of supervaluationary semantics, where instead of quantifying (as the standard supervaluationary account does) over two-valued specifications corresponding to each way of making predicates precise, we consider infinite-valued specifications. Each specification assigns a single value from the range [0, 1] to each sentence and the relations between complex and component sentences within that specification are as dictated by the truth-definitions. Different specifications can assign different values to the same sentence, and the range of values that a (possibly complex) sentence takes over those infinite-valued specifications gives the range of values to be assigned to it.[12] This possibility will be briefly considered in chapter 7, §7, where I shall argue that it holds no advantage over,

---

[12] Sanford only explicitly endorses this supervaluationary interpretation in his 1993, though it is strongly suggested in his 1979. The position is to be distinguished from the combination of degrees and supervaluationism found in Lewis and Kamp and mentioned in §5 above in relation to Edgington's account. The latter uses classical two-valued models and calculates degrees of truth on the basis of those models considered together.

and is in other ways inferior to, the standard two-valued super-valuationary account defended in that chapter.

Any theory assigning ranges of values rather than individual values must also face the following question: are sentences to be assigned *precise* ranges of values? If so, the move provides no advance in the treatment of higher-order vagueness and sharp boundaries. Objections are not met by replacing precise single values with precise ranges of them, for we can still ask what determines those exact ranges, and there will still be sharp boundaries, for example, between ranges that are strictly below 0.5 and those which are not. But how are we to understand vague ranges? At the very least, accommodating them would require a vague metalanguage so that not all metalinguistic sentences stating that some value is a member of that range need be determinately true or determinately false. But it would then be unclear why the move to *ranges* of values is advantageous; it would be the vague metalanguage that played the significant role in accommodating higher-order vagueness and the lack of sharp boundaries at higher levels. So I turn to the viability of an account with a vague metalanguage, putting aside the unpromising appeal to ranges of values.

(iii) *Vague metalanguages and iterated degrees of truth*

The link between higher-order vagueness and vague metalanguages was emphasised in chapter 1, §6: a many-valued theory may need to employ a metalanguage whose distinctive elements (namely the predications of truth-value) are themselves vague. I shall consider this suggestion first with degree theories and then with three-valued logics. Since, according to degree theories, a vague predicate is one that comes in degrees, this proposal will allow truth-value ascriptions themselves to hold to intermediate degrees. This might meet the objections about predications always being assigned exact values, since now there will not always be a first-order value of a sentence which can be uniquely and completely correctly assigned to a given sentence. And it could sometimes be true to an intermediate degree that a sentence takes a value strictly less than 1, or strictly greater than 0, which serves to 'fuzzify' the boundary between value 1 and values less than 1 and the boundary between value 0 and values greater than 0; and thus there is room for second-order vagueness. To accommodate still higher orders of vagueness, perhaps further iteration is required: ' "*p* is true to degree 1" is true to degree 1' might itself be true to an intermediate degree, as more generally might ' "*p* is true to degree *n*" is true to degree *m*', and so on.

No such theory has been worked out in detail and it is far from clear to what extent the approach is viable. Among those who imply (without showing) that iterating degrees of truth is unproblematic is Edgington: 'One *can* go higher order, and talk of the degree of truth of statements about degrees of truth . . .' (1993, p. 200). The onus is on proponents taking this line to show that it can work. I shall argue that any attempt will fail.

Suppose, for a given *p*, '*p* is true to degree 0.8' is true only to degree 0.9, and this is the highest value of any sentence of the form '*p* is true to degree *x*' for the specified *p* (so, e.g., it is not also degree 1 true that *p* is true to degree 0.9). Can it be appropriate to assign *p* any (first-order) truth-value? The best candidate value must be 0.8, but the same faults are evident in saying (without qualification) that *p* is true to degree 0.8 as there are in saying that *q* is true simpliciter when *q* is only true to degree 0.9. The degree theorist argued that because '*x* is *F*' and ' "*x* is *F*" is true' can hold to intermediate degrees we should introduce new truth-values to reflect this and should thus reject classical logic since it cannot accommodate those values. Accepting the proposal that the degree theorist's truth-value predications *themselves* hold to intermediate degrees would, in the same way, demonstrate the inadequacy of that chosen set of truth-values and hence undermine the use of the infinite-valued logic built on it. So the proposal that we adopt a degree theory with a vague metalanguage cannot be sustained. I will reinforce this objection and reject possible replies in what follows.

The parallel with the degree theorist's original rejection of classical logic can be pursued further. Once it is admitted that not all meaningful declarative sentences receive classical values, classical logic is rendered inappropriate for the language. It is still the case that $p \vee \neg p$ is true whatever classical value is assigned to a substitution for p – but this does not show that the law of excluded middle is *always* true if we accept the degree theorist's claim that not all sentences have classical values. But we can mirror this argument for a degree theory with a vague metalanguage: although $p \vee \neg p$ takes a value of at least 0.5 whatever value p takes from the range [0, 1], this does not show that $p \vee \neg p$ is *always* more than 0.5 degrees true if we accept that (because the metalanguage is vague) not all sentences can be correctly assigned a value from that interval. And take a complex formula, A, that is true whatever values from the set $[0, 1]$ are taken by the sentences substituted for the schematic letters in the formula. If we allow that sometimes *no* value in $[0, 1]$ can be truly assigned to a substituted sentence, there is no guarantee that A will always be true, and so, contrary to the degree theorist's practice, it should not be called a logical truth. So the degree theorists' account of logical truths and of logic in general is incompatible with the claim that the metalanguage is vague. And they cannot modify that account by also requiring that for A to be a logical truth, A must also be true if its substituted sentences *cannot* be truly assigned a value from the range. For the system can give no method of calculating the value of A in such a situation (just as classical logic cannot determine values for conjunctions with conjuncts that lack classical values).

Suppose, on the other hand, that a theorist introduces new values without the assumption that they are exhaustive, and takes logical truth as truth on all infinite-valued valuations but without endorsing the explanation that this condition must capture truth on all possible valuations. If viable at all, the justification for such an attitude must be that the model it delivers − in particular of logical truths and valid inferences − is appropriate to the phenomenon and our reasoning in vague language etc. Such a theorist would, I claim, be committed to rejecting the realist approach presented in chapter 2 − the model would assign all sentences some value though it cannot capture the actual distribution of values. So an instrumentalist attitude to the assignment of degrees of truth would have to be adopted. But then it is not clear why the metalanguage needs to be vague, since the commitment to sharp boundaries seems already to be avoided by the refusal to take seriously the actual assignment made. The instrumentalist option is considered as option (v) below.

To summarise: the use of infinite-valued logic works on the assumption that sentences each have a degree of truth, so that the set of values represented by $[0, 1]$ allows an exclusive and exhaustive classification of sentences according to their degree of truth. If, as is maintained on option (iii), those values themselves only hold to intermediate degrees, then the same objections can be raised as the degree theorists themselves raised against classical logic when they claimed that the true/false classification holds only to intermediate degrees.

Could we accommodate the need to iterate degrees of truth by introducing a full range of new values of the form 'degree n to degree m' where we distinguish between a value 'degree n to degree m' and 'degree n to degree $m^\star$', when $m \neq m^\star$? This is not enough if we accept that there is vagueness at still higher orders; the iteration would then need to be repeated, allowing values of the form 'degree n_1 to degree n_2 to . . . to degree n_k', for any k, which could be represented by the sequence $\langle n_1, n_2, \ldots n_k \rangle$. (Such values should be distinguished from Goguen's proposal for n-tuple values which was designed to meet problems of multi-dimensionality, rather than the idea of *iterated* degrees.) We would need to settle the treatment of various central matters in such a theory and it is likely to result in a considerable departure from standard degree theories and a huge increase in complexity. For example, it is no longer clear that sentences will only be appropriately assigned one value, for there is no conflict between p having both values $\langle 0.8, 0.7 \rangle$ and $\langle 0.7, 0.3 \rangle$. Moreover, the new system will face all of the same problems as the original version regarding the imposition of sharp boundaries, the denial of higher-order vagueness and the assignment of exact values. For example, the assignment of *more* numbers – degrees of truth for ascriptions of degrees of truth, then degrees for those degrees etc. – cannot defuse the objections raised above regarding the assignment of exact values to sentences. And how plausible is it to suppose that the meanings of our vague expressions (together with the facts) could determine values of the new iterated kinds for any predication?

The above theory would be one which admits not a *vague* metalanguage, but a metalanguage with an expanded set of truth-value predicates, and so objections to theories without a vague metalanguage are again applicable. Whatever the set of values a many-valued theory admits, if the metalanguage is precise there will be precise sets of sentences taking each of the values from the set and so sharp boundaries where there should be none.

As a special case, note that a three-valued theory is unable to admit a vague metalanguage in the above way: postulating one would lead to all the same criticisms as the infinite-valued version. It would amount to allowing sentences of the form 'p is indefinite' sometimes to be indefinite themselves. Tye considers this suggestion and remarks (in agreement with my above discussion) that it would require introducing a new truth-value 'indefinitely indefinite' taken by p when 'p is indefinite' is itself indefinite (1990, pp. 554–5). He describes this move as 'extending' his semantics, implying that it is an optional extra which could be pursued without threatening the suitability of his original three-valued system. But the three-valued theory would be undermined by the need to introduce a fourth value, just as classical logic must be rejected if we accept Tye's claim that a third truth-value is required. The move should be seen not as defending a three-valued logic with a vague metalanguage, but as adopting a four-valued logic. But, as I argued at the beginning of §9, all the same problems face a four-valued logic as face a three-valued one.

In short, a many-valued theory with a set S of truth-values cannot consistently admit that a metalinguistic sentence assigning some given intermediate value to p itself receives an intermediate value. For this would imply that we must introduce new values to make an appropriate assignment to p itself, which would undermine the theory with the original truth-value set, S; and the introduction of new values has already been seen to provide no response to the cluster of questions and objections raised.

(iv) Tye's treatment of vague metalanguages

Although Tye briefly discusses the above strategy, it is not his favoured response to the kinds of questions I have raised: he considers the introduction of new values to be unmotivated and seeks to avoid iteration of 'is indefinite'. His own response also draws on a metalanguage that is not precise, but the treatment of the issue is different because Tye does not accept that there are metalinguistic sentences of the form 'p is indefinite' which are themselves indefinite.

Among the metalinguistic sentences Tye *does* declare indefinite (1994, p. 200) are generalisations such as

(★) every sentence is true, indefinite or false.

He attempts to show that (★) must be indefinite by the following argument. If true, (★) would commit us to sharp boundaries between the true sentences and the indefinite ones; but there are no such sharp boundaries (as the series of predications along a sorites series illustrates), so (⋆) cannot be true. On the other hand, he continues, its falsity would require the introduction of a new truth-value. Therefore (⋆) is not true or false, so must be indefinite. Notice, however, that in this very argument he assumes (⋆). For to argue that a sentence must be indefinite because it is neither true nor false is to make the very assumption in question. But then he is absurdly relying on assuming that (⋆) is true to argue that it is indefinite. His argument fails. He offers similar arguments for the indefiniteness of other metalinguistic sentences such as 'every conditional in the sequence of sorites paradox premises is either true or not-true (i.e. false or indefinite)' (1994, p. 199), and these can be similarly rejected for relying on the truth of (⋆) which is incompatible with his desired conclusion that a consequence of (⋆) is indefinite.

So Tye has not established that any particular metalinguistic statements are themselves indefinite. I deny, moreover, that his position is viable: it is undermined for similar reasons to those described above. The use of a three-valued logic for a vague language requires the assumption that the three values provide an exclusive and exhaustive classification of declarative sentences; if not, it suffers the same defects as the rejected two-valued system. The claim that the three values *do* provide an exhaustive classification of sentences would commit us to the truth of (⋆). Since Tye maintains that (⋆) is indefinite, we can assume that he would likewise claim that it is indefinite whether the classification is exhaustive. But this alone is unsatisfactory. A three-valued logic for a language is inadequate if it is not true that all its sentences take one of the three values. And if Tye's unargued assumption is that it is only if (⋆) is *false* that the introduction of new values is called for is correct, the indefiniteness of (⋆) implies that three-valued logic is inadequate *but* also that it is no help to introduce new values. We are left with no satisfactory treatment of vague language.[13]

For an infinite-valued analogue of Tye's position, the key feature

[13] Again, if the assumption that the values are exhaustive is to be avoided, the modelling approach is needed, whereby the many-valued model is seen as merely an instrumentalist device (option (v) below). Moreover, if this line is taken, there are no longer good grounds for the claim that the falsity of 'every sentence is true, false or indefinite' would guarantee that there were sharp boundaries between those categories of sentence. So even if the logic is claimed to justify the form of inference Tye uses to argue for (⋆) (where if both '*p* is true' and '*p* is false' lead to absurdity, we can conclude that *p* is indefinite), that particular application of the inference would not be warranted, since it has not been shown that the falsity of (⋆) is absurd.

would be that although it is not the case that there are particular sentences that (definitely) cannot be assigned a value from the range [0, 1], a quantified statement such as 'all sentences have truth-values from the range [0, 1]' would receive an intermediate value. (Though how should we decide which one?) But the problems facing Tye's own approach would all arise again: if it is not true that all sentences take a value from the chosen range then a logic employing that range of values is inappropriate.

To summarise, Tye's response and infinite-valued analogues of it cannot be sustained. I conclude that commitment to a vague metalanguage on a many-valued scheme serves to undermine that system itself.

(v) Instrumentalism about the assignment of degrees

Perhaps we should see the assignments of numbers in degree theories merely as a useful instrumental device, rather than taking a realist attitude to them. If it turns out that by assigning numbers to sentences we can model vague predicates without paradox and while respecting certain truths (e.g. about the gradations of *F*-ness among borderline *F*s), this could justify employing that apparatus. It may be that the exact choice of values does not affect a number of important matters such as whether an argument is deemed valid, and this could account for a theory that assigns numbers being explanatory even though there is nothing privileged about the numbers chosen. Problems with the assignment of unique exact values and questions about what determines them will then be avoided by denying that there are such unique values to assign.

This is to adopt what, in chapter 2, §3, I called the modelling approach to a theory of vagueness which I showed to be apparent in the writing of many degree theorists, including Goguen, Machina and Edgington. But, as I argued in that section, we need to raise questions such as the following: what are we to say about the *real* truth-value status of borderline case predications if, as the modeller claims, they are not the values assigned by the theory? Being told that for some purposes it is useful to treat them in such-and-such a way does not answer that question. The modeller's approach as it stands is mere hand waving and an unsupported insistence that the problems raised concerning exact values assigned are not really problems for the theory because we can ignore the features of our theory that create them. But how can we ignore those features and still take the theory seriously – surely the assignment of numbers is central to it?

In chapter 2, §3iv I argued that a theory defended within the modelling approach is compatible with a different theory meeting the criteria of a successful realist theory. Modelling with numbers could be a useful guide in reasoning, for example, while some other account captures the reality behind it (which, it would be hoped, is also able to explain within its framework the effectiveness of the instrumental model). I suggest that Edgington's story of verities in particular is best seen in this light. That account is compatible with supervaluationism where, as explained above, verity is a measure of the proportion of specifications on which the sentence is true. And it is compatible with the epistemic view, where verities could be equated with degrees of belief, her other example of a probabilistic structure. Sentences are either true or false as the epistemic view has it, but we typically have intermediate degrees of belief about border-line predications and the degree-theoretic structure models those degrees. She rejects both of these combinations of theories. But, as I have indicated, her reasons for rejecting supervaluationism fail; and I also believe, though I will not argue it here, that an epistemic theorist could meet her challenges to explain the apparent differences between the roles of degrees of belief and of verities in guiding action (Edgington 1997, pp. 312–15).

On the assumption that degree theorists would generally reject the interpretation of their theory as compatible with (and subsidiary to) another theory of vagueness, I suggest that there is one, and only one, relatively promising route they could take in response to the general questions I raised above. They could claim that it should be a merely ordinal scale that represents the instantiation of values by sentences, and that the problems that I have been discussing throughout §9 arise because representing those values numerically suggests more structure than is exhibited by a merely ordinal scale. In the next chapter I examine this suggestion.[14] The framework introduced there allows me to inflict my final, fatal, blows on degree theories of vagueness.

---

[14] Note that the appeal to ordinal scales is incompatible with three-valued logics, so their proponents cannot take this line (see chapter 2, §3ii). I have argued that none of the approaches taken in (i)–(iv) is acceptable, and so I maintain that we should reject three-valued theories of vagueness at this stage.

5

Vagueness by numbers

This chapter has two main aims. As promised at the end of chapter 4, I shall argue against a specific response to the degree theorist's problems concerning the assignment of exact values (see §3 below). The other more general aim is further to undermine the prospects for degree theories of vagueness, which rely so heavily on numerical resources. In §1 I outline the widely accepted representational approach to measurement, showing how numbers can be used to capture a physical attribute (see e.g. Krantz et al. 1971). This will be used to compare measurement theory and degree theories of vagueness, and through that comparison I shall expose severe flaws in the degree theorist's approach.

I. MEASUREMENT THEORY

Krantz et al. capture the essence of measurement as follows: 'When measuring some attribute of a class of objects or events . . . we associate numbers with the objects in such a way that the properties of the attribute are faithfully represented as numerical properties' (1971, p. 1).

When an attribute P is suitable for measurement (e.g. temperature, weight), there will be a relation $\geq_P$ (e.g. *at least as hot as, as least as heavy as*), where $a \geq_P b$ is true iff a's quantity of P is at least as great as b's. We can formulate some non-numerical principles which govern that relation, and given an appropriate set of principles a *representation theorem* will be provable guaranteeing that numbers can be used to measure the attribute P. More specifically, consider the relational structure given by the ordered pair $\langle S, \geq_P \rangle$, where S is the set of objects or events that have P. A representation theorem states that there is a homomorphism, ϕ, from this relational structure into

$\langle R, \geq \rangle$ (where R is the set of reals and $\geq$ is the *greater than or equal to* relation), such that

(R) $a \geq_P b$ iff $\phi(a) \geq \phi(b)$.

Take the measure of temperature and the relation *at least as hot as*, $\geq_H$, holding between pairs of objects. Using ϕ, numbers are assigned to objects according to their temperature; $\phi(a) \geq \phi(b)$ then reflects the fact that *a* is at least as hot as *b*, i.e. $a \geq_H b$, so $\phi(a) = \phi(b)$ is true iff *a* and *b* have the same temperature.

Certain axioms are needed to prove any representation theorem. Among them is a *connectedness* axiom, stating that for all *a* and *b* in S,

(C) Either $a \geq_P b$ or $b \geq_P a$.

This is a necessary axiom, in the sense that if there is to be a representation theorem for P, then it must be true. It is not sufficient for proving the theorem − for example, a transitivity axiom is also necessary stating that if $a \geq_P b$ and $b \geq_P c$ then $a \geq_P c$ − but I single out (C) because of its importance in §2.

In general, the homomorphism or scale ϕ will not be unique (consider e.g. the use of different scales for measuring temperature). But a *uniqueness theorem* will be provable which states that it is unique *up to a certain type of transformation*. Such a theorem thus characterises the permissible transformations of any legitimate scale, and its breadth will depend on the principles governing $\geq_P$. Features of the numerical structure which correspond to genuine features of the attribute will be shared by all acceptable numerical assignments, and different uniqueness theorems lead to different answers to questions such as 'if two numbers add together to equal a third, does this correspond to a genuine relation between the objects assigned those numbers?'

Different uniqueness theorems determine different types of measurement scale; I shall describe the main types. With *ordinal* scales, the relation *greater than or equal to* holding between assigned numbers represents relations between objects, so the ordering of objects according to the number assigned must be preserved on any transformation of the scale. But it is *only* the ordering that matters for this type of scale, so if ϕ is a permissible homomorphism, any order-preserving transformation will also be permissible. In other words, we can allow a transformation $f(x)$ of the values assigned by ϕ whenever f is a strictly increasing function (i.e. one for which $f(x) < f(y)$

whenever $x < y$). For example, a transformation that squares the original values will be acceptable. Ranking a group of people according to their intelligence and assigning each of them a number accordingly would thus yield an ordinal scale where the only significant feature of the numbers is their ordering. A standard measure of hardness, the Mohs scale, is also an ordinal scale: the ordering is established given the principle that a is at least as hard as b iff a can scratch b.

For *interval* scales, intervals between assigned numbers also represent features of the attribute. If the intervals between two pairs of values are the same, they must remain the same under any permissible transformation, and other ratios between intervals are similarly invariant. This allows as permissible all and only transformations of the form $f(x) = \alpha x + \beta$. For example, compare the Celsius scale of temperature with the Fahrenheit scale: ratios between intervals are the same on the two scales, but the choice of zero is arbitrary and the ratio between values assigned to two objects can differ (suppose a is at 5 °C or 41 °F, and b is at 10 °C or 50 °F; the numbers assigned on the Celsius scale stand in the ratio 1 : 2, while the associated Fahrenheit numbers do not).

With a *ratio* scale, in addition to ordering of values and ratios between intervals, ratios of values are also significant and invariant across the permissible numerical assignments. So if $\phi(a)/\phi(b) = p$ for some permissible ϕ, then $\phi^\star(a)/\phi^\star(b) = p$ for any permissible $\phi^\star$. Choice of unit is generally still arbitrary (consider scales employing metres and feet), and the permissible transformations are all of the form $f(x) = \alpha x$. Sums of values are also significant here: suppose $\phi(a) + \phi(b) = \phi(c)$, then $\beta\phi(a) + \beta\phi(b) = \beta\phi(c)$ for any β, so $\phi^\star(a) + \phi^\star(b) = \phi^\star(c)$ for any permissible $\phi^\star$; $\phi(a) + \phi(b) = \phi(c)$ represents a genuine relation between a, b and c themselves. For example, summing length-values captures the relation which holds when c is as long as a and b would be if laid end to end.

2. REPRESENTATION THEOREMS FOR VAGUENESS

With this general account of measurement, I turn to ask whether it can be applied to degree theories of vagueness which depend on a numerical structure supposedly capturing truth to different degrees, and where these numbers are crucial for the definitions of the

127

connectives, accounts of validity etc. Here a representation function
φ would map sentences into the interval [0, 1], and φ(*p*) is con-
ventionally written as | *p* |.

We can use $>_T$ to express *true to a greater degree* and $\geq_T$ for *true to the
same or a greater degree*. For example, if *a* and *b* are both borderline *F*
and *a* is *F*-er than *b*, then *Fa* $>_T$ *Fb*. If real numbers are to play their
representational role, $\geq_T$ should be captured by the numerical relation
$\geq$, so there should be a function from *p* to | *p* | such that

(R$_T$) $p \geq_T q$ iff $| p | \geq | q |$.

I shall argue against degree theories by showing there is no relation
$\geq_T$ that both is suitably related to the phenomena of vagueness and
satisfies a representation theorem. In other words, there are no
numbers a degree theorist could assign to sentences that could be
used in a successful theory. This shows that we should reject degree
theories of vagueness.

I shall focus on the connectedness axiom, since this must be true if
there is to be a representation theorem. It states that for all sentences *p*
and *q*:

(C$_T$) either $p \geq_T q$ or $q \geq_T p$.

But is this true? If we were to follow Black and claim that the
numerical assignment for a sentence is determined by the ratio of
those who assent to those who dissent to it (see above, p. 114, note
11), the connectedness axiom would automatically be true, since the
proportions giving degrees of truth are already numbers and hence
automatically obey the axiom. But, as I noted in chapter 4, such
calculations do *not* yield the right relationships of 'true to a greater
degree' and Black's account fails. On other degree theories there is no
such guarantee of the truth of (C$_T$). It would imply that any two
sentences are comparable with respect to their degree of truth: is this
plausible?

There are some classes of sentences for which (C$_T$) does hold; take
those of the form p_n = '*n* is a small number'. Either *n* is at least as
small as *m*, so $p_n \geq_T p_m$, or *m* is at least as small as *n*, in which case p_m
$\geq_T p_n$. But (C$_T$) does not hold in general. I showed in chapter 1, §2
that in many cases of a vague predicate *F* there are indeterminate
instances of '*a* is *F*-er than *b*'. These are cases where neither *Fa* $>_T$ *Fb*
nor *Fb* $>_T$ *Fa* is true, and *Fb* $=_T$ *Fa* cannot be true either (else '*a* is

F-er than *b*' would be determinately not true), so the instance of (C_T) *Fa* $\geq_T$ *Fb* or *Fb* $\geq_T$ *Fa* fails. In particular, multi-dimensional predicates (e.g. 'nice' and 'intelligent') give rise to such indeterminate instances (e.g. in the comparison of two people who are both fairly nice, but in different ways). Even with 'is of medium height', where the relevant height scale is, we may suppose, one-dimensional, the comparison of the degree of truth between predicating it of someone who is borderline tall–medium and someone borderline medium–small may be indeterminate.

The connectedness axiom is thus incompatible with a feature of many vague predicates. Accepting the axiom – as the degree theorist would be obliged to do to make numerical assignments – thus badly misrepresents those predicates. And the corresponding comparatives (e.g. 'nicer than') will also be misrepresented, since the connectedness axiom together with the degree theorist's claim that if *Fa* $\geq_T$ *Fb* then *a* is at least as *F* as *b* implies that '*F*-er than' can have no borderline (or indeterminate) instances.

Finally, consider the case where *p* = '*a* is tall' and *q* = '*b* is red'. Here we have no single comparative on which 'true to a greater degree' can piggy-back. The comparison may be read as '*a* is more clearly tall than *b* is red' and if, for example, *a* is clearly tall and *b* is clearly not red, then this will be true. But in a wide variety of cases (e.g. with a 5-foot 10-inch man and a reddish-orange patch), neither disjunct of (C_T) will be true. I claim that again the connectedness axiom is incompatible with the nature of the vagueness of these comparisons: we cannot assume that there is always a fact of the matter about which of two borderline sentences is more true.

3. UNIQUENESS THEOREMS AND TYPES OF SCALES APPROPRIATE TO VAGUENESS

It remains open for degree theorists to insist that there *are* suitable numerical assignments which capture vagueness. They might claim, for example, that problems with comparability are merely epistemic – we sometimes cannot easily tell which of two sentences is true to a higher degree, but there is, nonetheless, a fact of the matter about this. Machina comments (1976, p. 77, note 8) 'it seems to me . . . that the difficulties about comparability are really just difficulties about how to assign degrees of truth to propositions'. He gives no reasons for this claim, which resembles an epistemic theorist's insistence that the unclarity in borderline monadic predications is really just an epistemological difficulty in assigning (classical) truth-values. But while proponents of the epistemic view usually take care to offer detailed explanations of the ignorance characteristic of vagueness, degree theorists make no such attempt (compare the criticism of certain degree theories in chapter 4, §9i). Nonetheless, given the availability of this dogmatic response, it is worthwhile pursuing the issue of the uniqueness theorem, the companion to the representation theorem. It also provides the best context in which to complete the discussion of the last of the suggested responses to the cluster of objections raised in chapter 4, §9.

What uniqueness theorem should we expect for the modelling of degrees of truth? What type of scale is appropriate? One reason why these questions are important is because their answers will determine which statements about degrees of truth are meaningful – namely only those that have the same truth-value across all permissible transformations of the scale.

Degree theorists often imply that an ordinal scale is sufficient for the representation of vagueness. For example, Machina writes (1976, p. 61) 'the assignment of exact values doesn't matter much . . . what is of importance instead is the ordering relation between the values of various propositions'. And Goguen's claim that 'any not identically zero function which is continuous decreasing and asymptotic to zero' would be appropriate for the representation of 'short' (1969, p. 331), implies that it is only the ordering of the values that matters. The only features of a numerical assignment that we should then take seriously are the relations *greater than* and *smaller than* holding between the assigned numbers. So although any given representation function will assign particular numerical values, it provides only one way of doing so, and worries about the specific numbers themselves (or the ratios between them) are misplaced. In this section I shall examine the viability of this proposal.

Let us assume, along with all the participants to the debate, that we fix the interval as [0, 1], with 1 as the maximum value (assigned to definitely true sentences) and 0 as the minimum value (for definitely false ones). We are then forced to make the assumption that all permissible numerical assignments agree on the degree 1 cases, and similarly on the degree 0 cases: any sentence assigned degree 1 (0) in one assignment must be assigned degree 1 (0) in *all*. For we can assume that on any scale some sentences receive the value 1 (0): to deny that any sentences are completely true (completely false) would badly misrepresent the language and fail to give the semantics of our predicates as they actually are, according to which, for example, someone of 6 feet 8 inches *is* definitely tall (see chapter 4, §4 above). But then the same sentences must receive value 1, else there will be sentences that are of equal value on some scales but not on others, which would violate the requirement of preserving ordering. Note that this fixes an unwanted sharp boundary between the borderline cases and the definite cases, apparently incompatibly with higher-order vagueness. So the recourse to an ordinal scale does not avoid the conflict between assigning numerical values and accommodating higher-order vagueness: it still encounters it in connection with the values 0 and 1. I shall ignore this problem here.

One consequence of the fixed endpoints which will be important below is that the only transformation of the form $f(\mid p \mid) = \alpha \mid p \mid + \beta$ is the identity transformation $f(x) = x$, because $f(0) = 0$ requires that $\beta = 0$ and then $f(1) = 1$ requires that $\alpha = 1$. But there may be transformations of other forms.

The defender of an ordinal scale may insist that we can we shift the values of borderline cases monotonically in any way (keeping the endpoints fixed). I shall argue against this claim. As an initial point, consider a judgement to the effect that a vague sentence is 'nearly true'. This is intuitively meaningful and seems appropriate for describing some borderline case predications. It also plays a central role in the degree theorist's solution to the sorites paradox which typically claims that we find the inductive premise so compelling because it is nearly true. But on an ordinal scale whatever margin were decided to be near enough to 1 to count as 'nearly true', there would be transformations of the scale that placed any not completely true sentence outside that margin. So no sentence is nearly true on all transformations permitted for an ordinal scale, which counts against the suggestion that such a scale is appropriate. It *might* be possible to meet this objection by reinterpreting 'nearly true' in non-numerical terms, for the same sentences will be high in the ranking of sentences even when the scale assigns them lower values, so counting as 'nearly true' could depend on that ranking among sentences, rather than on the number assigned. It is not clear, however, quite how the interpretation could work (e.g. would it just depend on the actual values of sentences?). I turn to considerations in which numerical matters must be paramount.

We need to explore what restrictions on transformations are imposed if we are to respect the truth-definitions of the connectives on every permissible scale. If & and ∨ are given the standard Łukasiewicz truth-definitions then they impose no further restrictions. For if a transformation keeps fixed the ordering of all atomic sentences, the maxima and minima of all pairs, and hence their conjunctions and disjunctions, will slip into the scale in the appropriate way: the ordering of sentences, including those compound ones, will not vary between transformations. But the definition of negation does impose further constraints. Suppose on one scale, $| p | = 0.2$ and $| q | = 0.6$; after a transformation that preserves the order of atomic sentences, the values can become $| p | = 0.4$, $| q | = 0.8$. But according to the first scale and the standard definition of negation, $| p | < | \neg q |$, while according to the second, $| p | > | \neg q |$. But then it cannot be the case that the old scale and the transformed scale both represent the ordinal facts about instances of the relation $\geq_T$ among (possibly compound) sentences.

We can show that $| p | = 0.5$ iff $| p | = | \neg p |$. For if p and $\neg p$ are equally true, this fact must be recognised on every permissible scale, and so p must always take the value 0.5, ensuring that $| \neg p | = 1 - | p |$. So for any permissible transformation $f(0.5) = 0.5$. As well as this fixed point, the definition of negation imposes a symmetry requirement: any transformation of the values must be symmetric about the value 0.5. So for a transformation f:

(N) $f(1-x) = 1 - f(x)$.

(N) is required to ensure that $\neg p$ and p are still related as the truth-definition requires after a transformation f of each of their values.

These requirements severely restrict the permissible transformations. The following discontinuous transformation would still be permissible though:

(F) $f(x) = x/2$ for $x < 0.5$;
$f(x) = x$ for $x = 0.5$; and
$f(x) = (1 + x)/2$ for $x > 0.5$.

Once the conditional is introduced, however, still further restrictions are imposed (and an account of the conditional is important for dealing with the standard version of the sorites paradox). According to the most common (i.e. Łukasiewicz) definition, $| \ p \supset q \ | = 1$ if $| \ p \ | \leq | \ q \ |$ and $1 - | \ p \ | + | \ q \ |$ otherwise. This rules out the transformation given by (F), for suppose that $| \ p \ | = 0.6$ and $| \ q \ | = 0.4$, so that $| \ p \supset q \ | = 0.8$. The transformation (F) yields $| \ p \ | = 0.8$ and $| \ q \ | = 0.2$, and sentences with value 0.8 are mapped to 0.9. But the truth definition for the conditional as operated on the new values for its components implies that $| \ p \supset q \ | = 0.4$, so the ordering of conditionals with respect to other sentences will not be preserved.

In fact, the definition of the conditional requires that if the interval between the values of two pairs of sentences is the same, then that equality is maintained across all transformations. For suppose $| \ p \ | > | \ q \ |$ and $| \ p \supset q \ | = | \ r \supset s \ |$ then $1 - | \ p \ | + | \ q \ | = 1 - | \ r \ | + | \ s \ |$ and hence $| \ q \ | - | \ p \ | = | \ s \ | - | \ r \ |$, so the intervals between the two pairs of values must always be the same to ensure that the corresponding two conditionals always share the same value. Such constancy of intervals is a typical feature of interval scales, and it requires transformations to be of the form $f(x) = \alpha x + \beta$. But we saw above that the only permissible transformation of this form is the identity function.

So the requirement of respecting the standard truth-conditions serves to ensure that there are *no* non-trivial transformations available. Hence if there is an acceptable assignment of truth-values at all, it must be unique. As a consequence, objections to the assignment of specific values cannot be alleviated by appealing to the non-uniqueness of the numerical scale.[1]

This stands, at least, as an argument against degree theorists such as Machina 1976 and Forbes 1983 who defend the Łukasiewicz definitions of the connectives. And shifting to other candidate sets of definitions will not solve the problem. Recall that the definition of

[1] The above argument could be generalised to avoid the assumption that the interval of values must be [0, 1]. If the interval were [n, m] the definitions of negation and the conditional would need to be changed to preserve normality. Negation would be defined by $| \ \neg p \ | = m - n + | \ p \ |$, which would impose a symmetry around $(m - n)/2$; while the conditional would be defined by $| \ p \supset q \ | = m$ if $| \ p \ | \leq | \ q \ |$ and $m - | \ p \ | + | \ q \ |$ otherwise, and the consequences about the need for an interval scale would be the same as for the standard definition. Also, the only linear transformation would still be the identity function given the interval $[n, m]$: since $f(n) = n$ and $f(m) = m$, any transformation of the form $f(| \ p \ |) = \alpha | \ p \ | + \beta$ would require $\beta = n(1 - \alpha) = m(1 - \alpha)$, which, given that $n \neq m$, ensures that $\alpha = 1$ and $\beta = 0$.

negation is universally accepted by degree theorists, and has no plausible rivals. Consider next Goguen's alternative suggestion for the conditional:

$$| p \supset q | = | q | \, / \, | p | \text{ when } | p | \geq | q | \text{ and } | p | > 0$$
$$= 1 \text{ otherwise.}$$

This imposes the requirement that any transformation f of the values yielded by one homomorphism must satisfy $f(x/y) = f(x)/f(y)$. This would be satisfied by transformations of the form $f(| p |) = (| p |)^n$ for some (not necessarily integral) n. But, given the requirement (due to the definition of negation) that sentences mapped to 0.5 are invariantly mapped to that value, the only possible value for n is 1, permitting only the identity transformation. Again, the value-assignment function must be unique.

To summarise, in giving their truth-definitions of the connectives, degree theorists typically commit themselves to a unique numerical scale on which sentences are placed. So the only remaining response to the objections raised in chapter 4, §9 fails: many-valued theories of vagueness must be rejected.

I shall now explain why accounts of vagueness that assign numbers have the initial plausibility that they do, and I shall offer a diagnosis of the fundamental error of which degree theorists are guilty.

4. DIAGNOSING THE ERROR

Consider again the vague predicate 'tall': I claim that any numbers assigned in an attempt to capture the vagueness of 'tall' do no more than serve as another measure of *height*. More generally, in so far as it is possible to assign numbers which respect certain truths about e.g. comparative relations, this is no more than a measure of an attribute related to, or underlying, the vague predicate.

In many paradigm cases of a vague predicate F there is a corresponding measurable attribute related to F in such a way that the truth-value status of Fx (the truth-value it takes, or perhaps its lack of one) is determined by x's quantity of that attribute. For example, the truth-value status of 'a is tall' is determined by, or supervenes on, a's height, and so the same truth-value is shared by 'x is tall' whenever x is of the same height as a. But although the measure of the underlying quantity may *determine* the applicability of the vague predicate, it does not follow that this measure is reflected in a non-classical numerical truth-value status.

Consider a scale for a measurable attribute; vague predicates are often so useful because we wish to pick out a rough range from that range (e.g. people in the upper region of the height scale for 'tall', ranges of temperature for 'lukewarm' or 'hot' etc.). But the feature of these predicates that constitutes their vagueness rests on the fact that it is only a rough, vague or indeterminate region of the scale, and numerical assignments based on the underlying measurable attribute do not capture that distinctive feature.

Are degree theorists thus mistaken in claiming that vague predicates come in degrees? I suggest that there is a *sense* in which F can be said to come in degrees – call it coming in degrees$_m$ – whenever there is a measure of the attribute F-ness, and where things have different degrees$_m$ of F-ness by having more or less of the attribute. The degree$_m$ of heat of an object will be a matter of its quantity of heat and we happen to call the measure *degrees* Celsius. And angle-size can be said to come in degrees$_m$ and again we use a notion of 'degree' for the measure. The connection emphasised by the degree theorist between the role of a comparative 'F-er than' and the supposed fact that F-ness comes in degrees would be appropriate if it was degrees$_m$ we were interested in, for the structure of F-er *than* relations generates a scale corresponding to degrees$_m$ of F-ness.

But the fact that many vague predicates come in degrees$_m$ is not enough for the degree theorist, who needs there to be implications for truth-values or degrees of truth, so that if F comes in degrees, predications of F can be true to intermediate degrees. Heat comes in degrees$_m$, but 'has heat' is a predicate which applies to things wherever they appear on the associated scale (i.e. whenever they have a temperature above absolute zero) and its predication is never anything but definitely true or false. Similarly the application of most predicates associated with degrees of angle-size are all-or-nothing (e.g. 'acute'), despite the fact that angle-size comes in degrees$_m$. So coming in degrees$_m$ is not the sense of 'coming in degrees' required by the degree theorist. The heat scale does indeed give scope for paradigm vagueness, as can be demonstrated with 'hot' and other related vague predicates that serve to pick out a rough section of the scale (with angle-size, such vague predicates are possible – e.g. 'is a large angle' – but they are less common). But this association is not enough to help the theorists in question: it does not show that to capture the truth-values of the sentences involving the vague predicate, we need to employ a numerical scale of degrees of truth or any of the distinctive features of degree theories.

Recall the Forbes-style argument for degree theories discussed in chapter 4, §4. The first three steps were as follows: for some *a* and *b*, (1) *a* is *F*-er than *b*; so (2) *a* is *F* to a greater degree than *b*; hence (3) *a* satisfies the predicate 'is *F*' to a greater degree than *b*. The sense of 'coming in degrees' that the degree theorist needs supports the inference from (2) to (3), but the inference from (1) to (2) is then questionable. By contrast, with the alternative sense, 'coming in degrees$_m$', the inference from (1) to (2) is valid, but we are not warranted in inferring (3). The argument, and the degree theorist's treatment in general, equivocates between these two senses of 'coming in degrees'. Distinguishing between them also helps with cases where *a* is more *F* than *b* but both are *F* and satisfy 'is *F*' to the same, maximum, degree (e.g. *a* is 6 feet 9 inches and *b* is 6 feet 8 inches and *F* = 'is tall'). This is a case where *Fa* and *Fb* can be assigned different numbers to capture the underlying quantity, but reflecting only the fact that *a* and *b* are *F* to different degrees$_m$; it has nothing to do with vagueness. Similarly with predications of non-vague expressions such as 'acute angle': relevant differences (reflecting 'more acute than') can be represented numerically, but this cannot be given the degree theorist's interpretation, only an interpretation in terms of degrees$_m$. I suggest that these cases are not significantly different from others in which the degree theorist does make numerical assignments: the assignments *never* reflect or represent vagueness.

Could the degree theorist reply that the numbers they assign to predications of 'tall' do not conform to the standard measures of height and that this shows that their numbers are not merely a measure of height or simply a matter of degrees$_m$? Height is measurable on a ratio scale, but the degree theorist's numerical assignments will typically not respect the ratios between values and the summation relations that are shared by all standard height measures. And there could be a maximum value for '*x* is tall' – degree 1 – though there is no maximum height (or if instead the values of '*x* is tall' were asymptotic to 1 as the height of *x* increases, this has no parallel for a height scale). But these observations will not help the degree theorist, since a scale can still operate as a measure of a quantity even if it does not reflect all the features of that quantity. Take the Celsius scale; it has an arbitrarily chosen zero and is not a ratio scale, but it is still a measure of temperature despite the availability of the Kelvin scale – a ratio scale with an absolute zero – which measures the same quantity. Similarly the degree theorist's assignments for 'tall' could still be legitimately classified as a measure of height, even though fewer characteristics of height are represented than with a metre-measure.

In the light of my diagnosis we can return to some of the problems raised above. Consider, for example, the difficulties with multi-dimensionality raised in §2. I claim that these arise because there is no measurable quantity underlying the corresponding predications in the straightforward way claimed for 'tall'. The measurement of other attributes that are apparently multi-dimensional, such as intelligence, faces difficulties comparable to those faced in assigning numerical truth-values to multi-dimensional vague predicates. Putative measures are often controversial, and one complaint may be that they impose an ordering when no such ordering is available. But from the point of view of measurement, it is often more valuable to have *some* measure that roughly approximates to the notion. Perhaps there is not really any genuine scale for 'intelligence'; there are measurable attributes (e.g. IQ, perhaps), and comparisons with respect to these will resemble judgements of intelligence in certain important respects. For scientific purposes, the vague notion of intelligence might then be put to one side in favour of these precise measurable ones. But this practice is not an option when we are interested in the vague expression 'intelligent' itself and its vagueness in particular. We cannot impose a measure that regiments the predications into an ordered scale and claim to be representing the expression and its vagueness, any more than we can impose a single sharp boundary to comply with classical logic and plausibly claim to be representing its vagueness in so doing.

So if, as I am suggesting, the numerical assignments are nothing more than measurement of attributes, then the lack of any underlying unified attribute corresponding to our intuitive (unprecisified) concept of intelligence explains the inability to assign numbers effectively in representing the vague predicate 'intelligent'. Moreover, suppose the degree theorist *could* assign such a range of numbers. Surely this would show that there *was* an appropriate measure of intelligence (at least for the borderline range of cases, and it seems reasonable to assume that the widely recognised problems concerning the measure do not only arise for clearly intelligent or clearly not intelligent people). A degree theorist who insists on such an assignment would thus be forced to deny widely accepted theses about the lack of a measure corresponding to certain expressions.

Next recall the problems encountered in comparing degrees of truth for predications of different vague predicates. Asking for an assignment of numbers for predications of 'tall', 'heavy' and 'clever' simultaneously is like asking for a measure of all of height, weight and intelligence at once, for which a's height is always comparable to b's weight etc. There is no kind of scale that can meet the latter challenge, at least not unless we construct one by arbitrarily deciding how measures of the three quantities should be compared. Similarly, comparisons of degrees of truth between borderline cases of different predicates would be undecided. And if the claim to be representing and illuminating natural language and its vagueness is to have any plausibility, the values must not simply be fixed arbitrarily.

In this chapter I have argued that degree theories, in their attempt to capture vagueness by assigning numbers to sentences, fail to provide an acceptable account of vagueness; in particular they must deny some important features of various classes of expressions. Moreover, they are, I argued, forced to make an implausible commitment to a unique numerical assignment for each sentence. Finally, I have explained why degree theories look plausible in a limited range of cases and argued that this is not because they are capturing *vagueness* even in those cases. In the next chapter, I move away from theories based on numerical assignments and examine pragmatic accounts of vagueness.

6

The pragmatic account of vagueness

In chapter 3 I rejected the epistemic view of vagueness which retains classical logic and semantics but commits us to a language in which our vague predicates have sharp meanings and vagueness is a matter of our ignorance. I then turned to the alternative strategy of treating vagueness as a semantic feature of our language that requires a revision of classical logic or semantics. Many-valued theories abandon classical logic, and, I have argued, they fail; while, as I shall discuss in chapter 7, supervaluationism calls for a revision of classical semantics. But are we forced to take either step, or could we avoid both of them by treating vagueness as a *pragmatic* phenomenon arising from features of our use of language? Could there be a pragmatic account of vagueness which retains both classical logic and semantics, but does not commit us to the unique, sharp meanings that the epistemic theorist accepts? Linda Burns hopes to provide such an account by taking up a suggestion of Lewis's: we are to consider a cluster of precise languages, where classical logic and semantics apply to each of them and vagueness arises from pragmatic factors concerning which of them we are using at any time. I shall argue that a distinctively pragmatic theory of this sort is not viable: at best it collapses into the semantic supervaluationary theory.

1. LEWIS'S PHILOSOPHY OF LANGUAGE AND THE PRAGMATIC ACCOUNT

Lewis's remarks about vagueness are made in the context of his general semantic theory (e.g. Lewis 1969, 1970, 1975). He treats languages as set-theoretic entities that assign meanings to the strings of symbols that qualify as their sentences. The meaning of a sentence in a language is a function from the specification of a context to a set

139

of possible worlds, namely the worlds in which the sentence would be true if uttered or inscribed in the given context; a context-specification is an *n*-tuple of indices including one for time, one for place, and so on for each of the other factors relevant in fixing the context. The semantic theory for a Lewisian language also specifies how the meanings of sentences depend on the meanings of their subsentential components (such as names, verbs and predicates), where these meanings are also functions (for example, the meanings of names are functions from contexts to possible objects, while predicates are ones from contexts to sets of possible objects).

So Lewis defines languages in abstraction from any actual use. The question then arises what picks out a language (conceived set-theoretically) as *the* language, or one of the languages, of a given community. Lewis replies that this is determined by the intentions and beliefs of the language-users of that community according to what they intend to convey when they utter sentences and what they understand when they hear sentences. (In this way the treatment of languages as abstract entities is reconciled with a Gricean account of meaning centring on the intentions of speakers; see e.g. Grice 1957.) Lewis describes the community's convention as a matter of the language-users conforming to a regularity of truthfulness and trust in a particular language L, expressing only what they believe true in that language and adopting beliefs on the assumption that other speakers behave likewise (see e.g. Lewis 1975).

Lewis's languages are precise: predicates are assigned clearly defined sets of objects at each world (for a given context), leaving no scope for the borderline cases typical of vague predicates. How is this compatible with the fact that predicates and other elements of our language seem to be vague? Lewis offers two types of answer, one treating vagueness within semantics and the other treating it as a pragmatic phenomenon. The former is a version of supervaluationism which will be examined in chapter 7; the latter I deal with here. According to the pragmatic account, vagueness arises in connection with the question *which* (precise) language a community uses (see Lewis 1969, pp. 200-2, 1970, p. 64 and 1975, pp. 34–5). The intentions, beliefs and habits of the members of a community do not determine a convention of truthfulness and trust in a single language; instead a cluster of largely similar languages is involved. Some of these will draw the boundary of 'tall' at 6 feet 0 inches, some at 5 feet 11 inches, etc., and the borderline cases of 'tall' are the cases classified differently by different languages of the cluster. So speakers are not restricted to a single language and may use different precise languages from the cluster at different times and in different contexts. This explains the discrepancies typical of the classifications of borderline case predications, since 'we are free to settle these indeterminacies however we like' by choosing different languages of the cluster (1975, p. 35). The convention can be redescribed as one of 'truthfulness and trust in whichever we please of some cluster of similar languages' (1975, pp. 34–5).

This is the account of vagueness adopted by Burns (see her 1991, e.g. pp. 36–41 and pp. 181–5, and 1995, pp. 43–5). There is no vagueness in languages themselves, nor need there be any vagueness in the world; instead it arises as a feature of the relation between language-users and languages. Burns judges Lewis to have given a successful semantic theory for the precise languages involved in the account; and this contrasts, she claims, with the repeated failure of philosophers' attempts to provide viable semantics for vague languages.

Note, any attempt to treat vagueness as an entirely pragmatic matter must be of broadly the same form as Burns's account. For if vagueness is a pragmatic matter, then languages are not themselves vague. But then if we were taken as consistently using a single non-vague language, the view would collapse into the epistemic view: our predicates would have unique, sharp meanings even if some of our linguistic behaviour suggested otherwise. So a cluster of precise languages must be involved (even if the Lewisian treatment of those languages is not adopted).

The pragmatic account of vagueness proceeds by reference to precise languages, but what are we to say about the vague language itself – the actual language of the community? Lewis and Burns may deny that this question is important since such a language plays no independent role in the account. Lewis casually suggests that 'an ordinary, open-textured imprecise language is a sort of blur of precise languages' (1975, p. 35). Elsewhere he describes the actual language of the community as a 'resonance hybrid' of the languages of the cluster (1969, p. 201), and though Burns promises clarification of this terminology (1991, p. 41), she fails to fulfil the promise. Burns's official position seems to involve denying that there is any such thing

141

as the vague communal language in addition to the precise ones (see 1991, chapter 2). Any talk about our vague, natural language should then be reducible to sentences about our (vague) use of precise languages.

Burns claims that her pragmatic account can succeed in accounting for the linguistic behaviour typically found in the face of borderline case predications: 'where there is a range of distinct precise languages to choose from, differing at just those points where questions about the application of vague predicates arise, individuals may be expected to dither occasionally, to be inconsistent and to differ from one another in the decisions they make about borderline objects' (1991, p. 182). She also seeks to use the idea of choosing a precise language to explain what she takes to be the legitimate practice of drawing sharp limits to the application of our vague predicates (e.g. 1991, p. 183; she criticises Wright for leaving no scope for such an explanation, 1991, p. 93). Such a practice of boundary-drawing is certainly acceptable for special purposes, for example in some legal contexts and in other situations when it is necessary to eliminate uncertainty and dispute over classifications. But in these cases, the sharpenings are fixed, shared and openly specified, and the boundary-fixing is then naturally seen as a form of stipulation which results in a change of meaning for the predicate in question (albeit a change that meets certain constraints on acceptable ways to make that predicate precise). *Pace* Burns, speakers are not usually free to draw precise limits to vague predicates without revealing their choice of boundary to the others taking part in the conversation.

Lewis seems to treat his two basic accounts of vagueness – the one locating it within semantics, the other treating it as a pragmatic matter – as alternatives between which we can choose at will (see e.g. 1970, p. 64). Perhaps there is no fact of the matter which one of his two stories gives the uniquely correct account of vagueness. Burns, by contrast, views the choice as crucial, maintaining that vagueness is a pragmatic phenomenon and that any semantic account is misconceived. But *is* the choice between the semantic and pragmatic accounts really a substantial one? Consider, as the supervaluationist does, a complete precisification of the language – one way of making all our vague predicates precise together. This will constitute a Lewisian precise language since each predicate will have a precise extension; and there will be a one–one correspondence between precisifications of the whole language and Lewisian precise languages in the appropriate cluster. So does the pragmatic account of vagueness coincide with the supervaluationary semantic theory, the only difference being whether they use the expression 'precisification of our vague language' or 'precise language of a cluster' to label the same entities? If so, we should not expect the pragmatic account to be of additional interest or to solve any problems and objections that face supervaluationism. But the pragmatic account *could* be a substantially different theory were it to give the precise languages a significantly different role from that which supervaluationism attributes to precisifications. To assess this issue, more details of the pragmatic account are needed: we may be clear about Lewis's account of what a convention of using a single precise language would be like, and acknowledge that the convention of language-use in a typical language-community involves a cluster of languages, but it still remains to be explained how the convention is to be understood once a cluster of languages is involved.

2. CONVENTIONS INVOLVING CLUSTERS OF LANGUAGES

Does following the convention require a speaker to be truthful and trusting in all the languages of the cluster? Or is it a matter of truthfulness and trust in *some* language(s) (where it is unspecified which)? Or do we have a cluster of conventions, one for each language, so we count as using all those languages? Or should we regard speakers as choosing, at any one time, some precise language or other in which to be truthful and trusting?

Before examining these alternatives I ask whether the relevant cluster of languages is sharply bounded. Borderline case predications are sentences over which there are disagreements among languages in the cluster, so if the cluster were sharply bounded then the borderline cases would be sharply bounded and there would be no room for higher-order vagueness. Burns recognises the importance of acknowledging higher-order vagueness and argues that the cluster of languages must not be seen as sharply bounded (1991, pp. 184–5) and similarly Lewis talks about 'a *fuzzy* region in the space of precise languages' (1970, p. 64, my italics). It is not enough, however, simply to assert this: a substantial account is needed of what a cluster with fuzzy boundaries would amount to. Burns's discussion is confusing:

she writes that 'the limits to the range of precise languages which may be spoken by a given population must be regarded as indeterminate', but very shortly afterwards she tries to meet the threat that this will yield a sorites paradox on 'language in the cluster' by concluding 'the linguistic behaviour of individual speakers will determine limits in practice, though the theorist has no way of specifying them in advance' (1991, p. 185). Why doesn't this last claim imply that the cluster has (albeit unknowable) sharp boundaries? Burns's remarks amount to no more than an assertion that we must accommodate the phenomenon of higher-order vagueness, without any indication of how this can be done, and we are certainly given no reason to believe that adopting a pragmatic account will *help* with higher-order vagueness. But I put this issue aside: however it is resolved, and perhaps in order to resolve it, we urgently need an account of the linguistic conventions involving clusters of languages. There seem to be four options.

(a) The first is to regard the convention as one of truthfulness and trust in *all* languages of the cluster. We should then count x as tall if x is tall according to all the languages, not-tall if x is not-tall according to all of them (i.e. if there is no language according to which x *is* tall) and borderline otherwise.

In this form the so-called pragmatic account would collapse into supervaluationism. As we have seen, the precise languages of the cluster each correspond to a supervaluationary precisification of the whole language, so following a convention that requires truth in all languages of the cluster amounts to the same as requiring truth on all precisifications. Could the difference between the positions rest with Burns's insistence that talk of 'the vague language' is not acceptable, since, by contrast, supervaluationism does provide truth-conditions for the vague language? I deny that it could: Burns has no grounds on which to maintain this insistence. For she endorses Lewis's account of the role of beliefs and intentions in fixing the language spoken and hence the meanings of sentences, and if we are seeking to be truthful and trusting in the whole cluster of languages then our beliefs and intentions are related in exactly the appropriate way to the corresponding language whose truth-conditions are given by the supervaluationist account. So on option (a) Burns would not be justified in rejecting the supervaluationist's formulation of truth-conditions and no difference between the accounts can be retained.

(b) Perhaps, instead, we should interpret speakers as aiming to be truthful and trusting in one or more languages from the cluster (not necessarily in all): they need not select a unique one provided they are truthful in at least one at any one time. This fits Burns's description of 'a single convention of truth in one or other of these precise languages' (1991, p. 39).

It might be explained that the convention involves more than a single language in this way because the convention-fixing beliefs and intentions are underspecific. In describing someone as 'tall' I do not have in mind a specific boundary height of 'tall'; rather there are a range of possible boundary heights and my belief is not specific about which one is relevant. Then, just as the underspecific statement 'Tek is in his thirties' can be re-expressed as a disjunction 'Tek is thirty or Tek is thirty-one or . . .', perhaps the content of the relevant beliefs and intentions could likewise be expressed as $p \vee p' \vee p'' \vee \ldots$ (for an appropriate set of disjuncts). But if our beliefs and intentions are underspecific, why is it not then appropriate to interpret the *language* as underspecific but not vague in the originally intended sense, with apparently vague sentences having truth-conditions in the form of disjunctions where each disjunct is a truth-condition of the sentence in one of the cluster of languages? The lack of specificity in the relevant beliefs and intentions would still allow a semantics for our language and does not warrant the adoption of a pragmatic account.

This mirrors the situation with (a), where there also turned out to be determinate truth-conditions for the vague language. Like (a), option (b) could also be presented within a framework of precisifica-tions, but with a different account of how truth simpliciter relates to truth on those precisifications, namely 'p is true iff p is true on *some* precisification(s)'. Instead of neither Fa nor $\neg Fa$ being true for a borderline case, *both* Fa and $\neg Fa$ will be true, and assuming we interpret 'p is false' as '$\neg p$ is true', there will be truth-value gluts (Burns 1995, pp. 30–1 defends such a view of borderline cases; see my chapter 7, §7 on Hyde's 'subvaluationary' account which is the dual of supervaluationism). For the purposes of this chapter the key point about option (b) is that it makes the appeal to a distinctive *pragmatic* account of vagueness unwarranted.

(c) In his final account of conventions, Lewis weakens the require-ment of *complete* conformity to the regularity: it is enough for the regularity to be followed by *most* of the people *most* of the time (see e.g. Lewis 1969, pp. 78–9). Can vagueness be accommodated by this slackening of the regularity condition?

The weakening allows for inevitable lapses by real-life followers of a convention. But it also seems to allow two different, but similar, regularities to count as conventions in the same community; in particular it could allow two different precise languages each to count as languages conventionally used. Consider a language L that draws the boundary of 'tall' at 5 feet 11 inches, and L' that draws the boundary at 5 feet 11.3 inches but is otherwise the same; the only differences between the conventions of using these languages would arise with assertions that people between 5 feet 11 inches and 5 feet 11.3 inches are or are not tall, and such assertions will constitute a minute proportion of linguistic behaviour. So the same body of linguistic behaviour would count as a convention of using L and equally a convention of using L'. More generally, each language of the cluster would count as being conventionally used by the population.

Lewis addresses the suggestion that we could have different conventions relating to the same behavioural regularities: he considers a situation in which there is a convention of truthfulness and trust in L and asks whether truthfulness and trust in L^- is also a convention of the population, where L^- is a language with a somewhat smaller vocabulary (Lewis 1975, pp. 31–2). His reply is that truthfulness and trust in L^- *should* also count as a convention, but that we are most interested in the 'most inclusive language' used, L not L^-, and so it can be misleading, but not false, to say that the community use L^-. But in the vagueness case there *is* no 'most inclusive language': the languages of the relevant cluster share the same range of expressions, though they conflict over the extension assigned to certain vague predicates; no single language in the cluster will be privileged. Can we accept a multiplicity of conventions assigning different extensions to the same predicates?

According to one of the precise languages of the cluster, 'tall' has a sharp boundary at 6 feet 0 inches. Thus if the use of that precise language counts as a convention it would count as a *convention* that there is a boundary to the tall people at exactly 6 feet 0 inches; and this is absurd. Moreover, since other precise languages of the cluster have the same conventional status but draw the boundary at different places, it would also be a convention that the extension of 'tall' is sharply bounded at 5 feet 11 inches and at 5 feet 11.5 inches and at all heights between. Surely these conflicting matters cannot *all* be conventions of our language use? Rather it seems that it is a convention that 'tall' has no sharp boundaries at all, in just the same way that other aspects of the meaning of 'tall' are conventional; which seems to imply, again, that vagueness should be treated as an aspect of meaning and so within semantics.

Options (a), (b) and (c) all ignore the idea of *choosing* a language, which is emphasised both by Burns and (to a lesser extent) by Lewis. Burns talks about 'a range of distinct precise languages to choose from' (1991, p. 182), and Lewis suggests that different languages 'may have different virtues and vices', and allowing speakers to choose among them will appropriately give them freedom to benefit from the different virtues according to the context (1969, p. 202; see also Burns 1991, p. 185). It is also the element of choice between languages that Burns relies on to account for typical linguistic behaviour surrounding borderline cases, namely conflict among speakers as they make different choices, and hesitation by individuals over their own choice of language (see §1). It may seem to be this element of choosing a language that sets the pragmatic account apart from semantic accounts. After all, none of the standard semantic theories uses such ideas, and these ideas may seem incompatible with the intuition that truth-conditions (which the semantic theory seeks to give) should not depend on choices we happen to make. By contrast, if we are also concerned with pragmatic issues such as when we choose to assert something, there is room for an element of choice in the account of vagueness. But despite this *prima facie* contrast, no sharp distinction between the two kinds of theories can be located this way: supervaluationists cannot allow choosing of *languages*, but they can replicate aspects of the pragmatic account. In particular, first, they can allow pragmatic rules concerning assertion in addition to (and not conflicting with) the semantic rules determining truth-values (e.g. stating when it is permissible to stipulate that a borderline case falls into or outside the extension, despite its not being strictly correct to classify it that way). And, second, mirroring the variation in language chosen, the precisifications that are quantified over could vary with context; and there could be semantic rules regulating this variation (see §3 on Lewis's account of vagueness-related context-dependence). I shall argue, however, that no account of vagueness based on a convention of choosing languages will work.

(d) According to this 'choice' option, taken literally, the convention of language-use would be a regularity by which, at any one time, a speaker or listener chooses one of the relevant range of precise languages in which to be truthful and trusting. But it is surely implausible to claim that speakers and listeners *always* pick a single language from the cluster, or that they operate at any one time with a (perhaps arbitrarily chosen) precise language with sharp boundaries to the extensions of all predicates. For a start, that would mean that we would never leave borderline cases unresolved at a particular time, as we so frequently do. And, as I argued in §1, though in certain specialised circumstances (e.g. legal ones) it can be legitimate to draw sharp boundaries, generally such a practice is inappropriate, contrary to this account of the convention.

Moreover, a convention involving an open choice of language could not be rationally sustained. Take the idea of 'trust in L', where this amounts to trusting that if someone utters S, then S is true in L. It is simply not a rational policy to choose a language in which to be trusting: we should attempt to be trusting in the language chosen by the people with whom we are conversing. A regularity in which we choose languages will not satisfy Lewis's condition on a convention that it must be rational to conform to the regularity given that others do: even if everyone else chose a language at will, our most rational ploy would *not* be to do just the same. (By contrast, recall the relatively rare case where a language is fixed by explicitly stipulating sharp boundaries: here the obstacle to communication is removed since the appropriate choice is then settled.) Relatedly, if I choose a precise language in which to be truthful and you choose a different one, we could disagree over truth-values without differing over the facts. I could mislead you by telling you that something was red because it counts as 'red' according to my language when it counts as 'orange' by yours. Lewis recognises a similar problem, but discusses it when he is primarily concerned with allowing unsharp analyticity (where the similar languages disagree over what counts as analytic, or true in all worlds). He observes that in these cases differences will only arise over how sentences should be assigned values in distant possible worlds and thus will rarely cause problems in general communication, where such possible worlds are irrelevant (1969, pp. 201–2). But once the account is extended to vagueness in general this defence will be unavailable: borderline case candidates, over which the languages disagree, are pervasive in the actual world.

Could the implausibility of supposing that we always choose a single precise language be avoided by maintaining that the 'choice' need not be a conscious one? Even if we do not (and probably could not) always consciously select a single language, aspects of the context can often narrow down the range of relevant languages (e.g. according to the relevant comparison class for classification as 'tall'). But it is still implausible to suppose that a single language is fixed even given such contextual factors. Suppose we have been talking about an election, and I say that some particular candidate is tall; there may have been no mention of tallness earlier in our conversation and yet according to the view in question, the context serves to identify a single language in which 'tall' has a sharp boundary.

We cannot provide a successful account of our language-use by taking it to be a convention of truthfulness and trust in a language we happen to choose from a cluster of precise languages, or by taking the 'choice' to be fixed by context.

To summarise: attempts to provide an account of vagueness in terms of a convention involving a cluster of languages either fail or collapse into a semantic supervaluationary account (or its subvaluationary dual). In the final section of this chapter I consider the denial of a single (vague) communal language.

3. THE VAGUE COMMUNAL LANGUAGE

One reason Burns (following Lewis) gives for denying that there is a single communal language is that otherwise we could not explain our language learning (e.g. Burns 1991, p. 39, Lewis 1969, p. 202). Someone learning the meaning of a predicate would be unable to identify the uniquely relevant extension of a communal language on the basis of their limited experience of others' use of that predicate. A cluster of extensions corresponding to a cluster of languages could be grasped more easily since the learner would not need to narrow the options down to one; latching onto any one language from the cluster would be enough. But that difficulty for an account committed to a single language only arises if that language is taken to be a precise Lewisian language which has no scope for vagueness. If the language is vague, learning the meaning of a predicate will not implausibly demand narrowing possible extensions down to one sharp extension. It is the precision that causes problems, not the uniqueness of the language. So, considerations of language-learning do not provide a reason for denying that there is a vague communal language. Moreover, such a denial creates further problems.

If we needed to talk about the meaning of vague predicates independently of their meanings within Lewisian precise languages then we could not accept (as Burns does) that Lewis's semantics of precise languages gives a complete account of meaning: we would be obliged to offer a semantics of the vague language too. Although Burns regards it as neither necessary nor indeed possible to provide such a semantics, she does not avoid the offending talk of meanings. Two types of case relevant here involve context-dependence and tolerance rules. Both – even in Burns's own treatments – seem to demand more from an account of meaning than can be given just by reference to precise languages, and this leads to problems for any pragmatic account of vagueness.

Within his *semantic* account, Lewis offers an account of certain forms of context-dependence related to vagueness: see chapter 7, §3. Here the effect of context on the truth-value of a sentence is treated as an element of its meaning which can be systematically specified and is typically grasped by those who have learnt that meaning. Burns hopes to adopt Lewis's treatment (e.g. 1991, pp. 189–91); but she cannot merely transplant his theorising within his alternative semantic account of vagueness into her pragmatic account. According to her account there *is* no communal predicate 'tall' to have rules of meaning reflecting context-dependence and determining how its applicability and extension varies with context; in the different contexts we are supposedly using different predicates with different meanings.

Finally, consider principles of tolerance for vague predicates. Accepting the tolerance of a predicate is clearly problematic because it allows the formulation of a sorites paradox; but nonetheless it is often argued that tolerance principles express an important aspect of the meaning of the corresponding vague predicates. Indeed, Burns maintains that tolerance rules, in some form, are vital to the meaning of vague predicates. Her solution to the sorites paradox rests on their careful reformulation in such a way, she claims, that does *not* lead to paradox (see Burns 1986, and 1991, chapter 6; for criticisms of her solution see Schwartz 1988 and Varzi 1995). But how can the claim that her principles are part of the meaning of our typical vague predicates be accommodated on the pragmatic account? Genuine and applicable tolerance rules are incompatible with the sharp boundaries found throughout Lewisian languages. Again, to maintain that tolerance principles reflect the meaning of our predicates, we need to talk about the meaning of the predicates of our language in such a way that requires more than a cluster of different languages used at different times or by different people: we should not dispense with a vague communal language.

Having seen that the pragmatic view does not fulfil its promise of retaining classical logic and semantics while accommodating vagueness, and having rejected the theories that offer a non-classical logic, it is time for us to explore the option of classical logic without classical semantics. I turn to the supervaluationist theory of vagueness in the next chapter.

7

Supervaluationism

In this chapter and the next I shall defend a supervaluationist theory of vagueness and seek its best possible version. I believe that, unfortunately, there is no straightforward argument for the correctness of this view – there is no simple demonstration that the truth-conditions of our vague sentences must quantify over precisifications, for example. The case for it must be made by showing the success with which it fulfils the tasks facing any theory of vagueness and the effectiveness of its reflective equilibrium in balancing our intuitions, judgements, explanations of our linguistic practices and theoretical considerations of simplicity and so forth. I claim that on this cost-benefit method of assessment, it does vastly better than its rivals. The main rivals have been rejected in previous chapters. Theories offering no modification to classical logic or semantics are unacceptable, I have argued (even if they deny that there is a vague language and characterise vagueness via our pragmatic relations to a range of precise languages). But theories offering a truth-functional many-valued logic are at least as bad. We should propose a non-truth-functional semantics and regard sentences that do not take classical values as falling into a truth-value gap instead. And the only viable way I can see of doing these things is with a supervaluationist theory. This leaves logical space for theories that I have not considered, in particular ones deviating from classical semantics in some other way and/or deviating from classical logic as well. In §7 I consider and reject some of those possibilities, namely those that can be seen as variants on the standard supervaluationary theory. I do not think that there is any hope for as yet undiscovered alternatives differing radically from all the considered options. So although I may not have eliminated, or provided comparisons with, every possible account of vagueness, I maintain that I have dealt with all those with any plausibility.

The aim of this chapter is to show how supervaluationism provides a natural and attractive story about our vague language, with the desired logic and a defensible semantics. I answer most of the most common objections, including (i) that its preservation of classical logic (especially the law of excluded middle) is undesirable, (ii) that classical consequence is not in fact retained, (iii) that the non-classical semantics are unacceptable, and (iv) that the appeal to precisifications is unjustified. Chapter 8 answers the final two popular objections to supervaluationism concerning the supervaluationist's notion of truth and higher-order vagueness. Potential developments and variants of supervaluationism are explored along the way, especially in §3 and in §7 of this chapter, and my own version of the account is developed in chapter 8 in particular.

As a starting point, we can take three things that the earlier chapters suggest we should seek from a theory of vagueness. First, we would like the theory to capture the thought that borderline case predications are neither true nor false, but that they do not each take some specific (numerical) value either. Second, and relatedly, we should avoid the commitment to sharp boundaries with vague predicates: for there is nothing in our language, its use, or the world that determines particular locations for such hidden boundaries. And third, we want a tried and tested logic, avoiding surprising and counter-intuitive consequences concerning principles or inferences that should be unaffected by the acknowledgement of vagueness: classical logic would surely be ideal.

How could the use of language consistently both determine that classical logic applies, and fail to determine specific classical extensions for our vague predicates (when nothing else can determine them either)? Supervaluationism has an answer and provides a semantics for the vague language. Though our practices do not determine a precise extension to 'tall', they do determine a (vague) range within which the precise extension would have to be if there were one. 'Tall' can be truly predicated of an object only if it falls into all of those extensions (no single extension, or subset of the range of candidates, is isolated); this leaves some cases indeterminate, but the demands of classical logic are still satisfied. Clearly, this is a simplified version of the story, but the resources of supervaluationism provide the means to fill it out into a complete theory. I begin, in the next section, by discussing the central aspects of supervaluationism in such a way as both to provide an exposition of those features and to show how they count in favour of the theory.

(i) Borderline cases

Let us review the central ideas. A supervaluationist theory can capture the distinctive nature of predications in borderline cases by allowing truth-value gaps. Replacing vagueness by precision would involve fixing a sharp boundary between the predicate's positive and negative extensions and thereby deciding which way to classify each of the borderline cases: this is to give a 'precisification' or 'sharpening' of the predicate. And there are *many* equally good precisifications corresponding to different positive and negative extensions. According to supervaluationism, by taking account of *all* precisifications we can provide the logic and semantics of vague language. It is proposed that a sentence is true iff it is true on all precisifications, false iff false on all precisifications, and neither true nor false otherwise.

To make an expression precise, uncontroversial truths involving it must be preserved. So with any precisification of 'tall', those objects for which the predication of 'tall' is intuitively true (false) must be members of its positive (negative) extension. 'Tall' is made precise by fixing a height boundary from among the heights of the borderline tall people, such that anyone above it counts as 'tall' and no one else does. Now, suppose Tek is a borderline case of tallness at 5 feet 10 inches. Some precisifications will place him in the positive extension of 'tall', and others will place him in its negative extension: 'Tek is tall' is neither true on all precisifications nor false on all of them, hence it counts as neither true nor false. The principle of bivalence thus fails, which fits our intuitions about borderline cases, our attitudes towards them and our associated linguistic behaviour (in particular, the typical hesitancy and disagreement over borderline cases). How we *should* respond to a sentence that is neither true nor false depends on quite what our rule of assertion is. Should we, for example, avoid asserting anything that is not true or only what is false? I suggest that we have in mind no clear-cut rule. In trying to assert what is true, the fact that neither Fa nor $\neg Fa$ is true could lead us to withhold judgement as to whether or not a is F, as in fact we frequently do. And if some pronouncement is required, often it will seem best to ascend to the metalinguistic level and explicitly say that the sentence is neither true nor false. On the other hand, pulling against that practice could be the recognition that we should deny what is not true, which, depending on whether we are concentrating on the lack of truth of Fa or of $\neg Fa$, could lead us to assert $\neg Fa$ or Fa respectively, as, again, we sometimes do.[1] Our practice of assertion cannot mirror intermediate cases – it would not be easy or helpful to make it neither true nor false that I have asserted something. And if we follow a binary rule of assertion or one formulated in terms of the classical truth-values, then hesitancy, silence, disagreement and even confusion are to be expected in the face of the lack of truth-value.

Supervaluationists can also accommodate the lack of sharp boundaries to the extensions of vague predicates: there would be a sharp boundary to the tall people if there were a height h which made true 'people of height h are tall but anyone shorter is not tall'. But, according to supervaluationism, there is no such h: different precisifications draw boundaries to the tall people at different heights and so for no h is it the case that on all precisifications people of height h are tall and anyone shorter is not. So no height is truly identified as marking a sharp boundary to 'tall' (see §5).

(ii) Semantic indecision and ambiguity

It is commonly said that vagueness is a matter of *semantic indecision* (e.g. Lewis 1986, p. 212). No single one of F's precisifications can be correctly identified as providing the extension of F, because the meaning of vague F is such as to leave the choice between them unsettled. Not only have we not consciously made the choice between these alternative extensions, but, as I have stressed, nothing about the world, or about our use of the word, picks out a unique extension, and in most cases it would be unwise or impossible in practice to do so. It is not merely a lazy indecision which is waiting to

---

[1] If there is a practice of rejection as distinct from the assertion of negation of the sentence (see e.g. Parsons 1984 and Smiley 1996), then the rejection of Fa would be appropriate. But generally that rejection would be communicated as 'a is not F' with a noticeable emphasis on 'not', which is hard to distinguish in practice from the assertion of the negation. The possibility of interpreting 'not' via rejection would also make sense of the not uncommon response 'a is not F but it is not not-F either', which would amount to the rejection of both Fa and $\neg Fa$.

be resolved. Though someone could stipulate a boundary to 'tall' at 6 feet, for example, and thereby make a decision on a semantic value, this would be to make a decision not as to its actual meaning, but as to how the predicate should subsequently be used by those party to the stipulation (and with an expression such as 'nice' no such precise stipulation could be made in our language, since there are no expressible and suitable precise conditions).

Clearly, supervaluationism is a theory that takes seriously the idea of semantic indecision, for it calls upon all of those alternatives between which we have not decided and declares a sentence true if it would be true on all of them. Lewis describes this as exploiting the fact that the unmade semantic decision does not matter: 'often what you want to say will be true under all different ways of making the unmade decision. Then, if you say it, even if by choice or by necessity you leave the decision forever unmade, you still speak truthfully' (Lewis 1993, p. 28).

Nonetheless, the characterisation of vagueness as semantic indecision can play only a limited role in the defence of supervaluationism. For the supervaluationist picture is not uniquely appropriate to capture reasonable descriptions of the phenomenon of semantic indecision. Take a claim that 'in using "tall" we have not (and could not have) selected between a range of precise meanings'. Not only is this clearly amenable to the pragmatic view's account of vagueness (chapter 6), but it fails to guarantee that the alternatives between which we are undecided contribute in any way to the semantics of our actual and vague assertions (cf. Tappenden 1993). And degree theorists could agree that we have not selected from among a range of precise meanings, but still defend their analysis invoking functions from predicates to truth-values.

Related to the description of vagueness as semantic indecision is the contention that supervaluationism captures vagueness as a form of ambiguity: 'tall', for example, would be taken as having a range of senses, each corresponding to a precisification of that predicate. In ordinary circumstances we do not (and often cannot) disambiguate, and instead we use a vague predicate without choosing its single precise sense from the possibly infinite set of alternatives. This contrasts with normal uses of an ambiguous expression when the speaker will typically have a specific disambiguation in mind. Nonetheless, Fine claims that 'vagueness is ambiguity on a grand and systematic scale' (1975, p. 282), and he maintains that the truth-conditions both of ambiguous sentences that have not been disambiguated and of vague sentences are given by the rule that any such sentence is true iff it is true on all disambiguations/precisifications. This account of ambiguous sentences is not widely accepted (see e.g. Tye 1989), which makes the analogy of limited use for defending the proposed truth-conditions of vague sentences. My own view is that vagueness and ambiguity are fundamentally different. For a start, ambiguous expressions have several *actual* meanings, whereas when there is semantic indecision between some precise extensions, those extensions reflect, at best, *hypothetical* (sharp) meanings: the actual meaning is vague and typically univocal. It is wrong to say that '[the supervaluationist's] idea is that questions of truth arise only relative to ways of making precise' (Sainsbury and Williamson 1997). The supervaluationist account gives the conditions required for truth simpliciter and thereby captures the vague meaning. Indeed, if we could only make sense of truth relative to a precisification ('truth-in-a-sense' as we might say), the supervaluationary conditions would not be *truth*-conditions, and the relevance of the account would be obscure. By contrast, it may be reasonable to claim that questions of truth for ambiguous sentences only arise relative to a disambiguation.

A common approach to ambiguity is to regard it as the having of several meanings or senses, where at the level of sentences this amounts to expressing (or having the ability to express) more than one proposition. There is, on this view, no such thing as the ambiguous *proposition*, just an ambiguous sentence related to two or more propositions. The corresponding line on vagueness would deny that there are vague propositions: all propositions are precise though we generally fail to express a unique one of them, uttering, instead, sentences whose truth-conditions draw on a range of different propositions. Is this rejection of vague propositions (and other vague meanings for sub-sentential expressions) tenable? This depends on one's views about propositions in general. On the one hand, it might be thought that the fact that each of our ordinary sentences has a meaning – a vague meaning – shows there must be vague propositions which are the meanings of those sentences. The view of propositions as *sui generis* items could be amenable to this acceptance of vague propositions. On the other hand, certain reductive accounts identifying propositions with, for example, (precise) sets of worlds may have no room for vague instances. But denying that there are vague propositions need not imply, absurdly, that vague sentences are meaningless. We may, for example, resist the inference from 'linguistic expression X has a meaning' to 'there is some item which is X's meaning'. Or 'X's meaning' may indeterminately refer to each of the relevant range of precise propositions. The question whether supervaluationists can allow vague propositions in addition to precise ones thus turns on highly controversial issues about the nature and status of propositions, and since the discussion of the supervaluationist approach can be conducted entirely without reference to propositions, I shall not pursue this question here.[2]

Regarding the logic of ambiguity and vagueness, the same approach may sometimes be justified in the two cases but for different reasons. If we did not know which disambiguation was intended in the various premises of an argument, then the safe strategy to follow regarding logical inferences would be the supervaluationary one (if each premise is true on all disambiguations, it does not matter for the argument which is relevant in the context). But usually the relevant disambiguations are known, when we can simply ban equivocations that use an ambiguous expression in different ways in different premises, treating them as misuses of the logical rules.[3] In the vagueness case my claim is that the supervaluationist framework is not merely a useful device given our ignorance, but the one that captures

---

[2] Schiffer 1998 objects to supervaluationism on the grounds that both views of the propositional content of a sentence – either as ambiguous or as itself vague – are unable to deal with (certain) sentences of the form 'X said that *a* is *F*'. Suppose '*a* is *F*' refers indeterminately to different precise propositions. Then, says Schiffer, for the report to be true it would have to be true for each such precise proposition *p* that X said that *p*. Clearly X asserted no precise proposition (let alone all of them), so the account allegedly misclassifies the report. But on various accounts of indirect discourse we are not obliged to accept Schiffer's truth-condition for the report. Consider Davidson's paratactic account (1968), whereby the report is to be understood as 'X said that. *a* is *F*' where this amounts to a claim that X made an utterance *u* such that *u* and the reporter's next utterance ('*a* is *F*') make them same-sayers. X and Y can be same-sayers by uttering sentences matching in their vagueness (perhaps '*a* is bald' and its translation into French). So the report 'X said that *a* is *F*' need not imply that X uttered any precise propositions at all.

[3] Lewis 1982 gives a logic of ambiguous sentences prior to disambiguation, though the type of cases he suggests where ambiguity might be ineliminable are 'all sorts of semantic indecision, open texture, vagueness and whatnot', and he offers no more discussion of the question whether the listed phenomena should be counted as genuine types of ambiguity. See §7 on a different approach, Hyde's, that treats vagueness as a form of ambiguity.

the truth-conditions of vague sentences and correspondingly their logic.

(iii) Precisifications of different kinds of expression

In the case of 'tall', we could stipulate some height boundary and thus carry out the process of making that predicate precise, and we have a way of picking out individual precisifications by the boundary height (though complications will be raised below). But these features are not necessary for the supervaluationist's quantification over precisifications. All that is needed for the truth-conditions is the range of precise extensions themselves, where each corresponds to a precisification in the sense that clear cases are preserved and borderline case predications are made true or false (subject to some constraints to be discussed below). Hence it is no objection that with most precisifications of 'nice' there are no terms in which we could describe the sharp boundaries or characterise the members of the positive extension. Similarly, though the precisifications of 'tall' form a neat one-dimensional array, that is not necessary for the supervaluationary truth-conditions either: multi-dimensional vague predicates cause no special problems.

The theory need not be limited to the treatment of vague monadic predicates either. The positive extension corresponding to a precisification of the vague two-place predicate 'is a friend of' is a precise set of ordered pairs, and if it is indeterminate whether a counts as a friend of b, $\langle a, b \rangle$ will be in some of the precise sets corresponding to precisifications and not in others. And the effect of modifying a predicate with an adverb such as 'quickly' can be made precise in a range of different ways, so this expression is also amenable to supervaluationary treatment. Whatever the classical interpretation of a given type of expression, the interpretation of a vague instance of that type is indeterminate between different candidate precise interpretations of that sort.

Consider next the singular term 'Toronto', which does not pick out a sharply bounded area of Canada. There are two ways for a supervaluationist to consider the semantics of such singular terms (each delivering the same classification of all sentences). The first of these is more natural within the framework. If it is assumed that there are no vague objects so all objects involved in the semantics have precise spatio-temporal boundaries, then precisifications of 'Toronto' can be taken to be the various different ways of drawing a spatial boundary to the city, and the interpretation of the name will be indeterminate between the objects so delineated. 'Toronto has an odd number of trees' is then indeterminate, since it is true only on some ways of drawing the boundaries, while 'Toronto is in Canada' is true on all ways, so counts as true simpliciter. (This example is from Mehlberg 1958.) Similarly, we may suppose that 'Tek' does not determinately pick out a unique precisely bounded object and this will make 'Tek is exactly 5 feet 10 inches' indeterminate – some of the candidate precise objects will be 5 feet 10 inches and others will not.

If, on the other hand, vague objects are admitted into the ontology and Toronto is taken to be one such object, the name 'Toronto' may succeed in picking out a unique object, though that object has fuzzy spatio-temporal boundaries. Because of those fuzzy boundaries 'Toronto has an odd number of trees' can still come out indeterminate, but this time the predicate 'has an odd number of trees' will count as vague since it is not determined whether the vague object Toronto is in its extension. Similarly, predicates used to express that something has a given exact height will also have borderline case (vague) instances, and so will not count as precise. Though there is no indeterminacy over the point on the abstract height-scale associated with the predicate 'is 5 feet 10 inches', there *is* indeterminacy over the members of the extension, since the fuzzy boundaries of Tek make it indeterminate whether he is 5 feet 10 inches. Doubts about the possibility of vague objects would clearly count against this second treatment of vague singular terms; and it is within the spirit of supervaluationism to put vagueness down to semantic indecision for singular terms – as the first treatment does – rather than postulating a world of vague objects. So I advocate the first of the accounts.[4]

This account is also the one chosen by Lewis in his discussion of Unger's 'problem of the many' (Lewis 1993; Unger 1980). Suppose Barney is a cat, with loose hairs, $h_1 \ldots h_{100}$, each of which is such

---

[4] Note that though there may seem to be a parallel choice between admitting vague properties and only precise ones, this distinction is not of interest to us since the semantics are not constructed by reference to properties themselves as distinct from the extensions of predicates. A predicate would still count as vague if it determinately picked out a vague property because it would still not have a precise extension.

that it is indeterminate whether they are parts of the cat. Consider the c_i, which have among their parts all the loose hairs except h_i. Each of the c_i are cat-like and, having different parts, they are not identical to each other. The problem is saying which is Barney. The solution is to say that it is semantically undecided – we have not decided that any one of them is to be the unique referent of that name. Similarly, the meaning of the expression 'cat' does not settle a unique one of the c_i for its extension. It is true that there is one cat on the mat when (as we would say) Barney is alone there, even though it is not (and could not be) determined exactly which object is to count as 'the cat'.[5]

I shall often take predicates as the central case in presenting further features of supervaluationism. But, in fact, much of the discussion will be at the level of sentences, where we need not ask which expression within the sentence is responsible for the sentence's indeterminate truth-value status.

(iv) The range of precisifications

My description of supervaluationism has so far left open the question whether there is a well-defined range of precisifications of e.g. 'tall' (a precise set of alternatives between which we are undecided), or whether that range is itself vague, with some candidate precisifications neither clearly counting as precisifications, nor clearly failing to count. This question ties in with issues of higher-order vagueness, for if there is a precise set of precisifications of 'tall', the borderline cases of that predicate will be sharply bounded and the phenomenon of higher-order vagueness must be denied (or, at best, accommodated as a phenomenon of a radically different character to first-order vagueness). If the range of precisifications of 'tall' is *not* precise, then the

---

[5] Should we object to the commitment to all the objects quantified over in the truth-conditions? I say not, since I am persuaded by Lewis's arguments for unrestricted mereological composition – for any set of things, there is an object composed of those things – but I cannot enter into this debate here (see Lewis 1986, pp. 212–13). The intuition that there are not so many objects in the region of Barney might be explained as being confused with the true thought that there is only one *cat* there. The counting of objects (without any restriction on type) is notoriously problematic, and supervaluationism gets right the counting of objects of particular types, such as cats. For example, it implies that there is only currently one person in this chair even though there is no unique object which is that person. Note that my sketch of the second account shows that supervaluationism is anyway not necessarily committed to an ontology of this kind.

expression 'precisification of tall' and the general notion of 'precisification' will themselves be vague. Since these are expressions of the metalanguage used to construct the theory, we reach the familiar conclusion that the key elements of the metalanguage must be vague. The form of supervaluationism that I will defend acknowledges that the metalanguage is vague. In chapter 8 I examine in detail this feature of the theory and its consequences, but I put that issue aside for now.

(v) Compound sentences

The constraint that sentences that are unproblematically true (false) before precisification should stay true (false) afterwards can be applied not only to simple predications like 'Bruno is tall', but also to general statements such as 'anyone taller than a tall person is also tall' and 'no one who is tall is also short'. These general statements certainly seem to be true. If the first is to come out as true simpliciter, there can be, for example, no acceptable precisification of 'tall' according to which people who are 5 feet 10 inches are tall but those at 5 feet 11 inches are not. For the second, it cannot be legitimate to sharpen 'tall' so that someone of 5 feet 10 inches counts as tall, while simultaneously sharpening 'short' so that someone of that height also counts as short. These two examples illustrate what Fine calls 'penumbral connections', which constrain how precisifications can fix determinate truth-values for the borderline cases of predicates. Such penumbral connections (or penumbral truths) may be 'internal', concerning instances of the same predicate (as in my first example), or 'external', involving several related predicates (as in the second one). External connections illustrate how we need to take expressions together and make them precise while respecting these penumbral connections. When all expressions are taken together in this way, a classical truth-value is assigned to every sentence giving an admissible valuation or, to use Fine's term, an admissible specification. (It corresponds to an *admissible* way of making the language precise.) The supervaluation quantifies over these admissible specifications: a sentence is super-true (super-false) iff true (false) on all of them; and truth simpliciter is identified with super-truth.

Now consider the disjunctive sentence 'the book is green or it is blue', said of a book which is on the borderline between green and blue. On the supervaluationist view this can come out true, since it is true wherever the sharp boundary between blue and green is drawn. But neither 'the book is green' nor 'the book is blue' is itself true; hence a disjunction can be true though neither disjunct is true. Supervaluationism thus rejects truth-functionality in the sense that the value or lack of value of a compound sentence is not determined by the values or lack of values of its constituents (other disjunctions with two indefinite disjuncts will not be true, e.g. 'the book is green or it is green'). On the other hand, if the constituents all have truth-values, those values do fix the truth-value of the whole compound. As Fine argues, the failure of truth-functionality (in the former sense) is a necessary feature of any theory of vagueness that rejects bivalence if penumbral connections are to be accommodated (1975, pp. 269–70). And they must indeed be accommodated. Some of the most persuasive examples were presented in chapter 4, §5: suppose, for example, that Tek is taller than Tim and consider the need to respect the truth of 'If Tim is tall then Tek is tall' and the falsity of 'Tim is tall and Tek is not tall'.

For the case of disjunction, suppose F, G and H are incompatible and a is on the borderline between being F and being G and is definitely not H: it would then be appropriate and informative to say 'a is either F or G'. (E.g. to the question 'is it red?' asked of a borderline blue–green patch, the reply 'no, it's blue or green' is appropriate.) Edgington cites some particularly strong candidates for disjunctions that are penumbral truths. With non-instantaneous sex changes, x can, at some time, be a borderline case of a brother and a borderline case of a sister, but a clear case of a sibling, where 'x is a brother or a sister' is true. And if the green-or-blue case is slightly less persuasive, then this may be because a category could be placed between the blue and the green – blueish-green, for example, or turquoise for some of those shades – in which case each pair of sharpenings of blue and green will leave cases between that count as neither, and the 'blue-or-green' disjunction will not come out super-true. (I would say that turquoise is a shade which is borderline blue and borderline green, but others may consider it neither blue nor green. A general theory of vagueness will not, of course, settle such a dispute, and either view about turquoise is compatible with super-valuationism.)

Next take the sentence 'either Tek is tall or he is not tall'. This is true, since it is true on all precisifications (even if Tek is actually borderline tall when, again, neither disjunct is true). More generally, $p \vee \neg p$ is true whatever the substitution for p and whatever value (or lack of value) p takes: the logical truth of the law of excluded middle is maintained. Equally, all other classical theorems are retained, for if a sentence is logically true according to classical logic, then it will be true on every complete specification (since they each obey classical logic) and thus, by supervaluationary principles, it will count as true simpliciter (see §4).

It could be objected that the conservatism about classical logic is inappropriate and unsustainable in the face of vagueness, and, in particular, that the law of excluded middle is a part of classical logic that should be given up because of vagueness. But, first, note that if a theory is to capture the truth of penumbral connections of the form '*Fa* ∨ *Ga*', for incompatible *F* and *G*, then it will also count as true '*Fa* ∨ ¬*Fa*': there is no reasonable way of counting one true but not the other. And the unassertability of the latter in contrast with the former is explicable, since, as explained, the former can be highly informative by saying something about the properties of *a*, in particular, implying that *a* does not have those properties that are incompatible with both *F* and *G* (e.g. that it is blue or green and not red), while '*Fa* ∨ ¬*Fa*' is entirely uninformative (saying that it is red or not-red does nothing to narrow the range of its possible shades). A statement which is similar to the trivial 'either *a* is red or not' but which would be informative (because sometimes false) is 'either *a* is definitely red or definitely not-red', and it could be that the two are sometimes confused: if someone were to assert the former, then, on the assumption that they are obeying the Gricean rule of being informative, it would be reasonable to take them to mean the latter. And the fact that the former is *never* informative could explain why it is so common for our judgements of both sentences to be dictated by our judgements of 'either *a* is definitely red or definitely not-red' and why we thus consider 'either *a* is red or not' to be not true.

Existential quantification displays behaviour similar to that of disjunction: 'something is *F*' can be true though no substitution instance is true. Although there is no *h* for which 'people of height *h* are tall while people 0.01 inches shorter are not tall' is true, the existentially quantified sentence formed from it, (H) 'there is a height *x* such that people of height *x* are tall while people 0.01 inches shorter are not tall', *is* true, since on each precisification some height or other makes it true. Similarly, we have the dual result that a universally quantified proposition can be false without any substitution instance being false. This is central to the treatment of the sorites paradox: the negation of (H) can be transformed into a quantified inductive premise of a sorites paradox for 'tall', namely, for appropriate series of x_i of gradually increasing height, 'for all i, $\neg(x_i$ is tall and x_{i+1} is not tall)'. This premise is false on the supervaluationist theory even though none of its substitution instances are false. (But objections to the supposed truth of sentences such as (H) will be considered in §5.) Versions of the paradox using a conditional instead of a negated conjunction similarly have a false premise. And when the sorites paradox is expressed in terms of a *series* of conditionals, there will be no one conditional which is false, but there will be some that are neither true nor false and on every precisification there will be one that is false. So again the supervaluationist will avoid the paradox by refusing to accept all of the premises. In short, supervaluationism solves the sorites paradox in all its forms.

(vi) The history of supervaluationism

We have seen that the supervaluationist approach lays claim to conserving classical logic and respecting penumbral connections while successfully accommodating the borderline cases and the lack of sharp boundaries distinctive of vagueness and also avoiding the sorites paradox. I finish §1 with a brief summary of the history of supervaluationism.

The technique was formally expounded, and the expression 'supervaluation' coined, in the influential work of van Fraassen (1966, 1968 and 1969). He developed the technique for applications other than vagueness, in particular for the treatment of non-referring singular terms and of the liar paradox.[6] Mehlberg had previously given what seems to be the earliest informal presentation of what is essentially a supervaluationist account of vagueness (1958, pp. 256–9). This drew

---

[6] Where there are putative truth-value gaps, supervaluationism can be, and often is, used for the semantics. There will be some appropriate notion of a complete admissible valuation which keeps all actually true (false) sentences true (false), but fills in truth-value gaps, and where the supervaluation captures what is common to all those valuations.

little attention (though see Przełecki 1969, 1976), but the basic ideas later occurred to a number of different philosophers apparently independently of Mehlberg and largely independently of each other. Dummett gave a clear, informal description of the position and its attractions, though he went on to reject it.[7] Lewis, at the end of his 1970 paper 'General semantics', defends such an account, albeit briefly, and subsequent discussions show that he still adheres to it (e.g. 1986, p. 212 and his 1993). And in 1975 Kamp proposed another version of supervaluationism in the context of a wider discussion of adjectives. The same year saw the publication of Fine's detailed treatment which is generally taken as the *locus classicus* of the supervaluationist theory of vagueness. I summarise his presentation and terminology in the next section; but note that his way of presenting the theory is not essential to it and the discussion following it does not rely on the details of his treatment.[8]

2. SOME FURTHER DETAILS OF FINE'S THEORY

Fine's formal account is built on the notion of a *specification space*, i.e. a set of points – specification-points – at which some or all sentences in a language L are assigned truth-values, yielding the specification. An appropriate specification space for L will consist of specification-points that each correspond to permissible precisifications of its vague expressions. Some specification-points are *complete*: these correspond to ways of making all vague terms completely precise. But other points are *partial*, where some or all expressions are left vague and some sentences remain truth-valueless.

Each space has an 'appropriate specification-point' or *base-point*; intuitively this is the point at which the atomic sentences of L receive their original valuation as assigned before any of the vagueness has been resolved (leaving truth-value gaps for all borderline cases). There is an *extends* relation on the space, where a specification-point b is said to extend another point a if, intuitively, b corresponds to a

---

[7] 1975, pp. 310–12, a paper written in 1970; his 1991 (e.g. p. 74) appears more sympathetic to the account.

[8] More recent endorsements of a supervaluationary framework can be found in Tappenden 1993 and McGee and McLaughlin 1995; but in both cases the role of the framework is different from the role in giving truth-conditions that Fine gives it.

(possibly partial) precisification of *a*. All points in the space extend the base-point. Fine formalises certain restrictions on his specification spaces to reflect their intended use. For example, his *Stability* requirement rules that the sentences true (false) at a specification-point must remain true (false) at any point which extends it (hence truth-value gaps may be filled, but previously settled values are never changed by further precisification). This ensures that the uncontroversially true (false) predications of a vague predicate at the base-point keep their value through all later precisifications. The requirement of *Fidelity* formalises the fact that the elimination of all truth-value gaps at complete specification-points must result in a classical valuation (compare normality conditions discussed in chapter 2, §2). And the *Completability* condition requires that every specification-point can be extended to a complete specification-point. There is thus always at least one way of making a sentence completely precise. This does not require that we could actually specify in some language the nature of the completion. All that is needed are the specifications themselves, whether or not we can pick out individual ones from among them.

Additional conditions are needed for further constraints on the values of compound sentences which are taken at partial specification-points. Stability ensures that if a (possibly compound) sentence is true at a partial specification-point *a*, then it is true at all complete points that extend *a*. As we have seen, Fine's chosen account of truth-conditions, the super-truth account, additionally guarantees the converse, so a sentence is true at *a* iff it is true at all complete specification-points which extend *a*. Truth simpliciter (or super-truth) is truth at the base-point, and since all complete points extend the base-point, a sentence is true there iff it is true on all complete specifications. Alternatives to the super-truth account of truth-conditions can be constructed within Fine's framework, and they result in different logical systems (see §7); I reserve the name 'supervaluationism' for the super-truth account, though many aspects of my discussion will be applicable to any theory within the specification space approach.

Fine elaborates his account by introducing a 'definitely' operator, *D*, into the object language (1975, p. 287). *DA* is true at a specification-point of a space iff *A* is true at the base-point, i.e. if it is true at all points. Consequently, *DA* is true at all specification-points of an appropriate space iff it is true at any. *D* is thus closely related to the metalinguistic truth predicate (since truth simpliciter *is* truth at the base-point). Given *D*, an 'indefinitely' operator can also be defined, where $Ip \equiv \neg Dp$ & $\neg D\neg p$. This allows us to express in the object-language the borderline case status of certain predications, e.g. *IFa* holds when *Fa* is neither true nor false. And having a *D* or *I* operator is necessary if, for example, we are to state in the object-language that a given vague predicate lacks sharp boundaries (see §5). Fine introduces such operators partly in order to pursue the issue of higher-order vagueness. But this may require complicating his original story to allow, for instance, for the possibility of cases in which *IIFa* is true, i.e. second-order borderline cases of *F*. Chapter 8 addresses the issues of higher-order vagueness.

Before further analysing the logic and semantics that an account such as Fine's delivers, I pause to consider the versions of super-valuationist theories offered by Lewis and Kamp, and the ways in which they attempt to develop and employ the framework.

3. COMPARATIVES, DEGREES AND CONTEXT-DEPENDENCE

In chapter 6 I examined Lewis's pragmatic account of vagueness and its relation to his supervaluationist account: I take up the latter account here. In Lewis's general semantic framework a central role is played by *indices* – sequences of co-ordinates (for time, place, possible world etc.) at which the truth-value of a sentence is evaluated and on which that truth-value might depend. He suggests building into the index what he calls a 'delineation co-ordinate', which specifies the way in which the relevant expressions are to be made precise by giving a sequence of boundary-specifying numbers (e.g. one specifying the boundary height for 'tall', one for the maximum temperature for 'cold' etc.; see his 1970, pp. 64–5). Rather than a single delineation being relevant in a given context, they are usually quantified over, so a sentence counts as true if true on all delineations and false if false on all of them, and in borderline cases different delineations assign different truth-values so that neither the sentence nor its negation come out true. The demand for a series of numbers to specify a delineation is unrealistic, however, for it would be impossible to capture a precisification of 'nice' with any number or series of numbers. Lewis should not make this demand, just as Fine does not: delineations can figure in indices even if they cannot be independently specified, just as we will often be unable to specify features that would individuate a possible world that figures in the index.

Lewis and Kamp show how the framework could illuminate the semantics of a number of locutions other than simple vague predications. One of Lewis's examples is the idiom 'in some sense': he suggests that 'in some sense p' is true just in case p is true on some specification or other. Using the D operator, this could be expressed as $\neg D \neg p$. A similar locution is '-ish' (as in 'reddish' or 'tallish') though Lewis does not state the exact semantic rule in this case. Again 'Tek is tallish' should be true only if 'Tek is tall' is true on some specification or other, but I suggest that it is also necessary that 'Tek is tall' is not true on *all* specifications (i.e. $\neg D \neg p$ & $\neg Dp$) – no one can be both tallish and definitely tall. It is appropriate that these locutions should receive a treatment that is bound up with the treatment of vagueness itself: for they are closely bound up with the vagueness of the expressions to which they are attached. 'Tallish' works by picking out the borderline cases of 'tall'.

Lewis and Kamp both also hope to explain the connection between a positive form, such as 'red' and its associated comparative 'redder than', proposing that 'a is redder than b' is true iff the set of specifications on which 'b is red' is true is a proper subset of those on which 'a is red' is true (see Lewis 1970, p. 65 and Kamp 1975, pp. 138–40). Their account can accommodate the various features of vague comparatives that I illustrated in chapter 1, §2. In particular, there can be borderline cases of a comparative, 'F-er than', since the set of specifications in which 'b is F' is true may neither be a subset of, nor have as a subset, the set of specifications on which 'a is F' is true. This will happen at least when the specifications are like those of a multi-dimensional predicate: different specifications can favour different dimensions rather than having the nesting structure of the specifications of 'small number'.

The Lewis–Kamp treatment of comparatives does face a problem, as both Lewis and Kamp recognise, in connection with cases such as 'Bob is taller than Bruno' when Bob and Bruno are both definitely tall (e.g. 6 feet 9 inches and 6 feet 8 inches respectively). 'Bob is tall' and 'Bruno is tall' will be true on the same set of admissible specifications - namely all of them – and so the specifications on which 'Bruno is tall' will *not* be a proper subset of those in which 'Bob is tall' is true. Lewis accepts the truth of 'Bob is not taller than Bruno if Bruno is definitely tall', though he remains neutral as to whether we should therefore call Bruno not definitely tall or deny that Bob is taller than Bruno (1970, p. 65). The second of these possibilities badly misrepresents the meaning of 'taller than': the 'taller than' relation rests on unproblematic facts about height comparisons, not just facts about objects classified as 'tall' and the vagueness associated with that word. But I also reject Lewis's alternative response of denying that, at 6 feet 8 inches, Bruno is definitely tall. I argued against accepting this in chapter 4, §4: an account on which 'Bruno is tall' is not definitely true (and, given that there is no theoretical limit to tallness, an account on which no one is ever definitely tall) has no claim to be an account of our predicate.[9]

It is not the *vagueness* of '*F*-er than' that causes the problem with two definitely *F* things, but the proposed relation between comparatives and positives. But the supervaluationist need not endorse an account of the comparative in terms of the positive and its precisifications; without one, instances of a comparative can still be true, false or borderline, with the last category, as usual, being of those sentences true on some specifications and false on others. The comparative is not like locutions such as '-ish' which are parasitic on vagueness (even if, as discussed in chapter 5, vague predicates will often have an associated comparative). So there should be no expectation of capturing it in terms of the framework designed to accommodate vagueness. There will however be penumbral connections between the predicate *F* and the comparative '*F*-er than'. In particular, it will always be true that $\neg(a$ is *F*-er than b & $\neg Fa$ & $Fb)$, so, appropriately, there can be no admissible specifications in which a is *F*-er than b but b counts as *F* and a does not. But this penumbral connection is

---

[9] Kamp (1975, pp. 138–40) offers a different response in which we allow the assessment of certain truth-values to depend on specifications which are not admissible in the original sense, but which we can call 'semi-admissible'. A specification where Bruno does not count as tall but the taller Bob does cannot be admissible because Bruno is definitely tall, and so tall in all admissible specifications, but it still respects the policy of selecting an exact height above which anyone counts as 'tall'. The only general distinction between semi-admissible and other non-admissible specifications seems, however, to be that if a is *F*-er than b, there are no semi-admissible specifications in which Fb is true and Fa is false. But if the only role semi-admissible specifications are called upon to play is in the account of comparatives, there is no gain in amending the supervaluationary account in this way.

compatible with comparatives not being reducible to positives, and it allows that '*a* is *F*-er than *b*' can be true, false or borderline when *a* and *b* are both definitely *F*.

I turn next to a different development of the basic supervaluationist framework. Lewis and Kamp both propose that we add a measure over the set of admissible specifications, where we say that a sentence is true to a degree according to the measure of the set of admissible specifications on which it is true. So, speaking loosely, predications true on most precisifications will come out true to a high degree. In this way, as on a degree theory, we can discriminate among sentences which are neither true nor false, rather than merely grouping them all together in an undifferentiated way. (See also chapter 4, §5 on Edgington's theory, which can be interpreted in this way.) Kamp emphasises how, on this approach, unlike with the degree theories of chapter 4, the degree assigned to a compound sentence can depend not only on the degrees of its component sentences, but also on the relation between those components. For example, $p \lor \neg p$ will be true on no valuations and so be true to no degree, though other disjunctions $p \lor q$ will be true to varying non-zero degrees, even given the same value for q as for $\neg p$. Such a supplement to the supervaluationist account is desirable, especially since (as noted in chapter 5) many philosophers have maintained that coming in degrees is a characteristic feature of vague predicates. (Simons 1996, for example, lists among his constraints on a theory of vagueness the requirement that it accommodates degrees of *F*-ness for vague *F*.)

In chapter 5 I argued against theories of vagueness constructed on a numerical basis, so I will now show that supplementing supervaluationism with a measure does not result in a theory subject to the same criticisms. First, the objections concerning vague comparatives and multi-dimensionality are resisted because, unlike degree theorists, supervaluationists are not committed to the claim that '*a* is *F*-er than *b*' is true iff '*a* is *F*' is true to a greater degree than '*b* is *F*'. The supervaluationist need not (and should not) defend such a relation between comparatives and degrees (Kamp briefly considers it but rejects it for reasons related to multi-dimensionality, 1975, pp. 140–1). Second, connectives are not given an account in terms of the numbers assigned – the account given on the unsupplemented supervaluationary account remains in place – so problems arising from the degree theorist's account of the connectives (chapter 5, §3) are avoided. More generally, the role of numbers is not central to the account; in particular, it is not by means of assigning numbers that logical behaviour is modelled. Indeed, I suggest that it *is* appropriate here to take a modelling approach to the degrees assigned. Unlike with degree theories, this is not to shirk questions about truth-values, since the numbers are not representing truth-values according to the supervaluationist. The degrees assigned are merely an instrumental device for modelling our loose use of 'truer'. And, for example, we need not suppose there is a single scale on which predications of all predicates can be modelled at once.

As Kamp and Lewis suggest, their notion of degrees of truth can be used to give a semantics for various other modifiers by rules that appeal to these degrees (Kamp 1975, pp. 145–7 and Lewis 1970, p. 65; Lakoff 1973 and Zadeh 1975 propose similar uses for their truth-functional degree theories). For example, '*a* is slightly *F*' is true iff '*a* is *F*' is true to some low (but non-zero) degree, while '*a* is rather *F*' requires that '*a* is *F*' is true to a higher degree. So such locutions have the effect of expressing within the object language something about a sentence (here '*a* is *F*') that would otherwise be expressed in the metalanguage by reference to degrees or by directly referring to proportions of specifications (albeit often in a vague way, capturing vague proportions or measures). This suggests a similarity with the *D* operator, which is a device for incorporating the metalinguistic 'is true' into the object language. Indeed, *D* can be seen as expressing the limiting case, equivalent to 'true to measure 1'. (These similarities explain why the effects on the logic resulting from the addition of the *D* operator are mirrored with locutions analysed in terms of the measure over the specification space: see §4 below.)

Finally, Kamp and Lewis also hope to illuminate context-dependence and its relation to vagueness. Lewis claims that the truth-value appropriately assigned to a vague sentence can depend on context and in particular on a 'standard of precision' in operation in the conversation – a standard which has been determined by the earlier course of the conversation (Lewis 1979, pp. 244–6). For example, the standard for assessment of 'France is hexagonal' would be higher in the context of a geography conference than when describing the shapes of countries to a child; and Lewis proposes that this standard be interpreted in terms of the degree of truth required for assertion. This will not, however, illuminate all instances of context-dependence related to vagueness. The classification of a thing can often depend on what it is being compared with, and variation in a contextually (and perhaps vaguely) determined comparison class is not a matter of changing the standard of precision. For example, certain features of context can push the red–orange boundary further towards the definitely red, which raises the standard of precision of 'red' but simultaneously lowers it for 'orange'. And context can alter the appropriate range of boundaries for a multi-dimensional predicate in a specific way that is not simply a raising or lowering of the degree of truth required for a sentence to count as 'true' (e.g. such that classification as 'a big man' depends only, or primarily, on height and not volume). So, though alteration of standard of precision is rightly seen as an aspect in vagueness-related context-dependence, there is a limit to the work it can do in an account of vagueness in general.

An alternative account of context-dependence which could be combined with the supervaluationary framework and which could deal with the various types of the phenomena outlined would be one in which the context determines what specifications count as admissible. On a lower standard of precision, precisifications with strict conditions for membership do not count as admissible (e.g. giving some relatively precise geometrical condition that no countries meet is not a way to make precise our loose idea of 'hexagonal' in the relevant context, because it does not preserve the truth-value of predications to things that do count as hexagonal in that context). Such precisifications are, however, relevant and admissible in the context of a higher standard of precision (when the fact that France is hexagonal on a range of loose criteria is not enough for it to count as hexagonal). And the sensitivity of 'tall' to the relevant comparison class will be captured by the crucial specifications being determined by that class: for example, if the comparison class consists of people all over 6 feet, then it may be that all the precisifications of 'tall' that are relevant in the context draw the boundary to 'tall' somewhere above 6 feet. There is still plenty room for vagueness and borderline cases in such a context, but the range of borderline cases will be different from its range with respect to another comparison class.

4. SUPERVALUATIONISM AND ITS LOGIC

I return now to central aspects of supervaluationism. This section on logic serves both to provide further details and discussion of the supervaluationist's account – illustrating more advantages of the theory – and to answer influential objections. First, I need to define validity in the supervaluationary framework. Standardly, B is a consequence of Γ iff for all models, if all members of Γ are true, then B is also true. With the supervaluationary account of truth, the definition of consequence becomes: $\Gamma \models_{SV} B$ iff for any specification space, if all members of Γ are true (i.e. true on all complete specifications of the space), B is true (i.e. true on all the same specifications).[10]

Supervaluationism's commitment to classical logic provides us with a guide to reasoning with vague language. Classical reasoning is to be trusted, but we should take care before accepting certain premises and should ask whether they would be true on all ways of making their components precise. This guide will not, of course, settle disputes over slippery slope arguments, nor should we expect the logic itself to do so. Two people can still disagree over the right response to a slippery slope argument with the premises 'if it is wrong to kill something at time t after conception, then it would be wrong to kill it at time t minus one second' and 'killing something nine months after conception is wrong' and the conclusion 'abortion is wrong any time after conception'. One party could believe that the case is just like that for 'red' – abortion is not wrong one day after conception, but is wrong nine months after, and there is no sharp boundary at which it suddenly becomes wrong. Such a disputant should not accept the premise of the argument for the same reasons as the supervaluationist tells us we should deny the sorites inductive premise for 'red'. The other disputant could think that abortion is wrong at any time after conception and that the premises and conclusion are true. (The relevant notion of an act of abortion being wrong could then be already precise.)

---

[10] This is Fine's condition for consequence. An alternative condition, labelled 'local validity' in Williamson 1994, is that an argument is valid iff in every specification, if the premises are true the conclusion is true. As Williamson emphasises, however, according to this definition validity is not a matter of preservation of what supervaluationists claim is truth, namely super-truth.

It might still be objected that we could be led badly astray by employing classical reasoning with vague language. Sainsbury considers an argument of the form '*Fa* or ¬*Fa*; if *Fa* then *Ga*; if ¬*Fa* then *Ga*; therefore *Ga*'. In his example *Fa* = '*a* is an adult'; *Ga* = 'watching the hard-porn movie will do *a* no harm'; the third premise is to be supported by the claim that if *a* is not an adult, he will not understand the movie (1988, p. 40). This argument counts as valid on super-valuationist terms, but Sainsbury suggests that it leads us to a false conclusion because the argument ignores the possibility that *a* is a borderline *F*, where if *Fa is* borderline then ¬*Ga* (the movie would harm the borderline adult). But I would argue that this example shows instead that we must be careful about the acceptance of certain premises, in this case the second and third ones. Even if *a* is G whenever *a* is a clear positive case of *F*, we must ask whether it is also true that 'if *Fa* then *Ga*' is true however *F* is made precise. To assess this we need to ask of a borderline *F* whether counting it as *F* would mean that it would count as *G* as well. In Sainsbury's problem case, the answer should be 'no'. ('If *a* is definitely *F* then *a* is definitely *G*' *is* true, but this must not be confused with Sainsbury's premise.) It is not the form of reasoning that would lead us astray here but the mistaken acceptance of two of the premises.

But is the logic yielded by supervaluationism really classical logic? Consider first a language with the usual connectives but lacking the 'definitely' operator. If its logic is to be genuinely classical, the supervaluationist consequence relation ($\models_{SV}$) must be classical, so that for any set of premises Γ and proposition B, $\Gamma \models_{SV} B$ iff $\Gamma \models_{CL} B$.

First, I show that

(a) If $\Gamma \models_{CL} B$ then $\Gamma \models_{SV} B$.

Suppose that $\Gamma \models_{CL} B$, so any classical valuation which makes all members of Γ true makes B true. Then, if every member of Γ is true at a complete specification-point (which, by the Fidelity condition, is classical), B must also be true there. So if every member of Γ is true at all the complete points of a specification space, B will be true at all these complete points too. So $\Gamma \models_{SV} B$.

Another argument establishes the converse:

(b) If $\Gamma \models_{SV} B$ then $\Gamma \models_{CL} B$.

If $\Gamma \models_{SV} B$, then in every specification space in which all the members of Γ are true, B is true. But any single classical model is a one-point degenerate case of a specification space (a space where there is a unique admissible specification, and which will trivially satisfy the requirements of Stability etc.). So B is true in all classical models in which the members of Γ are all true, i.e. $\Gamma \models_{CL} B$.

This pair of results shows that – at least in the absence of the D operator – the supervaluationary consequence relation coincides with its classical counterpart. And since logical truths are just those instances of the consequence relation with an empty set of premises, the (D-free) logical truths of supervaluationism coincide with those of classical logic.

The situation regarding classical reasoning changes, however, when the D operator is introduced. A number of commentators have emphasised how supervaluationist logic (now with the D operator) fails to preserve certain rules of inference or classical principles about logical consequence. For example, Machina (1976, pp. 51–3) argues that the rule of reductio ad absurdum cannot be retained.[11] Moreover, contraposition, conditional proof (or the deduction theorem) and argument by cases (or disjunction elimination) can also fail (see e.g. Williamson 1994, pp. 151–2). Take contraposition: it is not always the case that if $A \models_{SV} B$ then $\neg B \models_{SV} \neg A$. For $A \models_{SV} DA$: in any specification space in which A is super-true, DA is also super-true since DA is defined as true whenever A is true on all specifications (see also chapter 8, §1 on this entailment). But it is not typically the case that $\neg DA \models_{SV} \neg A$ (in a specification space where A is true on some specifications and false in others, $\neg DA$ is super-true while $\neg A$ is not). With classical conditional proof, we can infer $\models A \supset C$ from $A \models C$, but, as Fine himself notes (1975, p. 290), we have $A \models_{SV} DA$, but it is not usually the case that $\models_{SV} A \supset DA$ (for borderline A, there can be complete specifications on which A is true and DA false, so $A \supset DA$ is false too). Argument by cases usually allows you to infer $A \vee B \models C$ from $A \models C$ and $B \models C$. With supervaluationism and the D operator, however, we have both $A \models DA \vee D\neg A$ and $\neg A \models DA \vee D\neg A$ (from, respectively, $A \models DA$ and $\neg A \models D\neg A$ plus or-introduction). But we cannot infer $A \vee \neg A$

---

[11] Machina's argument is formulated in the supervaluationary framework with 'true' imported into the object-language. Given the relation between 'true' and 'definitely' noted above, this result can be run together with that in the body of the text.

$\models DA \lor D\neg A$ (the premise is true for borderline A, a paradigm case where the conclusion fails).

How is the failure of classical principles possible given the arguments outlined above which apparently show that supervaluationism's logic is classical? Do those arguments fail once a D operator is introduced? And if so, why?

To compare the supervaluationist consequence relation with the classical one when sentences involve the D operator, we must consider how D is to be added to classical logic. The minimal option is to keep the logic purely classical and to treat DA as in effect a new atom for any A. Then (a) will still hold: truth in all classical models still entails truth in all specification spaces; for example, introducing the D operator cannot invalidate substitution instances of tautologies. But (b) will no longer hold; for example $\models_{SV} DA \supset A$ but it is not the case that $\models_{CL} DA \supset A$. The previous argument for (b) fails because it is no longer the case that all classical models are (degenerate) appropriate specification spaces – a model in which DA is true and A is false is classically acceptable but not a specification space.

There are more natural ways of adding D to a classical framework. Consider a classical valuation as a one-point specification space, and take classical* logic to be classical logic plus D interpreted as it would be according to supervaluationism in this degenerate space, so that DA is true in the classical* model iff A is true. (D is therefore a redundant operator here.) On this interpretation, if $\Gamma \models_{SV} B$ then it *will* be the case that $\Gamma \models_{CL*} B$; the original argument for (b) will be reinstated, for the classical* models are all degenerate specification spaces. But this time the analogue of (a) is false: it is *not* the case that if $\Gamma \models_{CL*} B$ then $\Gamma \models_{SV} B$. For example, $\models_{CL*} A \supset DA$, but it is not the case that $\models_{SV} A \supset DA$. The original argument for (a) fails here because if B is a consequence of Γ in all of the classical* models, this does not guarantee that there are no specifications in which all the members of Γ are true and B false, for there are specifications that are not classical* models (e.g. specifications in which A is true and DA is not).

The situation is similar for a third way that D can be added to a classical framework, where it is treated as a modal operator, comparable to 'necessarily', whose logic, we would hope, can be represented by one of the standard modal systems. We can consider the classical valuation as the truth-values assigned to all sentences, including ones containing D (the equivalent of the actual world index). This time (b) fails again for similar reasons as in the first case. For example, $A \models_{SV} DA$ but A does not entail DA in the enriched classical system (just as A does not entail $\Box A$). Again, not all models of this enriched classical system are (degenerate) appropriate specification spaces. You can have classical models in which A is true and DA is false (comparable to ones with A true at the actual world and $\Box A$ false). But such models are not degenerate specification spaces, for if A is true at the only admissible specification, then DA must also be true there.

How important is the failure, in the presence of D, of certain classical principles governing logical consequence? How far is it a successful criticism of supervaluationism? To object to the way that contraposition, reductio ad absurdum and other classical principles fail in a supervaluationary framework requires assuming that these principles should *not* be challenged in the face of vagueness, perhaps because they are highly natural rules of reasoning on which we rely. Williamson, for example, describes reductio ad absurdum as 'the standard way of reaching negative conclusions' (1994, p. 152). My reply is that the described features of supervaluationism are acceptable since the cases in which these rules fail all involve the D operator (or similar such devices), and as Fine and Dummett both say, D is a non-classical notion (Dummett 1975, p. 311, Fine 1975, p. 290). Rather than being a criticism, I suggest that it is a *requirement* of any plausible regimentation of a 'definitely' operator that e.g. contraposition should fail: the failure cited above is exactly what we would expect independently of supervaluationism (at least given some reasonable assumptions and a non-epistemic D operator). For, as explained, A entails DA; but $\neg DA$ must not entail $\neg A$ (for $\neg DA$ can be true when A is borderline, so $\neg A$ is not true). If D were a classical notion, the fact that A entails DA and DA entails A would ensure that A and DA were everywhere substitutable salva veritate, but, instead, they can not be substituted for each other in embedded contexts: everyone should admit that $\neg DA$ is crucially different from A. Put in another way, the introduction of an operator that operates on a sentence s to give another sentence true in all the same situations as s would be redundant on an entirely classical scheme; but D is certainly not redundant. In effect, it brings to the object-language the non-classicality of the semantics, since it can be used to capture the fact that some sentence takes the non-classical indeterminate truth-value status: it is not surprising that this results in a deviation from classical logic.

Let us consider in more detail the classical rules that fail. They are rules which allow you to infer the validity of an argument from the validity of one or more other arguments. It is when one or more of the initial arguments contains the D operator (or equivalent device) that the inference can fail. I take the relevant rules one by one and suggest rules with which they might be replaced in such circumstances.

(i) *Contraposition.* Suppose $A \models C$. This guarantees that it is not possible for A to be true and C false, which appears to be compatible with the possibility that C is false while A is neither true nor false. So from the falsity of C (the truth of $\neg C$) perhaps we should infer just that A is not true, i.e. $\neg DA$, giving $\neg C \models \neg DA$. This suggests the following new rule:

Contrap*: From $A \models C$ infer $\neg C \models \neg DA$

The earlier counter-example to contraposition used the premise that $A \models DA$. With the new rule, we can only infer the trivial $\neg DA \models \neg DA$ (and not $\neg DA \models \neg A$). And we can show that Contrap* holds in the supervaluationist framework. If $A \models C$ then if A is true on all specifications, C is true on all specifications. But then if C is false on all specifications (so $\neg C$ is true) A cannot be true on all specifications, so $\neg DA$.

Note that when no D operator is involved in A or C, the old rule still applies, and from $A \models C$, we can also infer that $\neg C \models \neg A$. For the putative possibility that C is false while A is neither true nor false would mean that there were specifications in which A was true and C false. But when there are no D operators involved, some such specification would be a degenerate specification space, which is incompatible with the hypothesis that $A \models C$ (which implies that in no specification space is A true and C false).

(ii) *Conditional proof.* Suppose $A \models C$, where A or C contains the D operator. This shows that necessarily, if A is *true* then C, which can be captured as $\models DA \supset C$. If we adopt a new rule allowing us to infer only this weaker form of conclusion when D is involved in A or C, this does not allow the earlier counter-example. For from $A \models DA$ we can only infer $\models DA \supset DA$ (not $\models A \supset DA$). More generally, we have

$\supset$I*: From $A, B \models C$ infer $B \models DA \supset C$.

(iii) *Argument by cases.* If C follows from A, and also follows from B, this shows that the truth of A guarantees the truth of C as does the truth of B. This suggests the new rule

$\vee E^\star$: From $A \models C$ and $B \models C$ infer $DA \vee DB \models C$.

Using $\vee E^\star$, from the fact that A and $\neg A$ each entail $DA \vee D\neg A$, we can only infer $DA \vee D\neg A \models DA \vee D\neg A$, rather than the unwanted $A \vee \neg A \models DA \vee D\neg A$. And the rule can be shown to hold in the supervaluationist framework as follows. If whenever A is true on all specifications, C is too and whenever B is true on all specifications, again C is too, then since $DA \vee DB$ is true when either A is true on all specifications or B is, it follows that C is true on all specifications when $DA \vee DB$ is.

(iv) *Reductio ad absurdum.* Deriving a contradiction from A and B shows that A and B cannot both be *true*, so when B is true, A is not true, i.e. $B \models \neg DA$.

$\neg I^\star$: From $A, B \models C \,\&\, \neg C$ infer $B \models \neg DA$.

Williamson's counter-example to reductio (1994, p.152) showed that you can derive a contradiction from $A \,\&\, \neg DA$, though $\neg(A \,\&\, \neg DA)$ is not a valid formula. With $\neg I^\star$ we only infer $\models \neg D(A \,\&\, \neg DA)$ which is acceptable.

I suggest these four new rules for cases where a D operator (or similar device) is involved in the initial argument(s) (i.e. in A, B or C in the above formulations). These new rules are also, of course, applicable when no D operator *is* contained in the initial argument, but in those situations the original contested rules stand as well (e.g. from $A \models C$ we can infer both $\models A \supset C$ and $\models DA \supset C$). That the usual classical rules apply in these cases is guaranteed by the arguments for (a) and (b) above (pp. 175–6). So when the D operator is involved, supervaluationism needs to modify some classical rules of inference, but the new rules are reasonable, and when no D operator is involved normal classical inference rules remain intact.

Williamson considers the response that since classical principles are only threatened when the D operator is involved, 'our deductive style might not be very much cramped' (1994, p. 152). He replies that this underestimates the scope of the limitations: 'supervaluationists have naturally tried to use their semantic apparatus to explain other locutions. If their attempts succeed, our language will be riddled with counter-examples to [the cited classical rules].' Locutions relevant here include '-ish', 'in some sense', 'rather' etc., which are analysed by employing the framework (see §3). As with sentences containing *D*, the semantics of such locutions calls upon truth-values of sentences across the whole specification space, not simply at the specification in question. So there is no guarantee that classical logic governs them in virtue of the classical structure of each of the specifications. But it would *not* significantly cramp our deductive style to avoid the illegitimate reasoning using such locutions. Given that, as remarked above, using '*F*-ish' makes explicit and draws upon an element of the vagueness of *F*, it is neither surprising nor objectionable that it shares problems that arise when we use a formal means to express the vagueness of *F* within the language itself.[12] So I reject Williamson's description of the problem: according to supervaluationism the logic of the *D* operator is appropriately non-classical, and certain other casual locutions are appropriately affected, given their analyses within the supervaluationary framework.

5. SEMANTIC ANOMALIES

As I have emphasised, the supervaluationary semantics is not classical. The semantics of individual specifications is classical, and the semantics of vague language is based entirely on these specifications, but it is not itself given by any one of them or by any other classical interpretation. One striking departure from classical semantics is the way that there are, in Fine's phrase, 'truth-value shifts', where a disjunction is true though there is no answer to which disjunct is true because the true disjunct shifts from one to the other on different specifications, or similarly where the true instance of an existentially quantified statement shifts. We discussed this phenomenon in §1v with reference to 'either it's blue or it's green' said of a borderline blue–green object. The supervaluationist interpretations of 'or' and 'there is' have been a common source of objection to the theory, which is accused of distorting or misinterpreting those logical expressions. Some opponents object that truth-value shifts are never accept-

---

12 It might be more objectionable if classical rules failed when *comparatives* were involved: this suggests a further reason for rejecting the supervaluationary analysis of comparatives considered in §3.

able and that it is absurd to allow '*a* is *F* or *G*' when *a* is neither truly said to be *F* nor truly said to be *G*, or to allow 'there is something which is *F*' to be true when there is no *x* which is truly said to be *F*. (See e.g. Sanford 1976, Kamp 1981 and Tappenden 1993.) Super-valuationists must (and do) bite the bullet. Lewis, for example, considers the objection that it is 'peculiar' that 'although it is super-true that something is a cat on the mat, there is nothing such that it is super-true of it that *it* is a cat on the mat', and replies 'so it is. But once you know the reason why, you can learn to accept it' (1993, p. 29). There is a stand-off between opponents and proponents of truth-value shifts. I advocate the indirect argument that we should accept the phenomenon because of its role in an altogether successful theory of vagueness.

The opponent of supervaluationism might have gained the upper hand if the interpretations of 'or' and 'there is' affected not only the distinctive cases surrounding vagueness and the sorites paradox, but also other cases where issues of vagueness should be irrelevant. But this does not happen. For there to be truth-value shifts with $p \vee q$, p and q must both be of borderline case status, for if either were true there *would* be an answer to which disjunct was true, whereas if either were false that would not be the true disjunct on any specification. So there are no truth-value shifts for disjunctions when we remain in the realm of clear cases. Similarly for an existential quantification: for 'something is ϕ' to be subject to truth-value shifts there must be some indefinite cases of ϕx and all cases must be either indefinite or false.

Some have accused supervaluationism of changing the meaning of the existential quantifier rather than interpreting our quantifier. For example, Bertil Rolf considers sentences of the form 'there is a number n such that Tom was bald when he had n hairs on his head but not when he had $n+1$ hairs', saying that 'the very fact that we find [them] unacceptable shows that "there is" does not have the truth-conditions which supervaluationism says it has' (1984, p. 232). But this objection adds nothing to the previous one unless it provides a new reason for believing that supervaluationism fails to give the account of our actual quantifiers. And from the fact (if it is one) that supervaluationism disagrees with our intuitive judgement on certain sentences involving 'there is', it does not follow that it misinterprets that expression if (as I claim) it gives the best account more generally of our use of 'there is' (including the way we reason using it).[13]

A universally quantified sorites premise (U) 'for all i, $\neg(Fx_i$ & $\neg Fx_{i+1})$' is compelling – we are strongly inclined to assent to it – and yet on the supervaluationist account it counts as false. Similarly, the supervaluationist must accept its negation,

(E) 'for some i, Fx_i & $\neg Fx_{i+1}$',

but this seems to state that there are sharp boundaries to our vague predicates, and so it should be false.

I regard the supervaluationist's commitment to the falsity of statements like (U) and, in particular, to the truth of those of form (E) as one of the least appealing aspects of the theory. There are a number of different, but related, strands to the objection here and, correspondingly, my defence has several aspects, together showing that any costs are easily worth paying given the advantages of the theory.

First and most generally, we already knew that we would have to accept *something* counter-intuitive: the sorites paradox shows that we cannot accept all of our intuitions in this area (see chapter 2, §1), so admitting *some* counter-intuitive consequence in connection with the sorites paradox is a disadvantage which will plague *any* theory of vagueness.[14]

Second, it is not always the case that a sorites inductive premise would be assented to: when someone is aware of the slippery slope

---

[13] Williamson warns that 'the point of the enterprise is to give semantic descriptions of vague sentences as we actually use them' so supervaluationists cannot say that a sentence such as 'there is no n such that n grains make a heap and $n+1$ do not' does not mean what we think it does (1994, pp. 153–4). But again the enterprise might have to proceed via semantic descriptions of the sentence parts that do reflect our use of them in general but that deliver surprising consequences for occasional whole sentences.

[14] This also shows that we cannot straightforwardly read off cases of penumbral truths from our unreformed intuitions, for the sorites paradox inductive premise would then count as a penumbral truth which implies a relationship between penumbral cases of tallness (see Tappenden 1993 and Burns 1991). We cannot start with all sentences that are intuitively true (both atomic predications and compound sentences) and then construct the structure of specifications so as to respect all these truths by ensuring they are true on all specifications. The super-truth proposal that truth is truth on all complete and admissible specifications is incompatible with including sorites inductive premises among the repository of truths, since predicates must have sharp boundaries in complete specifications and so the premises involving them must be false.

down which the premise may lead us, a reasonable and common response would be to refuse to endorse that premise. In general, test our intuitions about p in contexts where the inferential consequences of p are salient, and the intuitions can be different from outside specific contexts of that kind. Similarly, if (E) were considered in terms of instructions on how to respond to a series of questions along a sorites series ('is x_i tall?'), then it would be appropriate to assert (E) – you must stop saying 'yes' somewhere, even though there is no particular point at which you must stop. Tappenden (1993) provides an elegant explanation of why we might utter the sorites inductive premise even if it is not true. In general, we can sometimes utter p to correct an error that would result from believing $\neg p$ even if p itself is not true (or not known to be true). He calls this practice 'articulation', in contrast with assertion. The articulation of the sorites inductive premise, Tappenden explains, can serve to stop someone settling a sharp boundary to the sorites predicate, or thinking that there must be one.[15] So the sorites premise is not always assertable and when we are inclined to utter it, this need not commit us to its truth.

The rest of my defence turns on the fact that supervaluationism can distinguish between the falsity of (U) and its having a false instance, and correspondingly, between (E) being true and its having a true instance. Avoiding the commitment to a false instance of (U) for which $Fx_i \,\&\, \neg Fx_{i+1}$ is true creates a major advantage over the epistemic theorist who both denies the inductive premise and *is* forced to accept that it has a false instance. In particular, the supervaluationist is not faced with theoretical considerations about what could determine where the sharp boundary lies and which instance of $Fx_i \,\&\, \neg Fx_{i+1}$ is true (see chapter 3, §3). These objections to the epistemic view rest not simply on the fact that the premise is true, but on the fact that the theory is committed to a true instance when there is nothing that could determine a unique such case. Similarly, typical arguments for tolerance, taken as objections to the denial of the inductive premise, are in fact arguments against the possibility of a

---

[15] He claims that *provided a given sentence is not false*, its articulation can be appropriate even if the sentence is not true, and so he judges the premise neither true nor false. But why couldn't the articulation of a *false* sentence be pragmatically justified in the same way as Tappenden explains? If I am interested only in preventing assertion or acceptance of false q, and the best way to communicate this is via p because it has the implicature that $\neg q$, then p could be a suitable thing to assert whatever its truth-value.

true instance of Fx_i & $\neg Fx_{i+1}$. For example, supervaluationism is not threatened by arguments which object to a first patch truly called 'red' in a sorites series for 'red' on the grounds that we could not recognise it. For that theory denies that there *is* a first such patch. So, although supervaluationism is committed to something counter-intuitive in maintaining that the *prima facie* plausible inductive premise is false, the best theoretical arguments for not accepting that consequence are ineffective against the theory.

Similar considerations can also be used to explain why we have the mistaken intuitions. Our belief that there is no true instance of the quantification gets confused with a belief that the quantified statement is not true. The more theoretical description of the lack of a true instance needs to be expressed using either the D operator or the truth-predicate, such as with the denial of (DE) 'for some i, DFx_i & $D\neg Fx_{i+1}$' or in the metalanguage with the denial of (TE) 'for some i, Fx_i is true and Fx_{i+1} is false'. (TE) or (DE) would also be the correct way to express the claim that F has sharp boundaries. Accepting (E) (or, equivalently, denying the sorites inductive premise) might *seem* to commit us to sharp boundaries, but that appearance is misleading. Now, (TE) would collapse into (E) if we had the thesis that 'p' is true iff p, for then the appearance of 'Fx_i is true' in (TE) could, without loss, be replaced with 'Fx_i', and 'Fx_{i+1} is false' with '$\neg Fx_{i+1}$' (on the assumption that the falsity of a statement is equivalent to the truth of its negation). But this cannot be done given the supervaluationist treatment of truth: see chapter 8, §3.

The confusion of (E) and (TE) is a confusion of scope, according to whether the truth predicate appears inside or outside the existential quantifier. It is thus like a confusion between saying that it is true that someone ought to do X and saying that it is true of someone that they ought to do X: the latter may be false while the former is true. We would run the two together if we thought the only way that 'someone ought to do X' could be true was if there was someone, y, who ought to do X. But instead we recognise that this is not so because, for example, the former could hold because X being done is a right of z's and so it ought to be done by someone, though it is no individual's *duty* to do it. For the vagueness case in hand, we tend to think that the corresponding two truth-conditions coincide, when in fact we should recognise that there is a distinction: 'for some i, x_i is F and x_{i+1} is not-F' can be made true without an instance making it true – vague meanings allow exactly this.[16]

Taking seriously the claim that truth is truth on all precisifications, the opponent could claim that not only is the sorites inductive premise false on this account, but a whole range of statements receive truth-values in such a way that is not only counter-intuitive but a simple denial of the fact that the relevant predicates are vague. Take, for example, '*F* lacks sharp boundaries': on every precisification this is false, so it should be false simpliciter. Similarly, for '*F* has borderline cases', since on every precisification there are no borderline cases. And even '*F* is vague' will come out false, since on every precisification *F* is precise. Moreover, the statements with which we described the supervaluationary account may themselves suffer the same fate: '*F* can be made precise in many ways' and 'there is no unique extension to *F*' are problematic since each precisification settles a unique way of making *F* precise and a corresponding unique extension. Statements about the multiplicity of precisifications will thus go awry and consequently there threatens to be a problem with even stating the theory if we accept it.

But the supervaluationist can answer these objections by claiming that these statements do not receive those alleged and counter-intuitive truth-values. For they are not in fact ordinary object-language sentences as assumed: they need to be interpreted either as metalinguistic statements which need formalising using the truth-predicate or in the object-language with the *D* operator. For example, the statement that *F* has borderline cases should be interpreted as 'for some *x*, *Fx* is not true, but nor is ¬*Fx* true'; and the denial of sharp boundaries is to be interpreted as (TE). Similarly, the assertion that *F* is vague is not assessed at specification *s* just by the behaviour of *F* at *s*; it also requires the quantification over specifications that *D* or the truth-predicate introduce. And talk of precisifications or ways of making predicates precise etc. cannot be straightforwardly assessed on each precisification as if it is ordinary

16 Williamson complains (1994, p. 154) that, according to supervaluationism, we are both recognising vagueness (hence rejecting (E) because we think there is no sharp boundary) and ignoring it (because we allow the inference from not-(TE) to not-(E) when it is in the presence of vagueness that this fails). But this could only be a reasonable criticism if we are assumed to *know* the semantic consequences of vagueness, and the supervaluationist need not suppose we do know them.

object-language talk – it would again need to be formalised using a truth-predicate or *D*. The metalinguistic interpretations of the cited problem sentences are reasonable, since each of those sentences does seem to be about the predicate *F* itself, and so to mention rather than use that predicate. Our *informal* statements can sometimes be ambiguous between the (*D*-free) object-language and metalanguage interpretations. Interpreting metalinguistically a sentence such as 'there's no *n* such that *n* grains make a heap and *n*+1 do not' (or interpreting it using *D*) makes that reasonable utterance true, and this is a good reason to take us as often intending that interpretation.

Further features and merits of this approach to the sentences in question can be seen by comparing and contrasting it with an alternative, namely that of narrowing the scope of the application of the supervaluationist rule, maintaining that, in particular, when a description of the theory is in question, the rule should be suspended. Lewis adopts this latter response to a similar difficulty facing his supervaluationary treatment of vague singular terms. He says that we should not apply the supervaluationist rule fanatically to every situation regardless of whether the relevant utterances make sense on such an interpretation. The rule is a 'defeasible assumption' that is sometimes suspended (1993, p. 30). Take the statement of the problem of the many. It is false on any specification, so false simpliciter, to say there are many candidates with equal claim to cathood, which shows that we cannot interpret the description of many cat candidates in that supervaluationary way. Its truth is not a matter of its truth on all specifications.

Applying Lewis's response across the board (and not just to singular terms) may allow us to regard as true the problematic statements such as '*F* has many precisifications' by denying that they are to be assessed within the framework via assessment at each specification-point. Lewis claims that there is nothing wrong with saying that there is a *sense* in which there are many cats when (intuitively) Barney is alone on the mat, provided we can accommodate a sense in which there is a lone cat there. But this strategy is unacceptable. For it introduces an unappealing lack of generality in the supervaluationist's theory, and it is unclear how to provide a reasonable and well-motivated specification of when we should or should not apply the supervaluationist rule. Moreover, we may even be left with certain sorites paradoxes intact, namely versions which are to be interpreted without the supervaluationary rule. And we cannot allow that there is a sense in which the inductive sorites premise is true when the supervaluationist response to the ensuing paradox is unavailable.

And yet there is something appealing about Lewis's response to the problems in hand. There does indeed seem to be a difference between maintaining that the supervaluationist rule is the proper rule governing ordinary circumstances – it makes sense of our linguistic and inferential practices, solves the sorites paradox etc. – and insisting that it is applicable even when we participate in the decidedly non-ordinary practice of reflecting on the multiplicity of precisifications and so on. Fortunately, the supervaluationist response I defended above can do justice to these thoughts without sacrificing the generality of the supervaluationary rule, namely by using the truth-predicate in the metalanguage or the D operator to express the sentences in question. The truth of any such sentence is still truth on all specifications, but its truth on specification s depends on the structure of the whole space of specifications, not just on the assignments of extensions to atomic predicates within s. Specifications then 'carry information about' other specifications, which allows them simultaneously to treat F as precise (with a sharply bounded extension in the model) and acknowledge its vagueness and lack of sharp boundaries.

6. THE ROLE OF PRECISIFICATIONS

Many commentators challenge more directly the basic appeal to precisifications. First, why should we think we can give a successful account of our vague language by considering how it *would* be if it were made precise? And various general considerations seem to show that tolerance is essential to the whole *point* of our vague predicates, which, in Dummett's phrase, are 'ineradicably vague' (1975, p. 312) in stark contrast with the precisifications at the centre of the super-valuationist account of vagueness. Objectors pursuing this line often claim that, in dealing only with precise structures, supervaluationism thus badly misrepresents our vague expressions, treating them 'as if they were vague only because we had not troubled to make them precise' (Dummett 1975, p. 258; see also e.g. Sanford 1976, Edgington 1997). There are a number of possible objections here. I consider first the claim that we should not believe in, or be committed to, the entities over which the supervaluationist quantifies. Then I reply to objections that even if precisifications/specifications are not objectionable in themselves, we should not employ them in our theory of vagueness.

Supervaluationism quantifies over complete and admissible specifications which are assignments of classical truth-values to all sentences. Are there any grounds for objecting to such entities? No: they are as unobjectionable as the assignment of truth-values represented by rows of a truth-table used in assessing the validity of an argument within propositional calculus.

The objection might be framed by reference to the precisifications of a vague predicate F, where Fa counts as true if a is F according to all of those precisifications. If these precisifications are assumed to be *properties*, in the sense of members of an elite category of natural properties (perhaps construed as universals or as sets of tropes) which 'carve nature at the joints', then there are clearly not enough such entities to qualify as precisifications of F. There is no natural property of *chairhood*, or of most precise replacements of our vague predicate 'chair' (cf. chapter 3, §3), and if all possible ways of drawing the boundary did correspond to a natural property, such properties would not be elite or scientifically significant. But supervaluationism is not committed to such an array of natural properties. All it needs are the specifications described above which, as I explained, are no more problematic as entities than any of the other combinatorial constructs regularly employed in formal semantics. And recall that the fact we cannot spell out precise requirements corresponding to specifications is no threat since supervaluationism demands no such grasp on the specifications: their existence is still guaranteed.[17]

Fodor and LePore (1996) offer a different argument against the call upon specifications. They could be seen either as objecting that there are no precisifications ('you cannot precisify English', they write, p. 523) or as objecting to the use of those precisifications. Either way their arguments fail. They claim that if 'Tek is tall' is neither true nor false, then it misinterprets 'tall' to call upon specifications in which that sentence *is* either true or false. More forcefully, if 'someone of height h is tall' is neither true nor false, then ' "someone

---

[17] Regarding our understanding, I agree with Fine (p. 282) that we typically grasp precisifications all in one go, and to grasp them all we need not have any way of distinguishing one from another.

of height *h* is tall" is neither true nor false' is a conceptual truth – true in virtue of the meaning of 'tall'. Any model of the language that falsifies that conceptual truth by counting 'someone of height *h* is tall' as true or as false (as precisifications do) violates the meaning of the predicate and so is illegitimate for modelling our natural language predicate.

But this objection misrepresents the role of precisifications: such valuations do indeed fail to capture all features of the meanings of our predicates – after all, the precisifications are not vague and our predicates are. But this constitutes no *objection* to the theory, for the claim is that it is the quantification over all precisifications that captures the meaning of the natural language predicates; the individual precisifications need not. The conceptual truth that ' "someone of height *h* is tall" is neither true nor false' indeed states a necessary truth (given an appropriate *h*) because in any possible situation 'someone of height *h* is tall' would be neither true nor false. The range of precisifications taken together would always guarantee this. Individual precisifications themselves do not represent possible situations and so need not respect all necessary truths.

Fodor and LePore's response to such a reply seems to be that precisifications could not then be valuations of our language. But we can admit that if, as they assume, a valuation of a language must respect all its meanings, then precisifications should not be called valuations of vague language. But precisifications can still contribute to determining the correct valuation without each *being* a correct valuation in this sense.[18] Fodor and LePore later complain that it is not then clear why valuations play their role in truth-conditions: this

---

[18] So we do not have to give up the contention that conceptual truths are preserved wherever meaning is (p. 522) since we can deny that meaning *is* preserved through precisification. I disagree that 'the very motivation that leads supervaluation theorists to postulate "penumbral connections"' is to allow that conceptual truths are respected by all classical models, including classical valuations (see their p. 521 and p. 527), rather what matters is respecting truths of meaning in the supervaluationary model as a whole. Fodor and LePore's discussion may suggest the more interesting question of how we determine of some conceptual truth whether or not it should be treated as a penumbral truth. But their own cases are not serious candidates since they are metalinguistic in referring to the truth-value status of certain sentences and do not concern logical relations between borderline cases as on Fine's original characterisation of penumbral connections. And note that had they chosen to express their case using the *D* operator instead of metalinguistically, the claim would have been that '¬*Dp* & ¬*D*¬*p*' is a conceptual truth. This *is* respected on all precisifications.

is not an objection to the existence of precisifications, rather it is the same popular objection to the *appeal* to precisifications that I reply to below.

Dummett's charge is that supervaluationism mistakenly treats vague predicates as if we could have made them precise if we had tried to. Single precisifications could indeed be semantic values of predicates, but Dummett's complaint is not about what abstract languages could be like, but about how *our* language could be in practice. And the contribution of specifications to truth-conditions has no implications about that. Supervaluationists can admit that it would be impossible in practice to impose complete precision or to use one of the precisifications, but this is no threat to a semantic account that quantifies over them. Dummett is unjustified in claiming that super-valuationism treats vague predicates as if we could (or should) have made them precise. The theory does not commit us to *anything* about how language could have been, whether vagueness could have been eliminated, whether eliminating it would destroy its point, or any such matters.[19]

A different type of objection considers the use, for other purposes, of precisifications or equivalent structures, and claims that the comparison undermines their use for typical cases of vagueness. Sainsbury considers 'incompleteness' in predicates, citing the example of 'pearl': there is no answer to whether 'a pearl-shaped lump of pearl-material that has somehow been synthesized outside of any oyster' should be called a pearl, but this, he claims, is not a matter of *vagueness* (1988, p. 37). Whereas, he maintains, such incompleteness results in some cases being left indeterminate, by contrast the meaning of a vague predicate *determines* that there is a borderline region and that predications in those cases are indeterminate. And he objects that supervaluationism 'cannot distinguish between vagueness and incompleteness, for it will offer the same treatment for any predicate which

---

[19] Edgington complains that supervaluationism presents vagueness 'as a relatively super-ficial phenomenon, eliminable in principle' (1997, p. 316). Given the vagueness of the metalanguage that I defend in chapter 8, the most damaging form of the superfici-ality objection is avoided. And why should the quantification over precisifications make vagueness superficial? Moreover, if the existence of specifications assigning a classical value to every sentence makes vagueness eliminable in principle, then such in-principle elimination is unobjectionable and should be accepted by non-superva-luationists.

can be associated with three sets as positive extension, negative extension and penumbra' (1995a, p. 38). I doubt that there is a significant difference between a meaning that determines that certain cases are left unsettled and one that determines an extension such as to leave certain cases unsettled. There may be pragmatic differences such as concerning how we would regard stipulations to settle the cases in question, but these do not undermine the parallel semantic treatment in the two cases. We should take on their own terms the suggestions that vagueness and incompleteness be treated within an apparatus of complete specifications. And supervaluationists can justify their use of this framework through the success of the resulting theory.[20]

Perhaps the most common form of objection to the use of precisifications is captured in the following quotation from Sanford 1976: 'grant then that a certain statement is true if its predicates are made completely precise in any appropriate way. Why should the statement thereby be regarded as true if its predicates are not made precise in any of these appropriate ways?' (1976, p. 206).[21] The justification for taking the supervaluationary approach to truth-conditions and employing precisifications is that it results in a successful theory of vagueness in all the ways already listed. This is enough to justify the use of precisifications within the theory, and since the advantages cannot be gained any other way, the appeal to them is indispensable. We can agree that it is not automatically true that there is a role in the semantics for facts about how a certain sentence *would* be if made precise: we do not need a prior justification of the use of the apparatus independent of the account it delivers. And even though precisifications do not in general cross the minds of the language-users in everyday use, this is no problem since a semantic theory need not offer a semantic apparatus which is invoked by

---

[20] A similar reply is available for Pinkal's parallel objection comparing the treatments of ambiguity and of vagueness (1983).

[21] Fodor and LePore's similar complaint is put in a misleading form since they take precisifications to belong to other languages, where the various precisifications of 'red' are to be seen as alternative (precise) words of other possible languages. They ask why reference to predicates of other languages should illuminate our own predicates. My reply to this form of the objection is the same: it can be phrased in terms of predicates in other languages, if desired. The representation of precisifications as predicates of other (hypothetical) languages can be found elsewhere; as we have seen it is certainly not necessary, and it can be misleading (cf. McGee and McLaughlin 1995, p. 239).

speakers. Speakers can directly employ the terms so analysed. In particular, they can use vague predicates without explicitly calling upon the precisifications of them, even if the truth of what they say requires truth on those precisifications. I doubt that many semantic theories can plausibly claim to mirror the psychological processes by which we assess values of statements. Indeed, the appeal to precisifications can be compared to Tarski's semantics for the quantifier which appeals to sequences of objects. That semantics is not to be rejected although few speakers explicitly consider such sequences of objects when they are assessing quantified statements.[22]

I have defended the employment of specifications for the semantics of vague language, and will continue the defence of my theory in chapter 8. But first I end this chapter by considering – and rejecting – specification-space approaches which deviate from the supervaluationary super-truth condition or which call upon non-classical specifications.

7. ALTERNATIVE ACCOUNTS WITHIN A FRAMEWORK OF SPECIFICATIONS

lternative accounts within Fine's framework differ over how truth-values are assigned to complex sentences at partial specification-points, and this results in different truth-definitions for the connectives. For example, it would be compatible with the conception of the specification space and Fine's conditions of Stability, Completability and Fidelity to take a disjunction always to be indefinite at a partial specification-point if both of its disjuncts were indefinite there (even if at all complete points extending it one or other disjunct is true). Now, the super-truth account delivers a uniform account of the truth-conditions of complex and simple sentences by the condition that p is true iff p is true on all specifications, but we could report the same information by giving, for each logical constant, the truth-conditions of compound sentences at a given (possibly partial) specification-point in terms of the values of its components at that and other points. First, negation can be summarised as follows:

---

[22] Compare also, perhaps, treatments of natural language by possible worlds theorists.

(N_1) $\neg B$ is true at specification-point t iff B is false at t
(N_2) $\neg B$ is false at t iff B is true at t.

The conditions for the truth and falsity of a conjunction at any specification-point t can be expressed by the following:

(C_1) B & C is true at t iff B is true at t and C is true at t
(C_2) B & C is false at t iff for all points v that extend t, there is some point u, extending v, such that B is false at u or C is false at u.

Both quantifications are needed in (C_2) because the falsity of B & C at a point t, by the standard super-truth condition, requires its falsity at all complete points extending t, which means that at each of those points at least one of B or C is false. This is not to say that for *all* points extending t either B or C is false, since there can be partial points extending t in which B and C are both indeterminate. But some complete point must extend each of those partial points and satisfy the classical condition for the falsity of B & C. Conditions for disjunction can be stated as:

(D_1) $B \vee C$ is true at t iff for all points v that extend t, there is some point u, extending v, such that B is true at u or C is true at u
(D_2) $B \vee C$ is false at t iff B is false at t and C is false at t.

This way of describing truth-conditions invites comparisons with many-valued theories for which none of the clauses on the right-hand side will refer to, or quantify over, any specification besides t itself. Such a presentation also encourages variations on the given set of conditions for the connectives (see Fine 1975, p. 273).

(i) Burgess and Humberstone

Burgess and Humberstone (1987) defend a system within the specification-space approach which is perhaps the most attractive of the specification-space alternatives to the standard supervaluationary account.[23] They share Fine's treatment of conjunctions, thus retaining the law of non-contradiction, but they diverge from Fine with regard to the conditions sufficient for the truth of a disjunction, replacing (D_1) with

---

[23] Burgess endorses it again in his 1997 and 1998, though he does not discuss the truth-conditions themselves in any detail in these papers.

(D$_1$*) $B \vee C$ is true at t iff B is true at t or C is true at t.

This means, advantageously they claim, that instances of the law of excluded middle can fail to be true since there are partial points at which neither p nor $\neg p$ is true. Thus the case for the Burgess and Humberstone system is that it can preserve what they see as the two central intuitions, namely that the law of non-contradiction is valid but that the law of excluded middle fails. By contrast, they stress, Fine's system can respect only the first of these intuitions, and many-valued theories only the second. But even if we grant the advantages of retaining these supposed intuitions (the second of which I have questioned above), they cannot be considered in isolation: we must also ask what other intuitions are preserved or violated. Burgess and Humberstone focus instead on the semantics, a natural deductive system and a completeness proof.

In giving up the law of excluded middle, Burgess and Humberstone are also forced to deny the truth of many of Fine's penumbral connections, such as 'the blob is red or pink' said of a borderline red–pink blob, or 'x is a brother or a sister' for Edgington's sex-change case. They *are* committed to the truth of 'the blob is not both not-red and not-pink', given their conditions for negated conjunctions, but this seems to be just saying that it is not neither red nor pink, which in turn seems to say that it is either red or pink, which is exactly what they must deny. This illustrates the fact that the standard interdefinability of & and $\vee$ is also lost, since $A \vee B$ is only true at t if at least one of A and B is true at t, while $\neg(\neg A \ \& \ \neg B)$ is true whenever in all complete specifications extending the base-point, A or B is true. The standard definitions of the conditional as $\neg(A \ \& \ \neg B)$ and as $\neg A \vee B$ are both rejected too, since on the chosen accounts of conjunction and disjunction neither alternative would support both conditional proof and modus ponens, and a different account of the conditional is chosen instead.

Classically valid inferential rules fail too. For example, reductio ad absurdum is not valid in full generality: when the assumption that A leads to a contradiction we cannot conclude $\neg A$ if A is a disjunction. An example of where this would go wrong on Burgess and Humberstone's system is with a standard proof by reductio ad absurdum of $p \vee \neg p$ by assuming its negation, for as we have seen, that classical law fails on the scheme in question. The restriction that Burgess and

Humberstone impose is that for reductio to be applicable, A must be 'a negated or unnegated propositional variable or else a formula of the form B & C' (p. 205). But this appears highly ad hoc and there is certainly nothing in our use of the rule to suggest any sensitivity to whether the assumption to be reduced is disjunctive. Burgess 1998 (pp. 246–7) emphasises that it is inevitable that some classical rules of inference fail given the failure of the law of excluded middle. But his assumption that we count only intuitions about sentences and not intuitions about what inferences are good is entirely unjustified. His claim to accommodate '*all* of the core intuitions' (1998, p. 234, his italics) rests on this ad hoc selection of which intuitions matter.

Burgess and Humberstone do note some odd consequences of their view. In particular, they acknowledge the unfortunate fact that on their system A & A can be false though A is not false. As an example, consider $\neg(B \lor \neg B)$ at point t. On their account of disjunction this can be neither true nor false when B is borderline, despite the falsity of that compound at all complete points extending t. Now, whether a conjunction is false at t is – according to (C_2) – assessed on the basis of the value of each conjunct at those complete points extending t and so, since $\neg(B \lor \neg B)$ is false at each of those points, the conjunction of that complex sentence with itself, $\neg(B \lor \neg B)$ & $\neg(B \lor \neg B)$, counts as false simpliciter. Similarly, conjoining an indefinite instance of $\neg(B \lor \neg B)$ with a definite truth will also deliver a falsehood; for example 'Tek is a man and it is not the case that either he is tall or he is not tall' will fulfil the right-hand side of (C_2) since the second conjunct is false at all complete points, so we have a false conjunction with one indefinite and one true conjunct. This is very different from the kind of cases that Burgess and Humberstone use for justifying the way that a conjunction can be false though neither of its conjuncts are false (p. 227). Those, they claim, arise when there is some incompatibility between the conjuncts themselves, whereas for cases of the above types, the two conjuncts can be entirely independent. It is surely undesirable that on their account, conjoining an unrelated indeterminate sentence with a true one can result in a false sentence. On no other theory can a conjunction be false with one indeterminate and one true conjunct, let alone when the conjuncts are unrelated. And on the super-truth account, unlike Burgess and Humberstone's alternative, we can stick to the motivated position that it is only when a conjunction reflects penumbral connections – i.e. logical relations between components – that it can be less true than either conjunct.

More generally, the super-truth account has a uniformity, simplicity and respect for our intuitions which far surpasses that of any alternative set of definitions of the connectives within the framework. The concise statement of truth-conditions it provides is elegant and philosophically well-motivated. Moreover, in retaining classical logic, it does not face the threat that, along with the intended changes to the logic, there are unpalatable failures of the theorems or principles that should not be affected by the presence of vagueness.

(ii) Hyde's subvaluationism

There is an alternative statement of truth-conditions built on specification spaces which has the simplicity of the super-truth condition while yielding very different results. But I shall argue that such an account fails on other grounds. It states that p is true (false) iff it is true (false) on *some* specification (cf. chapter 6). This results in truth-value gluts rather than gaps for borderline cases, since 'Tek is tall' is true on some specifications and false on others, so both true and false simpliciter on this account. Hyde 1997 has developed a version of this theory – labelling it subvaluationism – which is the dual of supervaluationism and a form of paraconsistent logic (i.e. it allows pairs of contradictory statements to be true, without entailing that every statement is true). Hyde hopes, at the very least, to be putting a paraconsistent theory of vagueness onto the menu of options for a theory of vagueness, as an alternative which is at least as promising as supervaluationism. But many philosophers would soon discount the paraconsistent option (almost) regardless of how successfully it treats vagueness, on the grounds of the unappealing commitments and features of the logical framework as a whole, in particular the absurdity of p and $\neg p$ both being true for many instances of p. At the very least, the cost of the paraconsistent framework is enough to favour supervaluationism over subvaluationism if other advantages and disadvantages are comparable. But I shall show more: Hyde's theory faces further considerable costs which have no counterpart for supervaluationism. Thus I need not address the general question whether paraconsistent theories are ever philosophically defensible. (See e.g. Smiley 1993 for criticisms of paraconsistency.)

There are very substantial deviations from classical logic on the subvaluationist picture, not least of which is the failure of adjunction. A & B does not follow from A and B, since those premises might be true by being true in different specifications and such that there are no specifications in which both are true. For example, when p is a borderline case, both p and $\neg p$ are true, and yet p & $\neg p$ is *not* true on any specifications, so not true simpliciter. Hyde shows, however, that although such a two-premise inference fails, we can easily prove that any *single*-premise argument that is classically valid is also valid according to subvaluationism, and, more generally, for any classically valid argument, the argument constructed by conjoining its premises is valid on the subvaluationist scheme (1997, pp. 647–8). For, if the single premise of an argument is true, then, by subvaluationism, it must be true on some specification; and if the conclusion classically follows, then that conclusion must be true on the same (classical) specification, which is enough to show it is true simpliciter. But, regardless of this, the failure of the very natural inference from A and B to A & B is an unacceptable consequence of the account. How can it make so much difference whether we say two acceptable things in succession as two separate sentences, or roll them into one with 'and'? Noting that the sentences are vague does not make the alleged difference any more plausible.[24]

Modus ponens is also invalid according to subvaluationism: again, the premises can be true because they are true in different specifications, where there is no guarantee that there are any specifications in which they are both true. (Hyde's example takes a sorites-like series in which there is no higher-order vagueness, so a single step arguing 'if Fx_i then Fx_{i+1}, Fx_i, therefore Fx_{i+1}', can take us from a predication, Fx_i, that is both true and false to one, Fx_{i+1}, that is just false. At

---

[24] Hyde draws a parallel, and claims that supervaluationism invalidates certain classically valid multiple-conclusion inferences. In particular, consider the argument with the premise A ∨ B and conclusions A and B: i.e. (V) A ∨ B $\models$ A, B. Given classical logic and semantics at least one of the conclusions must be true if the premise is true. This establishes it as a paradigm classically valid multiple-conclusion argument. But (V) fails according to supervaluationism, Hyde maintains, because the premise can be true without either conclusion being true. But we do not use multiple-conclusion arguments in ordinary life and it is reasoning in vague natural language that is in question. Multiple-conclusion logic is not intended as a logic of ordinary arguments (its study primarily has the role of providing a system for elegant analogies with multiple-premise logics) and its theses are questionably included among the body of 'traditional' logic. The contrast with the failure of adjunction is clear.

that step, the premise Fx_i is true on some specifications and the conditional is true on others, by having an antecedent false at them, but the conclusion, Fx_{i+1}, is true on no specifications, so false simpliciter.) According to Hyde, to use modus ponens within the sorites reasoning is to commit a fallacy of equivocation. For he regards vagueness as a form of ambiguity, where the different precisifications are different disambiguations (as described in §1ii, but with subvaluationist criteria for the valuation of sentences that have not been disambiguated). Thus when the premises are true in virtue of each being true in different specifications, they count as true in different senses, in which case to draw the conclusion is to equivocate. But in saying this, Hyde may be shooting himself in the foot. If this is to equivocate, then likewise saying that both p and $\neg p$ are true is to equivocate (anyone will accept that p can be true in some sense and $\neg p$ true in a different sense.) As I argued on p. 157 in relation to the remark that a supervaluationist must talk of truth-in-a-sense (or relative to a precisification), we need to allow that the supervaluationist/subvaluationist gives truth-conditions for univocal vague sentences; and if subvaluationism's truth is really *truth* then there is no equivocation in the modus ponens argument. The appeal to equivocation may provide some kind of a semantic explanation of the failure of modus ponens in the subvaluationist framework, but it cannot *justify* accepting that consequence without casting doubt on the subvaluationist account of truth.

The treatment of the sorites paradox also illustrates the dramatic and highly counter-intuitive difference the subvaluationist theory is forced to postulate between an argument with and without conjoined premises. Although the version consisting of a series of conditional premises comes out as invalid, a version conjoining all of those premises needs a different treatment. Since that latter version is classically valid, this will be valid on the subvaluationist scheme (by the result cited above about single-premise arguments); the premise will, however, be false. The situation is the same for the more common form of paradox which has a quantified premise in addition to a non-controversial definitely true premise (such as 'someone of 7 feet is tall'). The argument will again be valid and the quantified premise false. So we have to provide different responses to apparently equivalent forms of paradox. Hyde ignores all but the many-conditionals form of the sorites argument, and he even talks about his equivocation response as *the* paraconsistent resolution of the sorites paradox (p. 650), as if the same response can be given for all versions. This unappealing lack of uniformity in locating the blame results in denying most intuitions associated with the sorites argument: it is not valid, at least in some forms, one of the premises is not true, in other forms, and different ways of stating what is apparently the same argument are actually stating crucially different arguments.

(iii) Many-valued supervaluationist accounts

A final alternative to the standard supervaluationary account draws not on the same kind of specification space, but on a space of non-classical specifications in which sentences are each assigned one of a range of non-classical values. There is scope for a wide variety of theories of this form differing over the set of truth-values and over the relations between values at different specifications (in particular, how the values are assigned at the base-point).[25] One option was mentioned in chapter 4, §9ii where the specifications were taken as infinite-valued and the value assigned to a sentence (at the base-point) was the range of the values assigned in the admissible specifications. This seems to be the position proposed in Sanford 1993. Many of the advantages of supervaluationism are lost on this account, and many of the problems raised in chapters 4 and 5 will return. For example, the law of non-contradiction is less than true, and penumbral connections are not respected (when the blob is borderline pink–red 'the blob is pink or red' will not take value 1 in any of the specifications). And the problems with the various choices of truth-definitions for the connectives will also return, as well as the charge that any such choice is ad hoc.

What would be gained by adopting an infinite-valued version of supervaluationism rather than the standard two-valued variety? Sanford writes that 'any admissible many-value specification more accurately represents the actual ordinary use of the statement in

---

[25] Edgington's account could perhaps be interpreted in this way instead of in the way discussed in §3. Returning to an example from chapter 4, §5, when *a* and *b* are both borderline red and *b* is redder than *a*. The verity of '*a* is red' if *b* were (definitely) red could be one of a range of different values, each of which could be represented by an infinite-valued specification. Edgington may then supplement this account with some way of calculating a single value as the conditional verity given the values on that range of specifications.

question than any admissible two-value specification' (Sanford 1979, p. 179). But even if we were to accept this claim, it would not provide an argument for a supervaluationary theory with many-valued specifications, since individual specifications are not *required* to represent ordinary use. It is only at the stage when we have taken the valuations together to yield the supervaluation that ordinary use must be reflected, for that is the stage which offers the semantics of our language.[26] With these rather brief remarks, I leave many-valued supervaluationary theories in favour of their superior and more secure classical counterparts.

The alternatives considered in §7 all take seriously a framework of precisifications. Since a substantial proportion of the objections to supervaluationism turn on aspects of this framework in general, much of my defence of that theory in earlier sections and in chapter 8 could also be used by proponents of many-valued supervaluationist theory, a two-valued theory with different definitions of the connectives, or a subvaluationist theory. In chapter 8, I return to my defence of my supervaluationist theory.

---

[26] Sanford has also used the resources of many-valued semantics to provide a semantics for determinately and borderline operators which he hopes can be used in capturing higher-order vagueness (e.g. Sanford 1975), and this treatment may be compatible with the supervaluationary approach to those valuations. In particular, he suggests $|Dp| = 1 - (n$ times $|\neg p|)$, or 0 if this value is less than 1, for some $n \geq 2$. But the arbitrariness of the choice of n makes for an unacceptable treatment of a non-arbitrary feature of vague language, and the standard supervaluationary account of D is preferable regardless of whether or not the specifications are classical.

8

Truth is super-truth

'Truth is super-truth' can be the supervaluationist's slogan. One of the two main questions tackled in this final chapter is whether truth can really be super-truth or whether super-truth fails to have the definitive features of truth. I start with the other main question, which asks whether supervaluationism can accommodate higher-order vagueness or whether that phenomenon threatens the identification of truth with super-truth.

I. HIGHER-ORDER VAGUENESS AND VAGUE METALANGUAGES

Can supervaluationism accommodate – or be adapted to accommodate – the lack of sharp boundaries between the cases where a predicate clearly applies and the borderline cases, and between the borderline cases and the borderline borderline cases, and so on? This question has not been resolved by Fine and other advocates of supervaluationism, but the theory has the resources to succeed in this respect, I shall argue.

Consider the following quick argument against supervaluationism. According to the theory, a sentence is true simpliciter iff it is true on all complete and admissible specifications. But for any sentence, either it *is* true on all complete and admissible specifications (hence true simpliciter) or not (hence borderline or false). So there is no scope for avoiding sharp boundaries to the borderline cases or for accommodating borderline borderline cases. This argument is too quick as it stands, but it does encapsulate a popular line of objection to supervaluationism. We need to examine a key assumption on which it rests, namely that there is a precise and unique set of complete and admissible specifications. If 'complete and admissible specification' is vague, we should reject this assumption. (Compare the supervaluationist's claim that there is no precise and unique set of

202

all tall people because 'tall' is vague.) And there are good reasons to expect 'complete and admissible specification' (more particularly, 'admissible specification') to be vague: the notion corresponds to 'acceptable way of making all expressions precise', and it is natural to expect vagueness over what counts as acceptable here.

For example, it is acceptable to make 'tall' precise by drawing a boundary at 6 feet 0 inches but not by drawing one at 5 feet 0 inches, and there is no point between these two heights which determinately marks a point of sudden change from being an acceptable boundary to an unacceptable one.

So 'admissible specification' is vague and since it is in the proper part of the metalanguage, that metalanguage is vague in the desired way. There could thus be a borderline case admissible specification. Sentences that are false in such a specification but true in all definitely admissible specifications will be borderline cases of 'true on all complete and admissible specifications'; and '"p" is true on all complete and admissible specifications' will then be indeterminate. The truth-conditions provided by supervaluationism will not then definitely determine any truth-value for p or definitely determine that the sentence lacks a truth-value. For the indeterminacy over whether the truth-condition is fulfilled implies that we should not conclude that p is true, but nor should we call p neither true nor false as we would do if the condition (determinately) failed to be fulfilled. The truth-value status of p (whether it is true, false or lacks a value) remains unsettled. And sharp boundaries between the true predications and the borderline cases of 'tall' are avoided.[1]

The vagueness of the truth-condition does not, however, eliminate definite truths, since there will be clear cases of sentences true on all admissible specifications, which will be definitely true. And there will still be borderline cases which are true on some (definitely) admissible specifications and false on others. A sorites series can be described as starting with true predications, having borderline ones in the middle, and false ones at the end but being such that there are no sharp boundaries between those categories. There is no threat to the logic

---

[1] See the end of this section for an account on which admissibility is a relative notion (modelled via a relation between specification-points corresponding to the accessibility relations used in the semantics of modal logic). p might then count as true on all those specifications admissible relative to one point but not on all those admissible relative to another; the sketched argument against supervaluationism would then fail again.

of the (*D*-free) object language either. Consider the sentences declared logical truths by the theory. These are so classified because they are super-true (i.e. true on all specifications) in all possible situations. Now, a classical logical truth L is true on all complete specifications (since these are just classical models), and so whatever specifications count as complete and admissible, L will be true on all of them. The vagueness of 'complete and admissible specification' means that we may be unable to pick a unique determinate set of those specifications; but this is no threat to the status of the logical truths since we can be sure that the only complete specifications of any relevance to truth-conditions will be classical. For L to fail to be a logical truth according to supervaluationism, there would have to be *some* complete specification (in some possible situation) in which L was not true even if it were not determinate whether that specification counted as admissible. But if L is a classical logical truth there can be no such specification, so L cannot fail to count as a logical truth according to supervaluationism. Similarly, classical logical consequence relations are not challenged by admitting the vagueness of 'admissible specification'.[2]

Recall chapter 4, §9iii on the many-valued theory which is the counterpart of the above position and which acknowledges a vague metalanguage. One of my criticisms of that approach was as follows. A logical truth is true in all possible situations, but if the metalanguage is vague and sentences are not ascribed exact values, being true for all values in the chosen set does not capture truth in all possible situations. With supervaluationism this type of criticism is not applicable. Logical truth is (super-)truth (i.e. truth on all specifications) in all possible situations and this does not require a false assumption that the possible situations are each captured by a determinate set of specifications.

Note that although indeterminacy does not affect what sentences count as logical truths, there is scope for indeterminacy in those that count as penumbral truths. Penumbral truths are true in all admissible specifications, so corresponding to vagueness over 'all admissible specifications' there may be vagueness over whether certain sentences

---

[2] Compare Fine's passing remark that if we were to admit the vagueness of the true/false/indefinite trichotomy (something he is not, however, willing to do), this would not challenge the logic he has presented: 'validity is still classical on the super-truth view; for classically valid *A* is true in all complete and admissible specifications regardless of whether it is clear that a particular complete specification is admissible' (1975, p. 297).

qualify as penumbral connections. But it is appropriate that there should be vagueness over this notion, and this may reflect that there is no sharply bounded set of analytic truths.

The view that supervaluationism captures the nature of vagueness as semantic indecision is also compatible with the vagueness of the metalanguage. Vagueness arises because no choice is made between a number of alternative precisifications: but the range of those alternatives need not be determinate. Recognising that there is semantic indecision does not commit us to a determinate set of alternatives between which we are undecided. Rather, no precise set of alternatives is settled either – nothing in us or our language fixes a unique such set any more than it settles the first-level choice between precisifications.

There may, however, be the suspicion that the theory is circular or trivial in treating vagueness using a vague language. But 'truth is truth on all complete and admissible specifications' is certainly not trivially true, neither in the sense of being vacuously true nor in the sense of being obvious or uncontroversial. It would be rejected by theorists who were not supervaluationists, even if they were told that 'complete and admissible specification' was a vague notion.

The following question raises a more substantial triviality objection. What has the supervaluationist gained over stopping at the first stage and not giving truth-conditions in terms of specifications at all? We could simply say

(T) '*p*' is true iff *p*

and allow that both sides of the statement are vague, so that the vagueness of the truth-predicate matches the vagueness of the object language: let us call this the Simple Theory of vagueness. If supervaluationists are seen as objecting to the Simple Theory because it does not yield determinate truth-conditions, the same argument will apply against our truth-conditions once it has been admitted that there is no determinate set of 'all admissible specifications'. So it must be made clear that these are not the grounds on which the Simple Theory should be rejected and that supervaluationism is not trivial in the way this Simple Theory appears to be.[3]

---

[3] I am concerned here with the comparison with respect to triviality between what I

If we combine (T) with the commitment to classical logic, in particular the law of excluded middle, we can infer 'p is true or not-p is true' (cf. Williamson 1994, pp. 187–9). This leaves no scope for an indeterminate sentence, p, where neither p nor its negation is true; and if indeterminacy is thus to be epistemic, a form of the epistemic view is needed. Just stating (T), as the envisaged Simple Theory does, tells us nothing about vagueness. If, on the other hand, the possibility of abandoning classical logic is admitted, then the Simple Theory is of no help at all in revealing what logic should replace it, what truth-values we should allow etc.[4]

So the Simple Theory could fairly be criticised on the grounds of triviality – it does not illuminate vagueness at all in just *using* vague expressions and doing nothing more. But supervaluationism with a vague metalanguage can answer a parallel charge. For adopting truth-conditions in terms of admissible specifications opens up the possibility of non-epistemic indeterminacy. The theory (unlike the Simple Theory) provides an illuminating and non-trivial account of the central features of vagueness, namely borderline cases, the lack of sharp boundaries and the sorites paradox. The vagueness of its statement of truth-conditions does not threaten these achievements.

Sainsbury complains 'acknowledging vagueness in the notion of a sharpening . . . would mean that the real work of semantic description was being done in a vague language rather than in a set-assigning one' (1990). But, even if true, this constitutes no *objection* to the position. The semantic description is indeed being done *in* a vague language, but the work is done not simply *by* that language being vague, but by its reference to specifications.

There is no unacceptable circularity in the account either. We are not, of course, providing an account of vagueness using the *word* 'vague', nor is the primary aim of supervaluationism to provide an analysis of the word 'vague'. Rather it provides *truth-conditions* for vague sentences (and all other sentences) and does so in such a way as to illuminate the status of borderline cases, and the lack of sharp boundaries etc. If a definition of 'vagueness' is extracted, then it will

---

call the Simple Theory and the supervaluationist theory in question. I take up further discussion of the (T) schema itself in §3.

[4] The fact that the (T) schema commits us either to sharp boundaries and an absence of indeterminacy or to a radical revision of logic should make us question its apparent innocence: see §3.

explain when an expression is vague in terms of admissible specifications and not by circularly reusing 'vague'; and just because 'admissible specification' is vague, this does not mean that using it amounts to a (possibly disguised) use of 'vague'.

So any circularity charge must be based on the fact that the truth-conditions of vague sentences are given in vague terms. But I maintain that it is not, in general, objectionably circular to treat sentences which have a feature F by giving truth-conditions which are themselves F. It is fine, for example, to give truth-conditions of English sentences in English, or to give an account of what it is for a sentence to be grammatical that uses grammatical sentences. And, take a semantic feature with some similarities to vagueness, namely ambiguity: an account of the truth-conditions of ambiguous sentences which itself used (as well as mentioned) ambiguous expressions would not be objectionable for reasons of circularity, even if it would be undesirable because ambiguous truth-conditions should be avoided altogether. We have seen no reason to reject truth-conditions formulated in vague terms, and I claim that using them in one's theory of vagueness does not introduce any unacceptable circularity and is, indeed, necessary.

One objection, however, might be that using a vague metalanguage is *not* acceptable because vague languages are susceptible to sorites paradoxes. But that objection would be misplaced as long as we have a solution to the paradox, which the supervaluationist does have. The main premise of the object-language sorites is false; and its falsity but apparent truth is explained by ascending to the metalanguage. So if there are indeed apparent sorites paradoxes in the metalanguage itself, then their main premises will be false and *explaining* that solution will require ascending to a meta-metalanguage and reapplying the supervaluationist technique to the metalanguage itself. And other considerations may also call for such iteration. For if vagueness is, in general, to be understood in terms of a multiplicity of precisifications, then accepting the vagueness of 'admissible specification' will commit us to a multiplicity of *its* precisifications, which will be modelled in a meta-metalanguage. I argue that such iteration is innocuous.

The main premise of a metalanguage sorites paradox could be 'if there are admissible specifications which draw the boundary to "tall" at height h, then there are ones that draw it one hundredth of an inch lower'. That premise will be false even though there is no sharp boundary height which can be truly identified as the last acceptable place to draw a boundary. To explain the falsity of this premise, we do indeed need a meta-metalanguage; and the same considerations as raised with respect to the metalanguage will show that this meta-metalanguage must also be vague (its precision would bring sharp boundaries with it). And if this iteration were continued through a sequence of languages (each the metalanguage of the previous one), we would never reach a precise language at which to stop the iteration. But this is entirely acceptable. If there is no general objection to the claim that the sequence of metalanguages for metalanguages is potentially infinite, then what is the difficulty with adding 'and each of those languages is vague'? Moreover, we need not always take any notice of the hierarchy: in our account of the vagueness of the *object* language we need go no further than appealing to the vague metalanguage.[5] And, at that stage we will already have given an account of vagueness that can be applied to any language by treating it as the object language (even if it is itself a metalanguage for another language). There is no vicious infinite regress forced upon us. It is just that the vague is not reducible to the non-vague.

My presentation of the supervaluationist treatment of higher-order vagueness has been informal – what should we say about its formalisation? As stressed at the outset, my prime concern in this book is with philosophical justifications, and I do not seek to settle the details of its formal modelling here. Instead, I will survey the issues briefly and make some tentative suggestions. I have indicated that we can go up to a meta-meta-level and use the same framework for an account of the metalanguage and the vagueness of 'true'. What about the D operator, which provides a resource for capturing vagueness within the object-language?

[5] So, to return to a sentence p which is true on all definitely admissible specifications and not true on some borderline admissible ones. As explained, it is indeterminate whether p is true because it is indeterminate whether it is true on all admissible specifications. We do *not* assess p by ascending to the next level, observing that it is not true on all precisifications of 'admissible specification' that p is true on all admissible specifications and concluding that p itself is (determinately) not true. Admitting the hierarchy does not commit us to identifying super-truth with a condition to be stated in the meta-metalanguage or the meta-meta-metalanguage or via the limit of the sequences of metalanguages. Super-truth is the same notion we initially characterised and it is to express its vagueness that we use the higher metalanguages.

There is a tension here. First, a common expectation is that we can iterate that operator and thereby capture higher-order vagueness and reflect the vagueness of the metalanguage. We would then expect, for example, instances of p that make true $\neg DDp$ & $\neg D\neg Dp$, which express that Dp is of borderline status (just as at first level we have $\neg Dp$ & $\neg D\neg p$). But second, we characterised D such that Dp is true (i.e. true simpliciter, so true on all specifications) iff p itself is true on all admissible specifications. And so if Dp is true on any specifications (i.e. not false on all, so $\neg D\neg Dp$), then it is true on all and that leaves no room for the possibility that $\neg DDp$ & $\neg D\neg Dp$. Similarly DDp turns out to be equivalent to Dp: the possibility of higher-order vagueness looks threatened, at least if we assume it must be modelled with D itself.

Williamson's suggestion for the supervaluationist treatment of higher-order vagueness resists the above tension by rejecting the assumptions of the second half. His strategy mirrors that employed within the semantics of modal logic. Recall that the D operator can be compared to 'necessarily', whose semantics in terms of possible worlds resembles the quantification over specifications associated with D. The parallel to allowing that definiteness can be indefinite – as higher-order vagueness seems to require – is allowing that necessity can be contingent. The standard way for the latter is to use an accessibility or relative possibility relation, where p can be accessible from (or possible relative to) some worlds but not others. 'Necessarily p' counts as true at world w if p is true at all worlds accessible from w; so it can be contingent at w if there is a world, w^*, accessible from w and at which 'necessarily p' is true (because p is true at all worlds accessible from w^*) but there is another world w', accessible from w, at which 'necessarily p' is false (because p is false at some world accessible from w'). The comparable move for specifications is to introduce a notion of relative admissibility, where a specification can be admissible relative to some specifications but not relative to others. Dp is then true on a specification if true on all those admissible relative to it. Each specification, along with fixing sharp extensions, thus fixes which other specifications are to count as admissible; and it can be that p is true on all specifications admissible relative to s^* but not on all those admissible relative to s' making Dp indefinite. Just as different modal systems result from different requirements imposed on the accessibility relation, we can ask what features we should require of relative admissibility. (For example, plausibly it should be reflexive.) See Williamson 1994, pp. 157–61 and Williamson 1999 on this framework.

As Williamson discusses, hidden sharp boundaries still threaten this framework since if we define $D^\star$ such that $D^\star p$ is the conjunction Dp & DDp & $DDDp$ . . ., we will get $D^\star D^\star p$ always coinciding with $D^\star p$, and $D^\star p$ will then seem to be a sharp notion. But as Williamson also suggests, we can respond by admitting that we cannot express the vagueness of $D^\star$ using that very notion itself: 'it is like a cloud said to have an exact length because it is exactly as long as itself'. A new notion would be needed to capture the vagueness of $D^\star$; and again the new notion would not be capable of expressing its own vagueness; and so on. We will never reach a precise notion of 'absolutely definite'. As Williamson puts it, 'the term "perfectly straightforward application of a term" is itself vague. Not even iterating the supervaluationist construction into the transfinite will give it a precise sense' (1994, p. 161).

But the availability of this response suggests taking a parallel move earlier on, namely with D itself. Suppose we were to accept the initial interpretation of D whereby Dp is equivalent to DDp and there is no room for $\neg DDp$ & $D\neg Dp$. This does not preclude the vagueness of D if we deny that such vagueness is expressed using D itself. In chapter 1, §5 I warned against the assumption that in defining a D operator within some framework, we have to hand an operator that can capture its own vagueness. In introducing a technical operator D by drawing on features of the account of first-order vagueness, we cannot assume it will be appropriate to represent all aspects of all orders of vagueness. (If, on the other hand, we had introduced an operator which was *stipulated* to be appropriate to represent any order of vagueness, then we cannot assume it can be interpreted in the obvious way in the framework, even if such a notion is viable.)

It may be that the natural tendency is to capture second-order vagueness of p as 'not definitely definitely p and not definitely not definitely p'. I am suggesting that the formalisation of this is not $\neg DDp$ & $\neg D\neg Dp$ where the same operator is iterated in each conjunct. And this can still be compatible with a univocal account of the meaning of 'definitely', for its formalisation within a sentence can depend *systematically* on its position in an embedding. We have seen that sentences containing *D* can provide exceptions to principles of classical logic that are unproblematic within a *D*-free ordinary object-language. The suggestion that they also fail to slot into the usual formula for expressing vagueness in the obvious way may simply demonstrate another aspect of their non-conformity.[6]

To summarise: super-truth is vague because it is a matter of truth in all admissible specifications and 'all admissible specifications' is itself vague. *D* captures super-truth, but it cannot also capture the *vagueness* of super-truth. We need to ascend to a meta-metalanguage to capture the vagueness of our metalinguistic talk of 'all admissible specifications' and thus of super-truth, and this cannot be reflected in the object-language with the same *D* operator as is used to express the vagueness of *D*-free object-language sentences.

2. QUESTIONS WITHOUT ANSWERS

Another line of attack against the call upon a vague metalanguage is to say that even if the theory is not entirely trivial (as the Simple Theory of §1 is), it is still insufficiently informative. If appeal to all admissible specifications does not always settle the truth-value of a sentence, it might be objected, the theory leaves *unfinished* the central project of giving the truth-conditions of vague language. But, in reply, the supervaluationist can insist that there *is* no answer to be had beyond that given: that is the best statement of truth-conditions possible, because the nature and depth of vagueness ensure that not all indeterminacy can be removed (as shown by the arguments about higher-order vagueness in chapter 1, §6). The demand for truth-conditions that always deliver a determinate semantic status of some kind is a demand that cannot be fulfilled if we are to respect vagueness: the supervaluationist's use of a vague metalanguage allows as much illumination of truth-conditions as is possible while not striving for the unachievable elimination of vagueness.

These points can be made in the light of Horgan's 'forced march

---

[6] Note that on this interpretation of *D*, we can also retain the entailment $A \models DA$ which was called upon in the previous chapter. This entailment is guaranteed by the metalinguistic definition of *DA* in terms of all specifications. With a definition according to which the truth-conditions for *DA* at point *s* depend on the precisification of 'admissible' at *s* this would not be guaranteed.

paradox' (1994; see chapter 1, §4 above). Someone defending the theory I advocate must refuse to be marched down a sorites series assigning some semantic status or other to each member: no such series of assignments could accurately reflect the vagueness, and any shift of semantic status between adjacent members would impose sharp boundaries that my theory avoids. According to Horgan, this response reveals that I am advocating a form of transvaluationism, the essence of which is an acknowledgement that vague discourse is logically incoherent but nonetheless viable (see Horgan 1994, 1995 and 1998). He calls my sort of theory 'iterated supervaluationism' and argues that the only viable theories of vagueness are either epistemic views or transvaluationist ones. (His preferred version of the latter is a three-valued system very similar to Tye's: see my chapter 4 for criticisms.) I pause briefly to defend my version of supervaluationism against the charge of logical incoherence.

The distinctive feature of theorists that leads Horgan to classify them as transvaluationist is their refusal to assume that some semantic status or other is theoretically assignable to every member of a sorites series. There are, they maintain, semantic differences without a fact of the matter about the location of semantic transitions. But saying this does *not* commit them to logical incoherence. Horgan's forced march paradox should be seen as a *challenge* to any theory of vagueness, where accepting the incoherence should be a last resort, as I argued in chapter 2. Supervaluationism can meet the challenge. All the questions down the forced march may be meaningful and many of them have answers, but some do not. This is like the standard supervaluationist attitude to true disjunctions where sometimes the question 'which?' is unanswerable, though it is a reasonable question (one that often has an answer). Just as standard supervaluationism maintains that there is not always a suitable classification in terms of truth and falsity of all predications in a sorites series, so the current version maintains that there is not always a suitable classification of any kind, even if we include the category 'neither true nor false'. In other words, supervaluationism accommodates the distinction between there being semantic transitions and there being a fact of the matter about where those transitions are, as we saw with the difference between (E) and (TE) (see chapter 7, §5). So quite the opposite of being a theory that recognises the logical incoherence of vague language, supervaluationism shows how vague language is coherent despite the threat posed by sorites paradoxes and, in a more resilient form, by Horgan's relative of that paradox.[7]

The denial that there is an answer to certain questions about the truth-value status of various predications might suggest that my supervaluationist theory exemplifies the *modelling approach* with respect to substantial and important elements of the theory (see chapter 2, §3 on this approach). In chapters 2 and 4 I showed that the adoption of the modelling approach frequently amounts to producing a relatively attractive model without explaining its correspondence to the modelled phenomena, thereby ignoring a whole range of reasonable questions and merely gesturing at a theory of vagueness. But my version of supervaluationism is not guilty of this. It is not that the supervaluationist regards some assignments of values as merely *useful*: the description of truth-conditions it gives is true, not just useful; it is just stated using vague terms. In contrast with the modellers to whom I object, we can believe everything my theory says. And we need not take the modelling approach to precisifications themselves because the theory can accept that they are nothing more than a construct (see chapter 7, §6). They need not correspond to properties or languages, and their exact role according to the theory is perfectly clear.

3. TRUTH AND THE (T) SCHEMA

One popular criticism of the supervaluationist treatment of truth is that super-truth lacks features constitutive of truth. In particular, the supervaluationist must reject the Tarski schema:

---

[7] Horgan identifies two semantic requirements which he claims conflict with each other: the collectivistic one rules out facts about the location of semantic transitions and the individualistic one requires adjacent pairs of a sorites series to be classified the same way. The transvaluationist is portrayed as accepting logical incoherence and treating it as benign by claiming that one of those semantic requirements (the collectivistic one) *dominates* the other without *defeating* it. (This is compared to having an obligation to do *A*, and an obligation to do *B* where you cannot satisfy both, but where the obligation to do *B* dominates – that's what you should do – even though you have not shed the obligation to do *A* – that obligation has not been defeated.) But logical incoherence must be a matter of conflict among *truths* and, he claims, 'truth is correct assertability under *semantically dominant*, contextually operative, semantic standards' (1995, p. 111, his italics). So the existence of a requirement that is undefeated is irrelevant and the charge of logical incoherence unfounded.

(T) 'p' is true if and only if p.

This, like all other sentences, gets assessed by considering its truth-value at all complete and admissible specifications. Now, '"p" is true' counts as true at any point iff 'p' is true at all specification-points, and so the left-to-right conditional – (T$_1$) if 'p' is true then p – must always come out true at all points. But the right-to-left conditional – (T$_2$) if p then 'p' is true – is not always true at all points. For, suppose 'p' is neither true nor false, and so true at some but not all points; '"p" is true' will then be true at no points. At those points where 'p' *is* true, (T$_2$) is false, since its antecedent is true and its consequent is false; (T$_2$) and so (T) cannot be true simpliciter in those cases. Another reason why supervaluationists cannot accept (T) is that combined with the law of excluded middle, which they accept, it entails the principle of bivalence, which they reject (see e.g. Williamson 1992b, pp. 145–6 and Machina 1976, pp. 51–3).

Can we accept that (T) has instances that fail to be true, when it is often thought so central to the notion of truth? I reply that we can, and shall show that the observations that are typically cited in support of (T) actually commit us to no more than what the supervaluationist can allow. First, two results that show that the situation is not as serious as might first be thought.

First, (T) is never false, since when p is indeterminate there are specifications in which (T) is true – those in which p is itself false – as well as ones in which (T) is false; and so (T) is not false on all specifications and so not false simpliciter.

Second, it remains the case that p entails and is entailed by 'p is true'. For the super-truth of p, or its truth at the base-point, guarantees the super-truth of 'p is true', and vice versa. So we can retain the following principle of mutual entailment:

(T$\star$) from p we can infer 'p' is true, and vice versa

(a point noted in van Fraassen 1966; compare the mutual entailment of p and Dp, discussed above). The supervaluationist can argue that preserving (T$\star$) is all that our Tarskian intuitions require. But Williamson, for one, objects that a supervaluationist appeal to (T$\star$) would fail to deal with the original disquotational claim; he maintains that 'the availability of the mutual entailment reading is an irrelevance' (1994, p. 163). This, I shall argue, is unfair.

(T) is not as straightforward as Williamson and others imply. The substitution of liar-type sentences is clearly problematic and should cast some doubt on the reliability of our apparent intuitions about (T); but I shall limit my discussion to problems more closely connected to vagueness and the possibility of truth-value gaps. Objectors need to establish what they usually simply assert: namely that our notion of truth really commits us to the truth of all instances of (T). In fact, I claim, once the possibility of truth-value gaps is admitted, there is no such commitment.

Here are two possible scenarios regarding the sentence 'Tek is tall': first, Tek does meet the conditions of being tall, and second, Tek fails to meet those conditions. In the first, surely Tek is tall and 'Tek is tall' is true; and in the second, Tek is not tall, and 'Tek is tall' is false. Trying to express these two things at once by ' "Tek is tall" is true iff Tek is tall' (the relevant instance of (T)) would be appropriate if those scenarios exhausted the possibilities (as they would if bivalence held). But they do not, since Tek can be borderline tall in which case it is indeterminate whether Tek meets the conditions for being tall (for this is not just a way of failing to meet them). Similarly, consider Aristotle's slogan (cited by Tarski in support of the (T) schema): 'To say of what is that it is not, or of what is not that it is, is false, while to say of what is that it is, or of what is not that it is not, is true' (Tarski 1943, pp. 342–3). But what, we can ask Aristotle, if we say of what indeterminately is that it is (or that it is not)? His slogan does not speak to such a case.

But what *should* we say about (T) in those cases where p is indeterminate? ' "p" is true' surely cannot be true (and (T$_1$) would be false if it were), but this leaves the possibilities that ' "p" is true' is indeterminate or that it is false. Reflections on the notion of truth do not settle this case: there is a conflict between the inclination to call ' "p" is true' indeterminate to match the truth-value of 'p', and the inclination to call it false since in saying that p is indeterminate, we seem to be saying that it is neither true nor false and hence that it is not true. And so there are conflicting judgements affecting the valuation of (T) in such a case. With such a conflict, perhaps it can only be a matter of 'spoils to the victor'. Supervaluationism has a powerful story about truth and vagueness and we should, I recommend, accept the consequences regarding the value of ' "p" is true' and of (T) when 'p' is indeterminate.

Consider two more of the kinds of things that are said in support of (T) (or (T₂)), when anything *is* said to that effect. First, if I am in a position to say that *p*, then I can also say that '*p*' is true, since I know that inserting quotation marks and adding 'is true' adds nothing to the claim. And second, what it takes for 'TW is thin' to be true is just for TW to be thin, no more and no less (which Williamson (1994, p. 190) gives as the simple rationale for (T)).

Now, thoughts such as these do ensure that it cannot be the case that '*p*' is true while '"*p*" is true' is anything other than true. For if '*p*' were true but '"*p*" is true' were not, it would take more to ensure that '*p*' is true than that *p*, and the practice of adding quotation marks and 'is true' to a sentence we know to hold would not always be acceptable. This reflects the first two scenarios described. It is less clear what follows about the middle case in which '*p*' is indeterminate. Neither the indeterminacy nor the falsity of '"*p*" is true' would violate the claim that it takes no more for 'TW is thin' to be true than that TW is thin, for we are not dealing here with the situation in which TW *is* thin. Similarly, if '*p*' is indeterminate I cannot be in the position to assert *p* and go on to add quotation marks and 'is true', so the first justification dictates nothing about that scenario either.

So (T₂) will commit us to more than the cited reflections justify if it imposes more on the case where '*p*' is indeterminate than that '"*p*" is true' must not be true. And it does impose more, since on most accounts, the truth of the biconditional precludes the possibility that its left-hand side is indeterminate and its right-hand side false. Supervaluationists have a *diagnosis* of why (T₂) is sometimes not true, and their account does not threaten the above reflections on truth.

In order to capture only implications about the value of '"*p*" is true' when *p* is true or false without having consequences for the case where '*p*' is indeterminate, we can call on the mutual entailment reading (T★) – from *p* infer '*p*' is true and vice versa. Inferring *B* from *A* is a matter of concluding that *B* is true from the supposition that *A* is true, and this does not dictate what we should or should not conclude if *A* is indeterminate. (T★) best captures the key features of truth that are typically assumed to be expressed by (T). Even the stress that is placed on truth as 'disquotational' is amenable to the interpretation that this is a matter of the legitimacy of the inference from '*p* is true' to *p* and vice versa. We may not naturally state our intuitions about truth with (T★): it is, at best, a regimentation of our intuitions rather than a direct expression of them. But so is (T), as we must admit once we recognise the implications that 'iff' carries for cases involving indeterminacy. So, a theory rejecting (T) within a non-bivalent framework is not necessarily unfaithful to our notion of truth, at least not if it can respect (T*).[8]

What, however, if a predicate obeying the (T) schema could be added to the supervaluationist framework? Would the availability of such a predicate challenge the identification of truth with super-truth? Should truth be identified with the concept expressed by the new predicate?

Williamson claims that, given the supervaluationist framework, we can add a predicate 'true$_T$' that is disquotational in the sense that it satisfies the (T) schema. 'Let "'A' is true$_T$" be true on an interpretation if and only if A is true on that interpretation . . . In Fine's phrase, the vagueness of "true$_T$" waxes and wanes with the vagueness of the given sentence' (1994, p. 163). 'True$_T$', Williamson argues, has a far greater claim to being the real truth-predicate; and if we make that identification, he continues, the notion of super-truth and the appeal to precisifications fall out of the picture, leaving us with an epistemic view of vagueness.

But is the addition of a disquotational truth-predicate as simple as Williamson portrays it? First, can we afford to be so confident that anything can satisfy all its instances given that the liar paradox looms when 'this sentence is not true' is substituted for p in (T)? Just as the liar might make us suspicious of our intuitions about (T) in the full generality of its instances, so we should be wary of the claim that a predicate satisfying (T) can consistently be added to the language. Again, I put aside the liar paradox, however.[9]

Williamson's characterisation of 'true$_T$' states that whether '"A" is true$_T$' is true *on an interpretation* depends on whether 'A' is true on that interpretation. Are the interpretations referred to here the super-

---

[8] McGee argues that it is inference rules that are required for the typical work to which our notion of truth is put (1989, p. 534).

[9] Williamson mentions the liar paradox in a footnote: 'problems of self-reference and the like are too distant from those of mundane vagueness to make it plausible that the Tarskian condition cannot be met for a vague language without semantic vocabulary' (1994, p. 298). But Williamson instructed us to add the predicate 'true$_T$' to the object-language, in which case the object-language cannot *be* one without semantic vocabulary.

valuationist's specifications? The 'waxing and waning' of the vagueness of 'truth$_T$' which supposedly goes along with that of the sentences to which the predicate is applied would then correspond to the different values of those sentences at different specifications. But with this reading of 'true$_T$' we have not produced a candidate for the genuine or 'ordinary' notion of truth. 'True$_T$' is only defined relative to specifications, which, given the multiplicity of specifications, does not provide any notion of truth simpliciter. Our ordinary notion of truth allows us to say that sentences are true or not true without relativising the claim.

Truth-on-a-specification could be identified with truth if a single specification were singled out, or if it were assumed that there was such a uniquely relevant specification. But this is not to take seriously the supervaluationist framework. Either it would require singling out a specification arbitrarily, in which case truth in that specification cannot be identified with genuine truth, for it is no better than the alternative candidates. Or it is to assume that one specification is singled out by the meanings of the expressions, which is simply to assume something like the epistemic view, ignoring the supervaluationist framework again. Moreover, it is no good saying that there must be a unique specification because otherwise truth$_T$ will not be genuine truth, since this is just to assume that there is a predicate satisfying (T) which can be the truth-predicate. So 'true$_T$' understood this way is not a candidate for being identified with our ordinary truth predicate.

Given that we are still considering 'true$_T$' in the supervaluationist framework, perhaps the overall assessment of '"p" is true$_T$' should go by the quantification over specifications. Then '"p" is true$_T$' is true iff true on all specifications and false iff false on all specifications. If '"p" is true$_T$' is true on some specifications and false on others, it will count as neither true nor false, and this will be the case when 'p' itself is true on some specifications and not on others, i.e. when it is neither true nor false. This, perhaps, accounts for the described waxing and waning of the vagueness of 'true$_T$' with the vagueness of the sentences to which it is appended. I shall assume this reading for the rest of my discussion. On this understanding, however, it looks unlikely that 'true$_T$' can be understood without reference to super-truth. To grasp it, we need to know when a sentence involving it is true, false or neither and this needs to be stated using super-truth.

(And the claim that 'true$_T$' is disquotational rests on the super-truth of the (T) schema involving 'true$_T$'.) This throws doubt on Williamson's claim that supervaluationists can add 'true$_T$' to their framework and then entertain identifying it with truth. They cannot simply abandon the key notion used to characterise the application-conditions of expressions; and it is central to our ordinary notion of truth that it plays that role in characterising expressions, so they should not give up the identification of truth with super-truth.

Williamson notes that '*Fa* is true$_T$ or ¬*Fa* is true$_T$' holds for all *Fa*. For, just as at each specification either *a* is *F* or *a* is ¬*F*, so at each specification *Fa* is true$_T$ or ¬*Fa* is true$_T$; but then '*Fa* is true$_T$ or ¬*Fa* is true$_T$', like '*Fa* or ¬*Fa*', is true at all specifications and thus is super-true and true$_T$. For no *p* can we truly say that neither it nor its negation is true$_T$. If we understand the indeterminacy of *p* as 'neither "*p*" nor its negation is true' (equivalently '"*p*" is neither true nor false' if we assume the truth of '¬*p*' is the same as the falsity of '*p*'), then we cannot use truth$_T$ to characterise it. So, if we identify truth with truth$_T$, we are deprived of such a crucial notion as (non-epistemic) indeterminacy. And we thus cannot state in non-metaphorical terms what the supposed waxing and waning of the vagueness of '"*p*" is true$_T$' with the vagueness of '*p*' comes to, for we can no longer state that one is indeterminate if the other is.

Some sentences are indeterminate. 'Tek is tall', a paradigm borderline case, is among them. Our account of truth must accommodate this fact. Indeed, I suggest, in particular in the light of my discussion above, that this is far more important than allowing all instances of (T) to be true. So, even if the supervaluationist could make sense of the identification of truth and truth$_T$ within their framework, they have good reasons to resist it.

Let us see, anyway, how Williamson's argument proceeds. He argues that super-truth and the semantics of admissible interpretations drop out of the picture once 'truth$_T$' is introduced and identified with 'truth'. 'Of any admissible valuation, we can ask whether it assigns truth to all and only the true sentences of the language and falsity to all and only the false ones. At most one valuation has that property. But then any other valuation will assign truth-values incorrectly, so how can it be admissible?' (1994, p. 164). Now, we must agree that *at most* one valuation gets right all truth-values in the way described, for any two valuations disagree over the value of some sentences and both cannot be right. But how can adding true$_T$ to the supervaluationist framework suddenly produce the result that *any* of those valuations are correct? Supervaluationism starts from the assumption that none of them are. Williamson goes on: 'it might be replied that no interpretation is definitely the one with the desirable property.' But, he complains, 'if an interpretation does have the desirable property, why should it matter if it does not definitely have it?' (1994, p. 164). But this must assume that some valuation is correct (i.e. assigns truth to all and only the true sentences and falsity to all and only the false ones) and, in fact, none is. It may be that we cannot adequately express this fact using 'true$_T$', but so much the worse for that notion, at least as a candidate for truth.

As we have seen, true$_T$ does not allow us to make sense of 'determinately' or 'indeterminately', and so we cannot say of the valuations that each is (only) indeterminately correct. Unless, that is, those operators are interpreted epistemically; and Williamson suggests that we interpret the supervaluationist apparatus such that all specifications except the correct one are simply not known not to be correct – indeterminacy is then epistemic. But my response is to turn this argument back on itself. If true$_T$ allows no notion of non-epistemic indeterminacy, then it is not our notion of truth. Williamson writes 'if we cannot grasp the concept of definiteness by means of the concept of truth, can we grasp it at all?' I reply that we can grasp it by means of the concept of truth, so that concept cannot be truth$_T$.[10]

Williamson has not succeeded in showing that the supervaluationist's line is unstable. With (and only with) a notion of super-truth can we allow the required notion of indeterminacy. Supervaluationists can stand their ground. And if I have been successful in my defence of the theory in these two chapters and my criticisms of rivals in previous chapters, then they have every reason to do so.

[10] Williamson also gives as a reason for identifying truth with truth$_T$ that 'true$_T$' is conceptually prior to 'super-true' because the latter is definable in terms of 'true$_T$' and D (for a sentence is super-true iff it is definitely true$_T$; cf. Fine 1975, p. 296). But that definition is only reasonable within the framework if we assume a notion of definiteness that is unavailable if we identify truth with truth$_T$ rather than with super-truth, so the claim of conceptual priority is unwarranted.

References

Aristotle. *The Complete Works of Aristotle: the Revised Oxford Translation*, 2 vols. ed. J. Barnes. Princeton: Princeton University Press.

Armstrong, D. M. 1978. *Universals and Scientific Realism*. Cambridge: Cambridge University Press.

Barnes, J. 1982. 'Medicine, experience and logic'. In *Science and Speculation*, ed. J. Barnes, J. Brunschwig, M. Burnyeat, and M. Schofield. Cambridge: Cambridge University Press.

Black, M. 1937. 'Vagueness: an exercise in logical analysis'. *Philosophy of Science* 4: 427–55. Reprinted (with omissions) in Keefe and Smith 1997a.

Burgess, J. A. 1990. 'The sorites paradox and higher-order vagueness'. *Synthese* 85: 417–74.

1997. 'Supervaluations and the propositional attitude constraint'. *Journal of Philosophical Logic* 26: 103–19.

1998. 'In defence of an indeterminist theory of vagueness'. *Monist* 81: 233–52.

Burgess, J. A. and I. L. Humberstone 1987. 'Natural deduction rules for a logic of vagueness'. *Erkenntnis* 27: 197–229.

Burns, L. C. 1986. 'Vagueness and coherence'. *Synthese* 68: 487–513.

1991. *Vagueness: An Investigation into Natural Languages and the Sorites Paradox*. Dordrecht: Kluwer.

1995. 'Something to do with vagueness'. *Southern Journal of Philosophy* 33 (Supplement): 23–47.

Burnyeat, M. F. 1982. 'Gods and heaps'. In *Language and Logos*, ed. M. Schofield and M. C. Nussbaum. Cambridge: Cambridge University Press.

Campbell, R. 1974. 'The sorites paradox'. *Philosophical Studies* 26: 175–91.

Cargile, J. 1969. 'The sorites paradox'. *British Journal for the Philosophy of Science* 20: 193–202. Reprinted in Keefe and Smith 1997a.

Carnap, R. 1950. *The Logical Foundations of Probability*. Chicago: University of Chicago Press.

References

Chambers, T. 1998. 'On vagueness, sorites, and Putnam's "Intuitionistic Strategy"'. *Monist* 81: 343–8.

Cooper, N. 1995. 'Paradox lost: understanding vague predicates'. *International Journal of Philosophical Studies* 3: 244–69.

Davidson, D. 1968. 'On saying that'. *Synthese* 19: 130–46.

DePaul, M. R. 1998. 'Why bother with reflective equilibrium?' In *Rethinking Intuition: The Psychology of Intuition and its Role in Psychological Inquiry*, ed. M. R. DePaul and W. Ramsey. Lanham: Rowman and Littlefield.

Dummett, M. 1975. 'Wang's paradox'. *Synthese* 30: 301–24. Reprinted in Keefe and Smith 1997a.

1991. *The Logical Basis of Metaphysics*. Cambridge, Mass.: Harvard University Press.

Edgington, D. 1986. 'Do conditionals have truth-conditions?' *Critica* 18: 3–30.

1992. 'Validity, uncertainty and vagueness'. *Analysis* 52: 193–204.

1993. 'Wright and Sainsbury on higher-order vagueness'. *Analysis* 53: 193–200.

1997. 'Vagueness by degrees'. In *Vagueness: A Reader*, ed. R. Keefe and P. Smith. Cambridge, Mass.: MIT Press.

Evans, G. 1978. 'Can there be vague objects?' *Analysis* 38: 208. Reprinted in Keefe and Smith 1997a.

Fine, K. 1975. 'Vagueness, truth and logic'. *Synthese* 30: 265–300. Reprinted in Keefe and Smith 1997a.

Fodor, J. A. and E. Lepore 1996. 'What cannot be evaluated cannot be evaluated, and it cannot be supervaluated either'. *Journal of Philosophy* 93: 513–35.

Forbes, G. 1983. 'Thisness and vagueness'. *Synthese* 54: 235–59.

Frege, G. 1903. *Grundgesetze der Arithmetik, begriffsschriftlich abgeleitet*, vol. II. Jena: Hermann Pohle.

Giere, R. N. 1988. *Explaining Science: A Cognitive Approach*. Chicago: University of Chicago Press.

Goguen, J. A. 1969. 'The logic of inexact concepts'. *Synthese* 19: 325–73.

Goodman, N. 1954. *Fact, Fiction and Forecast*. London: Athlone Press.

Grice, H. P. 1957. 'Meaning'. *Philosophical Review* 66: 377–88.

1975. 'Logic and conversation'. In his *Studies in the Way of Words*. Cambridge, Mass.: MIT Press (1989).

Grim, P. 1982. 'What won't escape sorites arguments'. *Analysis* 42: 38–43.

Haack, S. 1974. *Deviant Logic*. Cambridge: Cambridge University Press.

1978. *Philosophy of Logics.* Cambridge: Cambridge University Press.

1979. 'Do we need "fuzzy logic"?' *International Journal of Man-Machine Studies* 11: 437–45.

1980. 'Is truth flat or bumpy?' In *Prospects for Pragmatism,* ed. D. H. Mellor. Cambridge: Cambridge University Press.

Halldén, S. 1949. *The Logic of Nonsense.* Uppsala: Uppsala Universitets Årsskrift.

Heck, R. G., Jr. 1993. 'A note on the logic of (higher-order) vagueness'. *Analysis* 53: 201–8.

Heller, M. 1988. 'Vagueness and the standard ontology'. *Noûs* 22: 109–31.

Hempel, C. G. 1939. 'Vagueness and logic'. *Philosophy of Science* 6: 163–80. Excerpted in Keefe and Smith 1997a.

Horgan, T. 1994. 'Robust vagueness and the forced-march sorites paradox'. In *Philosophical Perspectives, 8: Logic and Language,* ed. J. E. Tomberlin. Atascadero, Calif.: Ridgeview.

1995. 'Transvaluationism: a Dionysian approach to vagueness'. *Southern Journal of Philosophy* 33 (Supplement): 97–126.

1998. 'The transvaluationist conception of vagueness'. *Monist* 81: 313–30.

Horwich, P. 1997. 'The nature of vagueness'. *Philosophy and Phenomenological Research* 57: 929–35.

Hyde, D. 1997. 'From heaps and gaps to heaps of gluts'. *Mind* 106: 641–60.

Kamp, J. A. W. 1975. 'Two theories about adjectives'. In *Formal Semantics of Natural Language,* ed. E. L. Keenan. Cambridge: Cambridge University Press.

1981. 'The paradox of the heap'. In *Aspects of Philosophical Logic,* ed. U. Mönnich. Dordrecht: Reidel.

Keefe, R. and P. Smith 1997a. *Vagueness: A Reader.* Cambridge, Mass.: MIT Press.

1997b. 'Theories of vagueness'. In *Vagueness: A Reader,* ed. R. Keefe and P. Smith. Cambridge, Mass.: MIT Press.

King, J. L. 1979. 'Bivalence and the sorites paradox'. *American Philosophical Quarterly* 16: 17–25.

Kirk, R. 1986. *Translation Determined.* Oxford: Oxford University Press.

Kleene, S. C. 1952. *Introduction to Metamathematics.* Amsterdam: North Holland.

Klein, E. 1980. 'A semantics for positive and comparative adjectives'. *Linguistics and Philosophy* 4: 1–45.

Körner, S. 1966. *Experience and Theory*. London: Routledge and Kegan Paul.

Krantz, D. H., R. D. Luce, P. Suppes, and A. Tversky 1971. *Foundations of Measurement*. New York: Academic Press.

Kripke, S. A. 1975. 'Outline of a theory of truth'. *Journal of Philosophy* 72: 690–716.

Lakoff, G. 1973. 'Hedges: a study in meaning criteria and the logic of fuzzy concepts'. *Journal of Philosophical Logic* 2: 458–508.

Lewis, D. K. 1969. *Convention*. Cambridge, Mass.: Harvard University Press.

    1970. 'General semantics'. *Synthese* 22: 18–67.

    1975. 'Language and languages'. In *Minnesota Studies in the Philosophy of Science*, vol. VII, ed. K. Gunderson. Minneapolis: University of Minnesota Press.

    1979. 'Scorekeeping in a language game'. *Journal of Philosophical Logic* 8: 339–59.

    1982. 'Logic for equivocators'. *Noûs* 16: 431–41.

    1983a. 'New work for a theory of universals'. *Australasian Journal of Philosophy* 61: 343–77.

    1983b. *Philosophical Papers*, vol. I. New York: Oxford University Press.

    1986. *On the Plurality of Worlds*. Oxford: Basil Blackwell.

    1993. 'Many, but almost one'. In *Ontology, Causality and Mind: Essays in honour of D. M. Armstrong*, ed. J. Bacon, K. Campbell, and L. Reinhardt. Cambridge: Cambridge University Press.

    1994. 'Humean supervenience debugged'. *Mind* 103: 473–90.

Long, A. A. and D. N. Sedley, eds., 1987. *The Hellenistic Philosophers*. Cambridge: Cambridge University Press. Excerpted in Keefe and Smith 1997a.

Łukasiewicz, J. and A. Tarski 1930. 'Investigations into the sentential calculus'. In *Logic, Semantics, Metamathematics*, ed. A. Tarski. Oxford: Clarendon Press.

Machina, K. F. 1972. 'Vague predicates'. *American Philosophical Quarterly* 9: 225–33.

    1976. 'Truth, belief, and vagueness'. *Journal of Philosophical Logic* 5: 47–78. Reprinted in Keefe and Smith 1997a.

McGee, V. 1989. 'Applying Kripke's theory of truth'. *Journal of Philosophy* 86: 530–9.

McGee, V. and B. McLaughlin 1995. 'Distinctions without a difference'. *Southern Journal of Philosophy* 33 (Supplement): 203–51.

Mehlberg, H. 1958. *The Reach of Science*. Toronto: University of Toronto Press. Excerpted in Keefe and Smith 1997a.

Parikh, R. 1983. 'The problem of vague predicates'. In *Language, Logic, and Method*, ed. R. S. Cohen and M. W. Wartofsky. Dordrecht: Reidel.

Parsons, T. 1984. 'Assertion, denial and the liar paradox'. *Journal of Philosophical Logic* 13: 137–52.

1987. 'Entities without identity'. In *Philosophical Perspectives, 1: Metaphysics*, ed. J. E. Tomberlin. Atascadero, Calif.: Ridgeview.

Peacocke, C. 1981. 'Are vague predicates incoherent?' *Synthese* 46: 121–41.

Peirce, C. S. 1902. 'Vague'. In *Dictionary of Philosophy and Psychology*, ed. J. M. Baldwin, 748. New York: Macmillan.

Pinkal, M. 1983. 'Towards a semantics of precization'. In *Approaching Vagueness*, ed. T. T. Ballmer and M. Pinkal. Amsterdam: North Holland.

Przełecki, M. 1969. *The Logic of Empirical Theories*. London: Routledge and Kegan Paul.

1976. 'Fuzziness as multiplicity'. *Erkenntnis* 10: 371–80.

Putnam, H. 1983. 'Vagueness and alternative logic'. *Erkenntnis* 19: 297–314.

Quine, W. V. 1981. 'What price bivalence?' *Journal of Philosophy* 78: 90–5.

Raffman, D. 1994. 'Vagueness without paradox'. *Philosophical Review* 103: 41–74.

Rawls, J. 1971. *A Theory of Justice*. Oxford: Oxford University Press.

Read, S. and C. Wright 1985. 'Hairier than Putnam thought'. *Analysis* 45: 56–8.

Rolf, B. 1981. *Topics on Vagueness*. Lund, Sweden: Studentlitteratur.

1984. 'Sorites'. *Synthese* 58: 219–50.

Russell, B. 1923. 'Vagueness'. *Australasian Journal of Philosophy and Psychology* 1: 84–92. Reprinted in Keefe and Smith 1997a.

Sainsbury, R. M. 1988. *Paradoxes*. Cambridge: Cambridge University Press.

1990. 'Concepts without boundaries'. Inaugural lecture published by the King's College London Department of Philosophy. Reprinted in Keefe and Smith 1997a.

1991. 'Is there higher-order vagueness?' *Philosophical Quarterly* 41: 167–82.

1992. 'Sorites paradoxes and the transition question'. *Philosophical Papers* 21: 177–90.

References

1995a. *Paradoxes*. 2nd edn. Cambridge: Cambridge University Press.

1995b. 'Vagueness, ignorance and margin for error'. *British Journal for the Philosophy of Science* 46: 589–601.

1997. 'Easy Possibilities'. *Philosophy and Phenomenological Research* 57: 907–19.

Sainsbury, R. M. and Williamson, T. 1997. 'Sorites'. In *A Companion to the Philosophy of Language*, ed. B. Hale and C. Wright. Oxford: Blackwell.

Sanford, D. H. 1975. 'Borderline logic'. *American Philosophical Quarterly* 12: 29–39.

1976. 'Competing semantics of vagueness: many values versus super-truth'. *Synthese* 33: 195–210.

1979. 'Nostalgia for the ordinary: comments on papers by Unger and Wheeler'. *Synthese* 41: 175–84.

1993. 'The problem of the many, many composition questions, and naive mereology'. *Noûs* 27: 219–28.

Schiffer, S. 1998. 'Two issues of vagueness'. *Monist* 81: 193–214.

Schwartz, S. P. 1989. 'Vagueness and incoherence: a reply to Burns'. *Synthese* 80: 395–406.

Shapiro, S. C. 1998. 'A procedural solution to the unexpected hanging and sorites paradoxes'. *Mind* 107: 751–61.

Simons, P. 1996. 'Review of Williamson: *Vagueness*'. *International Journal of Philosophical Studies* 4: 321–7.

Smiley, T. 1993. 'Can contradictions be true?' *Proceedings of the Aristotelian Society*, supplementary vol. 67: 17–33.

1996. 'Rejection'. *Analysis* 56: 1–9.

Sorensen, R. A. 1988. *Blindspots*. Oxford: Clarendon Press.

Sperber, D. and D. Wilson 1985–6. 'Loose talk'. *Proceedings of the Aristotelian Society* 86: 153–71.

Tappenden, J. 1993. 'The liar and sorites paradoxes: toward a unified treatment'. *Journal of Philosophy* 90: 551–77.

1995. 'Some remarks on vagueness and a dynamic conception of language'. *Southern Journal of Philosophy* 33 (Supplement): 193–201.

Tarski, A. 1943. 'The semantic conception of truth'. *Philosophy and Phenomenological Research* 4: 341–75.

Tye, M. 1989. 'Supervaluationism and the law of excluded middle'. *Analysis* 49: 141–3.

1990. 'Vague objects'. *Mind* 99: 535–57.

1994. 'Sorites paradoxes and the semantics of vagueness'. In *Philosophical*

Perspectives, 8: Logic and Language, ed. J. E. Tomberlin. Atascadero, Calif.: Ridgeview. Reprinted (with omissions) in Keefe and Smith 1997a.

1997. 'On the epistemic theory of vagueness'. In *Truth (Philosophical Issues*, vol. 8), ed. E. Villanueva. Atascadero, Calif.: Ridgeview.

Unger, P. 1979. 'There are no ordinary things'. *Synthese* 41: 117–54.

1980. 'The problem of the many'. In *Midwest Studies in Philosophy*, vol. 5, ed. P. A. French, T. E. Uehling Jr. and H. K. Wettstein. Minneapolis: University of Minnesota Press.

van Fraassen, B. C. 1966. 'Singular terms, truth-value gaps, and free logic'. *Journal of Philosophy* 63: 481–95.

1968. 'Presupposition, implication, and self-reference'. *Journal of Philosophy* 65: 136–52.

1969. 'Presuppositions, supervaluations and free logic'. In *The Logical Way of Doing Things*, ed. K. Lambert. New Haven: Yale University Press.

1980. *The Scientific Image*. Oxford: Clarendon Press.

Varzi, A. C. 1995. 'Vagueness, indiscernibility and pragmatics'. *Southern Journal of Philosophy* 33 (Supplement): 49–62.

Walton, D. N. 1992. *Slippery Slope Arguments*. Oxford: Clarendon Press.

Wheeler, S. C. 1975. 'Reference and vagueness'. *Synthese* 30: 367–79.

1979. 'On that which is not'. *Synthese* 41: 155–73.

Williams, B. 1995. 'Which slopes are slippery?' In his *Making Sense of Humanity*. Cambridge: Cambridge University Press.

Williamson, T. 1990. 'Review of Sorensen: *Blindspots*'. *Mind* 99: 137–40.

1992a. 'Inexact knowledge'. *Mind* 101: 217–42.

1992b. 'Vagueness and ignorance'. *Proceedings of the Aristotelian Society*, supplementary vol. 66: 145–62. Reprinted in Keefe and Smith 1997a.

1994. *Vagueness*. London: Routledge.

1995. 'Definiteness and knowability'. *Southern Journal of Philosophy* 33 (Supplement): 171–91.

1996. 'Putnam on the sorites paradox'. *Philosophical Papers* 25: 47–56.

1997a. 'Imagination, stipulation and vagueness'. In *Truth (Philosophical Issues*, vol. 8), ed. E. Villanueva. Atascadero, Calif.: Ridgeview.

1997b. 'Reply to Commentators'. *Philosophy and Phenomenological Research* 57: 945–53.

1999. 'On the structure of higher-order vagueness'. *Mind* 108: 127–43.

Wright, C. 1975. 'On the coherence of vague predicates'. *Synthese* 30: 325–65.

References

1976. 'Language-mastery and the sorites paradox'. In *Truth and Meaning: Essays In Semantics*, ed. G. Evans and J. McDowell. Oxford: Clarendon Press. Reprinted in Keefe and Smith 1997a.

1987. 'Further reflections on the sorites paradox'. *Philosophical Topics* 15: 227–90. Reprinted (with omissions) in Keefe and Smith 1997a.

1995. 'The epistemic conception of vagueness'. *Southern Journal of Philosophy* 33 (Supplement): 133–59.

Zadeh, L. A. 1965. 'Fuzzy sets'. *Information and Control* 8: 338–53.

1975. 'Fuzzy logic and approximate reasoning'. *Synthese* 30: 407–28.

Zemach, E. M. 1991. 'Vague objects'. *Noûs* 25: 323–40.

Index

Index

Index

Printed in the United Kingdom
by Lightning Source UK Ltd.
117872UK00001B/19-36

9 780521 033893